ABOUT THE AUTHORS

TONY BENSON

Head Coach
1992 Australian Olympic team
1991 Australian World Championships team
1990 Australian Commonwealth Games team
1982 Philippines Asian Games team

National Coach
Philippines 1979-1983
Australia 1988-1993

IAAF/IOC Lecturer
Africa, Asia and the Pacific

Competitor
Olympic 5000m, 1972
Highest world ranking—5th, 1971
Sub-4-minute miler
Set Australian records in the 2000 and 3000m

Coaching Success
Olympians (5)
World Championships representatives (4)
World Cross Country representatives (2)
Commonwealth Games representatives (3)
National champions (5)

Qualifications
National distance coach—Education
Level 3 Track & Field
 • Middle Distance
 • Steeplechase
Level 2 Triathlon (Level 3 pending)

Tony Benson and Kip Keino in the DN Galan 5000m, Stockholm, 1971. Benson won at Stockholm, Oslo and Cologne that year and is the last Australian distanceman to win a Grand Prix-level race in Europe.

IRV RAY

Head Coach B.A., PE; M.A., Ed.
Head T&F & Cross Country Coach, California Baptist
    University (Men & Women), 1997-present
Cross Country & Distance Coach, Azusa Pacific, 1989-96

Lecturer
USA High School Coaches Association
Irv Ray & Steve Scott Developmental Athlete
    Camps, 1993-1997
Run With The Best National Coaches Seminars
Vigil-Ray National Coaches Clinics

Competitor
Collegiate middle distance runner
National age-group distance runner
Has competed in every running event—100m to
    ultra-marathons—to test his theories

Coaching Success
Olympians (2)
World Championships representatives (2)
All-Americans (49)
NAIA national team championships (6)
National individual champions (8)
Women's age-group world record holder (1)
U.S. mile indoor champion (1)

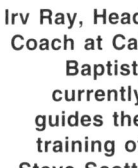

Irv Ray, Head Coach at Cal Baptist, currently guides the training of Steve Scott.

RUN WITH THE BEST

A Coach's Guide to Training Middle and Long Distance Runners
Based on the Cerutty and Lydiard Models

Tony Benson
Endurance Performance Systems

Irv Ray
California Baptist University

First published in 1998 by Tafnews Press,
Book Division of Track & Field News
2570 El Camino Real, Suite 606,
Mountain View, CA 94040 USA

Copyright © Tafnews Press

All rights reserved. No part of this publication may be reproduced or transmitted in any form or by any means, including photocopy, recording or any information storage and retrieval system, without written permission from the publisher

Standard book number: 0-911521-53-4

Printed in the United States of America

Production and cover design: Teresa Tam

Cover photograph by Victor Sailer/Photo Run

Publisher's Note: Although this book is addressed to coaches and athletes of both sexes, for the sake of readability, the male pronouns (he, his, him) are generally used throughout the book. This is done not because one sex is prioritized over the other, but strictly as a shorthand to avoid the constant and unwieldy use of "he or she," "his or her," and "him and her."

THE BENEFITS OF THIS BOOK TO THE COACH

1. **IT PRESENTS THE COACH WITH:**
   - A SIMPLE STEP-BY-STEP METHOD OF DEVELOPING AN ANNUAL PERIODIZED TRAINING PLAN TO ENSURE YOUR ATHLETE IS IN PEAK CONDITION TO REPRESENT HIS/HER TEAM IN THE MOST IMPORTANT CROSS COUNTRY AND TRACK RACES OF THE SEASON.
   - A PLAN THAT CAN BE INDIVIDUALIZED TO ENCOMPASS EACH INDIVIDUAL ATHLETE'S NEEDS AND GOALS IN TERMS OF:
     - VOLUME,
     - INTENSITY,
     - DURATION, AND
     - FREQUENCY.

2. **IT ASSISTS THE COACH TO:**
   - INTEGRATE THE MAJOR TYPES OF WORKOUTS, E.G., LONGER STEADY-STATE RUNS, SHORTER LACTATE THRESHOLD, MAXIMAL OXYGEN UPTAKE AND LACTIC ACID TOLERANCE WORKOUTS—WITH SPEED AND TECHNIQUE DRILLS, STRENGTH TRAINING REGIMENS AND STRETCHING ROUTINES TO MAXIMIZE THE ATHLETE'S:
     - ENDURANCE,
     - STRENGTH,
     - POWER,
     - SPEED,
     - TECHNIQUE, AND
     - FLEXIBILITY.
   - PROVIDE A MEANS OF ENSURING THAT THE ATHLETE DEVELOP HIGHER LEVELS OF MOTIVATION, EXPERIENCE LESS ILLNESS AND/OR INJURY, COMPETE FOR MANY YEARS, AND GET MORE ENJOYMENT FROM TRAINING AND RACING BECAUSE HIS GOALS ARE:
     - REALISTIC,
     - TANGIBLE, AND
     - BEING ACHIEVED SEASON BY SEASON.

DEDICATION

Raylene

My wife, mother of our three children,
Jacqueline, Christopher and Virginia,
and a lifelong teammate.
My competitive and coaching careers reflect
her unwavering support and assistance.
Run With The Best is dedicated to her.

My parents, Moya Ellen and Charles John Benson,
also have a special place in this book.

Tony Benson

My Family

To my wife Carol and my two sons, Chris and Ryan,
who sacrificed with me through two decades of coaching.
I am indebted to all my past and present athletes who
endured to help develop this system into today's format
and to my friend Steve Scott, whose advice and
experience kept me on the right track.

I wish to acknowledge all these people who have supported
my endeavors or trusted me with their training.

Irv Ray

Corinthians 9:24
Do you not know that those who run in a race
All run , but only one receives the prize!
So run and train in such a way
That you may win the prize!

CONTENTS

Foreword, by Irv Ray 9
Introduction, by Tony Benson 11

Section 1. The History and Philosophy of Coaching
    Chapter 1.   A Brief History Of Training Methodology 15
    Chapter 2.   The Importance Of A Coaching Philosophy 21
    Chapter 3.   The *Run With The Best* Program 22
    Chapter 4.   Periodization Of The Year 34
    Chapter 5.   The Major Training Components 37
    Chapter 6.   The Aerobic Training Components 39
    Chapter 7.   The Anaerobic Training Components 45
    Chapter 8.   The Auxiliary Training Components 50
    Chapter 9.   The Training Plan 53

Section 2. Training Tools
    Chapter 10.   Performance Indicators 61
    Chapter 11.   Training Indicators 64
    Chapter 12.   The Long Run: Speed Through Endurance 72
    Chapter 13.   Surge Intervals: Where Threshold Meets MVO$_2$ 74
    Chapter 14.   Sprint Intervals: Where MVO$_2$ Meets Lactic Acid Tolerance 76
    Chapter 15.   Will Power Training: Where The Will To Prepare Meets The Will To Win 77
    Chapter 16.   Race Practice Workouts: Putting It All Together 79
    Chapter 17.   The Hallmarks Of The Great Athlete: "So Run And Train In Such A Way
                         As You Might Win The Prize!" 83
    Chapter 18.   Running And Breathing Techniques: Getting The Most From Your Training 86
    Chapter 19.   Training For The Future: So You Will Not Be Left Behind 89
    Chapter 20.   Junior Athletes: Plan To Perform As Elite Seniors 93
    Chapter 21.   Age Group And Recreational Athletes: Create Your Personal Program 96
    Chapter 22.   Rehabilitation Exercising: The Price Of Sub-Optimal Training 99
    Chapter 23.   The *Run With The Best* American Program: A Dual Peak Season 101
    Chapter 24.   Sample Training Programs 104
    Chapter 25.   Training Guidelines 116
    Chapter 26.   Examples Of Various Types Of Workouts 120

Afterword: Using The *Run With The Best* Program In The American College
            And High School System, By Irv Ray 125
Extra Worksheets (from Chapter 3) 129

FOREWORD
By Irv Ray

I first met Tony Benson in 1993 and our relationship got off to a wonderful start because we shared the same excitement and enthusiasm for coaching middle and long distance runners.

Tony's experience and depth of knowledge is in many ways quite unique. Starting as a developing athlete who ran 4:20 for the mile at 20 years of age, he used the Lydiard and Cerutty programs to become an athlete who "ran with the best" from 1969 to 1972. During that time he ran a sub-four-minute mile, earned a world No 5 ranking, ran personal bests of 7:50.1 (3000m) and 13:36 (5000m) and gained Olympic selection.

In addition he has also had extensive contact with the Kenyan system through both competition and lecturing for the Olympic Solidarity Committee and the International Amateur Athletic Federation in Africa, Asia, and the Pacific.

Finally, he has held head coaching positions on Olympic, World Championship, Commonwealth and Asian Games teams and most importantly practiced what he preaches by coaching athletes onto these and World Cross Country Championship teams.

Up to 1993 it is probably fair to say I was a good coach, and like most coaches, gave long hours and maximum concentration to coaching my athletes. Because I loved what I did, I went to many clinics and seminars, read extensively and developed a successful training system—one that encompassed my philosophies and the best of what I had been exposed to.

However, in my heart of hearts, I also knew there were gaps in many aspects of my athletes' preparation. Many of them ran very well but some recorded good performances before the championship race, then failed to repeat them on the day. Others were capable of maintaining contact in their races but failed to find the speed they demonstrated in training when it counted in the final sprint. Still others showed obvious talent, ability and commitment, but failed to exploit these attributes, never reaching their goals or optimizing their potential.

I am always searching for better ways to coach and have never been afraid to ask questions or seek advice from any source, so when I met Tony I wasn't going to let an opportunity like this pass. The more Tony and I talked the more convinced I became that my "athletic angel" had walked into my office!

Over the next few days we explored training methods in general and the challenges many unique aspects of the American system presented for coaches. I discovered Tony had a system incorporating a key list of components integral to coaching middle and long distance runners and that this system was based on his knowledge of Lydiard, Cerutty and Kenyan training methods.

More significantly he had blended these ingredients into a working model that can be used to establish individual goals and then provide direction for athletes at every level.

Run With The Best is a system produced by two coaches based on respect for history and the most current information. It is based on two main concepts:
1. "Training to train," i.e., developing the organism to ever higher levels of physical fitness as occurs in the Lydiard system and is exemplified in the benefits gained from all their early years of activity by so many Africans, and
2. "Training to race," i.e., developing the organism for competition (or combat as it might have been!) as advocated by Cerutty and is seen in the way the Kenyans train once they become involved in competitive racing.

Central to the system is the understanding that the potential runners of today are not as naturally active as kids were in the years up to the mid-1970's and that care and patience is essential because it can take from four to ten years to develop athletes to their true potential.

As I have continued to refine my programs within the *Run With The Best* framework the more I have come to appreciate its benefits. Three of these benefits predominate:
1. The formation of a more successful coach-athlete relationship with each member of the team because athletes reach their true potential and perform at their best in the season's goal race or races.
2. The development of the complete athlete equipped with all the components necessary for successful middle and long distance racing. These components may be summarized as general endurance, speed, stamina and strength and all are developed to maximal levels within a periodized annual training plan that targets specific volumes, intensities, frequencies and

duration according to the agreed coach-athlete goals and the individual's current capacities;
3. The reduction of illness and injury within the team framework, plus an increase in athlete motivation toward, and enjoyment of, training and competing as a result of less time away from training, and the provision of a structure that allows the athlete to achieve realistic, tangible goals.

The challenge for me, then, was to adapt this system to the American season—in particular, the U.S. high school and collegiate season.

INTRODUCTION
By Tony Benson

I have successfully used the *Run With The Best* system for many years to assist athletes of all age and ability levels to reach senior national class and even achieve international representation.

By following the simple guidelines, which are modeled on Arthur Lydiard's conditioning theories, Percy Cerutty's naturalistic approach and my experiences in Kenya and with Kenyan athletes, a coach can develop any 14- or 15-year-old high school athlete of moderate ability into a national class junior and any 17- or 18-year-old of similar ability into a competitive senior by the time that athlete reaches 22-24 years of age. Given more time with these athletes a coach could well see many of them gain international representation.

The *Run With The Best* system would have remained merely a system I used and a set of notes I handed out at various seminars and courses around the world had it not been for Irv Ray. At the very time I had finally documented my ideas for presentation, I had the good fortune to meet Irv. With his boundless enthusiasm fired by his excitement at finding something he had been seeking both from within himself and a wide variety of external sources, my bland pile of lecture notes were quickly christened the "Lydiard/Cerutty/Benson Training Model" and headed for the publisher under the title of *Run With the Best*.

Without Irv this manual would not exist and I thank him sincerely

Before publication, the challenge became to produce a clear, concise manual that would be easily understood by coaches and athletes and which would be kept on the coach's desk, not filed away on some shelf.

Run With The Best is intended to be a working manual for coaches. It will assist them in applying proven training principles to help a great number of athletes reach their full potential and to perform at their best *when it counts the most*. It is a manual that aims to help the coach work with the grass roots school and club athlete who forms the foundation of track & field, as well as provide a resource that will significantly boost the performance of even an elite athlete who has not been previously exposed to its concepts.

The manual encourages coaches and athletes to take a step back from an environment constantly inundated with new theories and/or alterations to previous theories. It recommends coaches do not deviate from carefully prepared long-term plans as a result of reading articles which describe a famous athlete's short-term training routine or imply major physiological gains can be achieved in short blocks of training.

This training system does not claim to invent any new type of training or offer any "quick-fix" training schemes. Nor does it try to supply training examples of world class runners. Rather, it recommends that coaches revisit training principles and methods that, with some refinement due to perceptive insights and changing world competitive conditions, have a proven record of success in the modern era and have been verified by innumerable scientific studies. We therefore dedicate this book to four men from four different countries who we believe significantly influenced modern distance running and three other coaches who influenced either one or both of the authors during either their competitive or coaching careers.

Arthur Lydiard

Eschewing the massive interval training workloads advocated by the European coaches of the 1950's, Lydiard introduced the concept of marathon training during the Preparation Period for all runners from 800m to the marathon. His methods produced world-beating New Zealand athletes, led by Peter Snell and Murray Halberg in the 1960's and the successes of athletes from other countries he worked in, such as Mexico and Finland. These methods provided the foundation for most present-day training principles.

Percy Cerutty

Like Lydiard, Cerutty also rejected the European approach and his successes in Australia paralleled Lydiard's. He was the first coach to thoroughly discuss strength training, technique and diet. Herb Elliott, considered the greatest miler/1500m runner of all time, was produced by an approach that valued long runs as much as Lydiard did, along with varied pace running which is so common to the Kenyan approach.

John Velzian

John has lived in Kenya since the 1950's and coached, among others, the great Kip Keino. His administrative and coaching input have became an integral part of a tradition that is continually growing in Kenyan runners.

Bill Bowerman

Bowerman brought Lydiard's concepts to America and adapted them to the U.S. college-based system. In particular, he stressed the concept of overcompensation in relation to the balance between training and rest. University of Oregon athletes from Dyrol Burleson to Steve Prefontaine benefited from his knowledge.

Pat Clohessy

An All-American 3-miler while on scholarship at the University of Houston, Pat knew both Cerutty and Lydiard, but was philosophically more attuned to Lydiard. He has coached or advised many top athletes, including Billy Mills, Robert De Castella, Simon Doyle (a 3:31/1500m runner) and, more recently, Shaun Creighton, who has run 27:31 for 10,000m.

Joe Vigil

His coaching at Adams State University has consistently transformed average high school runners, such as Pat Porter, into national and international-caliber athletes and his scientifically documented training programs have strongly influenced distance running in America.

Fred Wilt

Wilt advised Buddy Edelen, a former world marathon record holder. His *How They Train* books were invaluable to two generations of athletes and coaches. He was also perhaps the first coach to present the physiology of coaching in easy- to-understand layman's language.

Over the years the alterations and adaptions made to Lydiard's and Cerutty's theories by some astute coaches have led many other coaches into misunderstanding the original concepts that underpinned the Lydiard and Cerutty methods, which in turn means these coaches are ignoring training systems that produced world records and Olympic medals!

As you read *Run With The Best* we suggest you revisit the times and performances of athletes such as Elliott, Snell, Halberg, Mills, Clarke, Ryun, Gammoudi, Keino, Lindgren, Dellinger, Clayton and Prefontaine and note the common threads between the philosophies of Lydiard and Cerutty, the adaptions made by many great coaches to suit specific environments, and the way the African athletes train.

We hope you can use the manual to benefit your athletes and increase the satisfaction you gain from track & field.

Bill Bowerman

Arthur Lydiard

Percy Cerutty

SECTION 1

THE PHILOSOPHY OF COACHING

CHAPTER 1
A BRIEF HISTORY OF TRAINING METHODOLOGY

It is difficult to imagine coaching an athlete to his potential without knowing something of the history of middle and long distance training. At some point in every athlete's career he must pass through a training zone already experienced by some past champion.

If Fig. 1-1 below is reviewed it is obvious that any athlete who has world record ambitions has to better the times of all the previous world record holders in that event. This means a knowledge of what types of training have produced these previous world records is useful.

Based on the available information it appears that the great professional runners prior to 1900 concentrated on steady mileage and time trials or races—a pattern not dissimilar to the one espoused by Arthur Lydiard and Ernst Van Aaken some 60 years later. Some like Alfred Shrubb, who held the world one-hour record for nearly 50 years, were running twice a day though not necessarily all year round. Walking was also used regularly, a practice the legendary Finn Paavo Nurmi continued into the 1920's.

Before 1940

The years between 1912 and 1940 basically belonged to Finland, Great Britain and the United States. Britain's Albert Hill, Douglas Lowe and Tom Hampson and Americans, such as James Meredith, John Paul Jones, Abel Kiviat, Norman Taber, Ben Eastman, Bill Bonthron, Glenn Cunningham, and Elroy Robinson, all set middle distance records between 800m and one mile and/or won Olympic medals, while Finnish runners like Hannes Kolehmainen, Paavo Nurmi, Ville Ritola, Taisto Maki, Gunnar Hockert, Lauri Lehtinen, Imari Salminen and Viljo Heino were preeminent from 3,000m to 10,000m.

An interesting footnote to running during this period was that five Americans were also among the twelve runners to register marathon best times. Very little has been written about the training programs of the middle distance runners of the era but what is available indicates they relied on their 400m speed, 10- to 40-minute runs, sprints and repetition runs, e.g., 6-8 x 200m, 3-4 x 400m, 1-2 x 600-800m with a walk recovery over similar distances. Occasionally the 1500m runners/milers would run a hard 1200m or 1320y time trial effort.

Their annual volumes were undoubtedly very low by modern standards, probably not more than 1500 miles or 2500 kilometers in their peak years. Glenn Cunningham, for example, competed for about 13 years and it was estimated he ran approximately only 10,000 miles (16,000km) in this time.

The Finns on the other hand gradually increased their volumes to very high levels by pre-World War II standards. Firstly they trained twice a day most days. The morning was initially a walk plus some 50-100m sprints but gradually walking gave way to running prior to the sprints. The evenings were usually 3-8k tempo runs with the last 1-2k at a faster pace. During this period the concept of extending workouts by alternating work and rest periods was introduced.

FIG. 1-1: MEN'S MIDDLE AND LONG DISTANCE WORLD RECORD PROGRESSIONS

Men's Events	1900	1912	1940	1965	1990	1997
800m		1:51.9	1:46.6	1:44.3	1:41.73	1:41.11
1500m	4:10.4	3:55.8	3:47.8	3:35.6	3:29.46	3:27.37
1 Mile	4:12.7	4:12.7	4:06.4	3:53.6	3:46.32	3:44.39
3000m	9:18.2	8:36.8	8:09.0	7:39.6	7:29.45	7:20.67
2 Mile	9:17.6	9:09.6	8:53.2	8:26.4	8:13.45	7:58.61
5000m	15:20.0	14:36.6	14:08.8	13:16.6	12:58.39	12:39.74
10,000m	31:40.0	30:58.8	29:52.6	27:39.4	27:08.23	26:27.85
3,000 S/C			9:03.8	8:26.4	8:05.35	7:55.72
Marathon		2:42:31	2:26:42	2:12:00	2:06:50	2:06:50

The interesting thing about the period from 1912 to 1935 is it seemed basically "athlete driven." Coaches either did not exist in any numbers or they contributed so little to the athlete's success that they were rarely mentioned. All this was about to change however. Woldemar Gerschler of Germany and Sweden's Gosta Holmer were adapting the Finnish approach to suit their own environments. The most dramatic record of the era was Rudolf Harbig's 800m time of 1:46.6. It would last until 1955, the longest of any pre-1940 record.

Harbig's times over 400m (46.0) and 800m focused attention on training and this in turn put the spotlight on his Gerschler, his coach. Gerschler became famous as the coach who introduced interval training, based on set recoveries that related to heart rate.

But there was more to the Harbig-Gerschler program than this. Harbig regularly ran between 1:30 and 3 hours on Sundays, he included calisthenics, gym work and light weights in his program, and he paid careful attention to diet and rest. Gerschler later coached the 1952 Olympic 1500m champion Josy Barthel and England's Gordon Pirie, the first man under 13:40 for 5000m and the 1956 Olympic 5000m silver medalist.

Gerschler & Pirie

Training focus changed dramatically in the late 1930's and 1940's. In Sweden Gosta Holmer introduced the concept of fartlek or "speed play," whereby athletes ran uninhibitedly through the glorious Scandanavian forests, surging repeatedly over distances from 50m to 3k and taking as much or as little rest as they felt like.

The immediate impact of this method was to bring greater speed endurance to the 1500m and mile races and the result was that Arne Andersson, Gunder Hägg and Lennart Strand reduced the 1500m record from 3:47.8 to 3:43.0 (a time basically equal to a 4-minute mile) and the mile from 4:06.4 to 4:01.6. In the longer distances, Henry Kälarne and Gunder Hägg took the 3000m record from 8:14.8 to 8:01.6 while Hägg became the first sub-14-minute 5000m runner.

The Post-War Explosion

By 1946 with Europe slowly returning to normal fartlek was coming under challenge from interval training. First espoused by Gerschler in the 1940's with Harbig, it was now extended into the longer distances by the self-coached Emil Zatopek of Czechoslovakia who used prodigious workloads such a 60 x 400m for up to 10 days at a time to lower Hägg's 5000m time to 13:57.7 and, over a 10 year span, to reduce Viljo Heino's 1944 world 10,000m record of 29:35.4 to 28:54.2.

By 1954 interval training was the totally dominant method of training and the race for the first sub-four-minute mile was in full swing. It is now history that the Englishman Roger Bannister, coached by the former Austrian, Franz Stampfl, beat Wes Santee of the United States and Australian John Landy to this mark. Stampfl, who was coaching at Oxford University, also produced Chris Chataway, who dueled with the Russian Vladimir Kuts for the 5000m world record, and Olympic steeplechase gold medalist Chris Brasher.

These records were in turn bettered by Mikhail Iglói's athletes. Iglói, the great Hungarian coach who would later train American athletes such as Bob Schul and Jim Beatty, was responsible for the performances of Sándor Iharos, Lászlo Tábori and István Rózsavölgyi as they brought the 1500m and 5000m towards 3:40 and 13:40.

Iglói was the first coach to develop the idea of workout sets. He initially prescribed workouts such as 3 sets of 10 x 100m, but then moved to training sessions like 2 miles of 15 x 100m shake up with 100m jog; 4 x (4 x 400min) in 64, every 4th 400m run in 60 with 200m jog between reps and 400m between sets; 1200m jog; 14 x 200m fresh swing with 100m jog; 800m jog; 6 x 175m (alternate 2 x 100%, 2 x 90%); 15 x 100m shake down with 100m jog.

Iglói, with American protégés Max Truex and Jim Beatty.

This was the era of big mileages, contrary to the more popular belief that it was started by New Zealand's Arthur Lydiard. Iglói's athletes ran only interval sessions and the reader will note the workout described above totals 24km (15 miles). Workout volumes as high as 23 miles (35 kms) were not uncommon and many weeks were in excess of 120 miles or 180 kilometers. Pirie, Kuts (who set world records of 13:35 for 5000m and 28:30.4 for the 10,000m and won both these events at the 1956 Olympic Games), and Pytor Bolotnikov (the 1960 Olympic 10,000m Champion) all ran in excess of 100 miles per week regularly—most of it on a twice-per-day interval regimen.

The Thunder Down Under

1958 was something of a turning point. The 800m record belonged to Roger Moens of Belgium and interval-trained athletes now held every record up to 10,000m. But the Australians and New Zealanders were coming. John Landy had been a forerunner with his 3:57.9 mile in 1954, a time that was later reduced to 3:57.2 by Derek Ibbotson in 1957. Landy was basically a self-coached interval trained athlete but, at the instigation of the controversial Australian coach Percy Cerutty, he also trained regularly in natural surroundings.

Cerutty, whose most famous pupil was Herb Elliott, preached a doctrine of 60-mile (100-kilometer) weekends of intense fartlek, race simulation surges, sand running, long runs of up to 30 miles, 100-200 mile hikes through mountainous terrain, very heavy weight lifting, sound nutrition, complete aeration of the lungs, power running techniques and mental toughness. In fact it was Cerutty's contention that a 5-minute mile could be achieved on proper breathing and running techniques without any recourse to training by anyone with some natural ability—something he could still do at 55 years of age.

Across the Tasman Sea in New Zealand, Arthur Lydiard took a simpler approach. After extensive research, much of the practical aspects of it demonstrated on himself, he determined that the backbreaking anaerobic training then in vogue could be replaced by establishing an enormous aerobic base, making the transition from the Base Period to the Competition Period by using carefully planned speed and hill repetitions. In many ways Lydiard and Cerutty were the first to really periodize a year. Before them it was basically a matter of changing from one form of interval training to another.

Both Cerutty and Lydiard agreed on approximately six months of Base Training. In Cerutty's case the athlete was instructed to employ long runs, fartlek, hills, resistance work in sand, and heavy weights, and in general develop a high level of all-round strength. The next three months, or Pre-Competition Period, of a Cerutty program advised the athlete to develop speed using wind sprints over 70 to 100m, to develop mental and physical stamina using occasional ultra-long runs and regular visits to the sand hills.

In addition the athlete spent a considerable amount of time running hard repetitions over all types of terrain for the time they hoped to achieve in a race. For example a runner aiming at a 4-minute mile was told to run repetitions of 1:50 for his 800m race and 4:00 for the mile. In the final Competition Period the athlete concentrated on racing, doing only as much training as was necessary to maintain form.

Lydiard was more precise. The entire year's training was based on the date of the athlete's first major race, normally considered to be between 10 days and two weeks before the major race of the season. Lydiard's schedules preceded this race with a two week taper and a 6-10 week Pre-Competition period in which the athlete did moderate amounts of intervals to develop rhythm and enhance aerobic fitness and many controlled pace runs over race distances.

Leading into this race-focused period was a six-week hill running phase aimed at gradually developing speed, power and correct running technique. Prior to the hill work was the core of it all—the 10 weeks of 100 miles (160km) per week.

Many who have not fully studied Lydiard's methods have mistaken this period as something akin to long slow distance. It was not. Two days were run at around 85% effort and one day was assigned a hard fartlek workout. All the other days were composed of 15-22 mile (24-35km) runs at 75-80% effort. Finally if there was time left over before starting the 10-week block the athlete either ran large amounts of steady aerobic miles or did a cross country phase.

Over a whole year the volumes that Lydiard and Cerutty advocated were probably no more than their predecessors, but a much higher percentage of the aerobic training was continuous and at threshold pace. They also favored race-specific repetition running rather than intervals in the Pre-Competition.

Olympic medals and world records to Elliott, Albie Thomas, Dave Power, Murray Halberg, Peter Snell, John Davies, Bill Baillie and Barry Magee turned the world's attention to the Southern Hemisphere.

Developments in America and Europe

The United States was rejuvenating itself and Germany was re-emerging. Iglói had relocated himself in Southern California and coached Jim Beatty, Bob Schul, and others, while the University of Oregon's coach, Bill Bowerman, took the Lydiard

Lydiard coached Murray Halberg to a 5000m Olympic gold medal in 1960.

message back to Oregon and started a dynasty beginning with Bill Dellinger, Dyrol Burleson, and Jim Grelle and culminating with stars like Steve Prefontaine and Albert Salazar.

Meanwhile Ernst Van Aaken, a quiet German doctor, was also advising athletes to reduce their intensity in favor of prolonged steady running and race-specific speed work. Franz Josef Kemper (a former world 1000m record holder), Bodo Tummler (Olympic 1500m bronze medalist in 1968) and Harald Norpoth (Olympic 5000m silver medalist in 1964) were all outstanding athletes who were guided by this philosophy.

Meanwhile Lydiard was having the last say in the era of great coaches. He moved from New Zealand to Mexico and later Finland and both countries soon became very prominent in distance running. Finnish runners such as Lasse Viren, Pekka Vasala, and Juha Vaatainen had spectacular results during the early to mid-1970's.

After that it is fair to there has not been very much new in coaching. Great athletes such as Carlos Lopes, Steve Ovett, Steve Scott, Seb Coe and Steve Cram emerged in the late 70's and 1980's but nearly all were either self-coached or are the lone products of their coaches. On the other hand, just as the influence of coaches such as Gerschler and Holmer influenced Stampfl, Iglói, Cerutty and Lydiard, so too have they influenced future coaches.

For example, Coe's program features many of the elements espoused by Cerutty, e.g., the use of fartlek, running steep 100m hills with slightly uneven surfaces, developing the ability to vary pace at will or as Peter Coe put it, having "repeatable 400m speed," averaging 40-60 miles (70-100km) each week for the 800m-1500m runner, developing a high level of general strength using weights and circuits. In fact the longevity of Coe's 800m record could well be the type of performance Cerutty was alluding to when he said "I am convinced that for future superior performances running alone can never be the answer. Strength per medium of the gymnasium, the barbells, the sand hill, the steep hill (grass or road), or in the cities the flights of stairs in buildings. Anything for hard, sweating continuous effort."

On the other hand, Peter Coe has also stated he uses hills of "up to 800m quite often" while 6 x 800m hill bounding on a slope that is gentle enough for the athlete to also run down at a fast pace was an integral part of Lydiard's program.

A major change in the middle and long distance balance of power was coming however. The signs had been there for some time but the British "Big 3" of Coe, Ovett and Cram plus the American Steve Scott held it at bay until the mid-1980's.

Sebastian Coe

Out Of Africa

The origins of this change dated way back to 10th of July 1954. A Kenyan athlete, Nyandika Maiyoro, led the first mile of a 3-mile race in which Chris Chataway and Fredrick Green set a new world record of 13:32.2. His time at the mile was 4:23, which equates to a 13:09 pace for 3 miles, or about 13:35 for 5000m. Maiyoro then finished fourth in the 3 miles at the 1954 Empire Games and went on to represent Kenya at three Olympics.

Ten years on Wilson Kiprugut won Kenya's first Olympic medal, taking bronze in the 800 behind Peter Snell at the Tokyo Olympics, and in 1965 the great Kip Keino became Kenya's first world record holder, establishing global standards in the 3000m and 5000m. Keino went on to win Olympic gold medals in the 1500m (1968) and 3000m steeplechase (1972). Behind him came Naftali Temu and Amos Biwott, the 1968 Olympic Champions in the 10,000m and 3000m steeplechase.

This era was also highlighted by Abebe Bikila's 1960 and 1964 gold medals in the marathon, and by Mohamed Gammoudi of Tunisia and Mamo Wolde of Ethiopia, each of whom won full sets of Olympic

FIG. 1-2: WOMEN'S MIDDLE AND LONG DISTANCE WORLD RECORD PROGRESSIONS

Women's Events	1940	1965	1990	1997
800m		2:15.3	2:01.1	1:53.28	1:53.28
1500m		4:41.8	4:19.0	3:52.47	3:50.46
3000m			9:44.0	8:22.62	8:06.11
5000m			16:45.0	14:37.33	14:28.09*
10,000m				30:13.74	29:31.78
Marathon		3:40:22	3:19:33	2:21:06	2:21:06

*Wang Junxia ran the last 5k of her 10k world record of 29:31.78 in 14:26!

Kenya's first international distance star, Kip Keino.

distance medals—gold, silver and bronze.

Despite Kenya's Olympic non-participation in 1976 and 1980, Kenyans set world records in 1973 (Ben Jipcho, three times in the steeplechase), 1977 (Samson Kimobwa, 10K), 1978 (Henry Rono in the steeplechase, 3000m, 5000m, and 10k), and 1981 (Rono, 5000). Miruts Yifter of Ethiopia was a double gold medalist at Moscow in 1980. And Filbert Bayi started a brief flurry of Tanzanian middle distance heroics in 1974 with a world 1500 record. He added the mile record the following year.

The world distance scene has changed radically. Currently all the male world records from 1500m to the marathon are in African hands. Kenyans, Moroccans, Algerians and Ethiopians dominate the men's world ranking lists every year while countries like Tanzania, Burundi, Somalia and others have all produced outstanding athletes. No country however can match the Kenyans for sheer depth of talent. They continually win the World Cross Country individual and teams honors and have won a totally disproportionate number of Olympic and World Championship medals in relation to their population.

Why Are They So Good?

Many theories have attributed the success of the Africans—the Kenyans and Ethopians in particular—to factors such as genetics, altitude, heat tolerance (despite the fact most of the best athletes come from climates made temperate by altitude), diet and lifestyle. These facts are important but each new generation of African runners surpasses the performances of the previous generation every three to five years. With the Kenyans, for example, the story is usually one involving an unknown athlete surprising one of the champions, then having his 3-5 years at the top, then being surpassed by another unknown and moving on to the U.S. road circuit. This suggests contempory factors are more important than environmental ones.

The most significant difference between the very best Africans and their European and Asian opponents (as well as the many other fine African athletes we never hear about) is basic speed. The 1500m runners have world class 800m speed, the steeplechasers and 5000m runners have world class 1500m speed, and so on. This aspect is full discussed in Chapter 10.

The Africans are often driven by a fierce nationalism and the belief they can be the best. The easy friendships that develop between athletes from western countries rarely occurs between Africans. National rivalry is often intense. The tradition of other team members joining the gold medalist in a victory lap began with the Kenyans.

Finanical reward is another major motivating factor. Developing athletes have seen the rewards gained by the previous generations and they know winning will guarantee the same rewards for them. When their work ethic is geared to beating their own best athletes, beating the athletes from other countries can be taken for granted.

There are many parallels in the Kenyan approach and Cerutty's methods. The diet is basic, natural and nutritious with an emphasis on unprocessed grains. Weak tea, heavily supplemented with sugar and often milk, is a common drink called "chai." Training camps are a common feature. Like Cerutty's, the training at these camps is rigorous and often done three times a day. Africans go to bed early and so did anyone who wanted to survive a Portsea weekend.

Training conditions also have much in common. At Portsea the surfaces were natural, varied, and the terrain designated for some workouts was often extremely formidable. The younger Africans develop on similar surfaces. Descriptions of the workouts and the terrain on which the work is done at the more publicized Kenyan camps suggest they are equally challenging!

The situation of African athletes having to beat the best in the world in domestic competition is also comparable to Australia and New Zealand of the 1960's. The hardest races were often club races in Melbourne, Adelaide or Auckland. If the athlete could win at home, Americans, Europeans and Africans were considered eminently beatable.* This was the outlook of Australians and New Zealanders at the time—just as the Kenyans feel today. Often their

---

*Co-author Tony Benson remembers contesting a one-mile race early in his career at the Victorian State Championships where the 12-man field contained Ron Clarke (world 5k and 10k record holder), Ralph Doubell (the future 800m record holder), Derek Clayton (the future marathon record holder), Kerry O'Brien (the future 3000m steeplechase record holder), Trevor Vincent (at the time the Commonwealth Games steeplechase champion) and John Coyle (who would run 8:24 for 2 miles).

Former Kenyan national coach John Velzian and co-author Tony Benson. Benson lectured at the IAAF Centre in Nairobi in 1987, 1989 and 1991.

toughest races are the ones at home that select their Kenyan national teams.

A distinction could also be made between the Cerutty/Kenyan approach and the Lydiard/Ethiopian one. The Ethopians appear to execute a Lydiard-type long run more regularly than the Kenyans and they favor methods that lean more to threshold work. The Kenyans appear to include a higher percentage of maximal oxygen uptake workouts. This may explain the relative strengths of the two nations in terms of performance between 800m and the marathon and the fact that their greatest contests are often at 5000m. It may also partly explain the greater longevity of the Ethopians when it comes to "time at the top."

Women's Distance Running

Things are not as clear cut when comes to women's running. Due to a combination of the following factors, the women's record progression below is not nearly as consistent and regular as the men's.
1. The inclusion of a full complement of women's middle and long distance races into the Olympic program did not occur until the 1980's.
2. The International Amateur Athletic Federation (IAAF) has a list of marathon bests dating back to 1926. It also recognized records in the 800m as early as 1922. However, records were not recognized in the 1500m until 1967, the 3000m until 1972 and the 5000m and 10,000m until 1981.
3. Times such as North Korea's Sin Kim Dan's for 800m of 2:01.2 (1961), 1:59.1 (1963) and 1:58.0 (1964) were not recognized because the GANEFO Games were not affiliated with the IAAF.
4. The influence of drugs.

The most consistent feature in the coaching of elite female athletes is that most of the outstanding athletes have been the product of an individual athlete-coach relationship and that the females whose training has most closely approximated the volumes and intensities of their male counterparts have been the most successful. Even the majority of the great athletes from the former Soviet Union and East German eras had individual coaches. The only real exception to this was the success enjoyed by Chinese coach Ma Junren's squad of athletes which included Qu Yunxia, Zhang Lirong, Zhong Huandi, Wang Junxia and Zhang Linli. Those athletes burst onto the world scene in 1993 with a series of incredible performances but only Wang Junxia was able to sustain the effort and claim an Olympic championship in 1996.

After some time in limbo, Ma's troops and others resurfaced in 1997 at the Chinese National Games in October; one women's world record fell (5000), as did several world junior records in the 1500, 5000 and 10,000m.

One final point needs to be made in relation to women's performances and it concerns drugs. Clearly those countries, like the Russians, Romanians, East Germans and Chinese, who have produced outstanding female athletes but have not managed to produce male athletes of anywhere near the same caliber must be suspect in relation to their methods. However it is also reasonable to assume that women can perform within 10% of their male counterparts. An analysis of the records through 1996 shows this is the case in all events except the 5000m. The 800m is 89.80% of the men's record, the 1500m is 89.98%, the 3000m is 90.65%, the 5000m is a low 87.21% (90% would be 14:10), the 10,000m is 90.17% and the marathon is 89.88%.

In the same way that Florence Griffith Joyner's 200m time of 21.34 is now merely 90.5% of Michael Johnson's 19.32 it is possible that what appears to be an unbelievable performance by a female athlete in a middle or long distance race merely means that the men's record is in need of revision- as was true of the men's 200m and is currently true of the men's 100m, because FloJo's 10.49 aside, even a 9.5% improvement on Merelene Ottey's number two all-time 100m time of 10.74 suggests the men should be running 9.71!

In this context 1:53 for 800m, 3:50 for 1500m, 8:06 for 3000m and 29:31 for 10,000m do not look unreasonable and the facts seem to indicate that the women's 5000m is overdue for improvement, even after taking the 1997 improvements into account.

This means that if any record that comes within 10% of a man's is suspect then all such performances become suspect. It is simply not logical to say women can perform within 10% of a man in one middle or long distance event but only 13% in another. Even if drugs have been used it seems that hard work and a close athlete-coach relationship have been very important ingredients.

CHAPTER 2
THE IMPORTANCE OF A COACHING PHILOSOPHY

An easily observable characteristic of all great coaches is that they have developed a personal philosophy upon which to base their training schedules. Put another way, a coach without a philosophy is like an author without a theme—the material may be interesting but the ending will be inconclusive.

This manual believes:
- a program must develop a healthy athlete, one who is fit for life as well as for competition, because the unhealthy athlete is prone to regular injury and illness,
- the only way to maximize an athlete's potential is to establish an extensive aerobic base so the muscular, skeletal, ventilatory and circulatory systems are strong enough to withstand the rigors that the training sessions oriented toward anaerobic competition will impose on the athlete, and
- speed development is essential and must be incorporated into the athlete's program on a year-round basis.

The philosophy of this manual recommends duplicating the active lifestyle of America, Australia and New Zealand of the 1960's or of current-day Africa by encouraging the athlete to develop a huge aerobic capacity, adequate muscular and skeletal strength, and a high level of pure speed before introducing significant amounts of stressful anaerobic work into their programs.

The manual also stresses that the athlete and coach must:
- work together to set measurable, realistic and tangible long-, medium- and short-term goals,
- ensure they integrate the appropriate training volumes and intensities into a year-long training cycle that centers on achieving specific annual mileage goals that will ultimately become appropriate to their event, as well as achieving specific annual training and competitive cross country & track goals, and
- have enough confidence in themselves, both individually and as a team, to continue the process from year to year, following a regimen of progressively increased workloads, until the athlete's potential has been accomplished or the athlete's goals have been satisfied.

The theory of general adaptation is well known to all coaches. Arthur Lydiard has often quoted the example of Milo, the Greek strongman, who could lift a full grown bull overhead—a feat of strength no other athlete could emulate—because he had been lifting the animal every day since it was a newborn calf. Lydiard's point was that, like Milo, his athletes were superior because, over time, they adapted to the stress of an endurance training program no one of that era thought possible.

The goal of all athletes and coaches must be to adhere to the principles of general and specific adaptation so that the athlete not only performs well in team-oriented competition but that he or she finish their careers knowing they maximized their potential and performed at their best when it counted the most. Successful coaches regularly achieve the former, but *great* coaches get it *all* right. We hope *Run With The Best* will help every athlete and coach get it all right!

CHAPTER 3
THE *RUN WITH THE BEST* PROGRAM

When an athlete retires it is possible to quantify all the aspects of his training: the number of years in the sport, the number of miles/kilometers run in his first and last year—and in all the years in between, total mileage, the amount of aerobic, anaerobic and speed work done, the number of competitions, competition results in terms of placings and times, the periodization of the training throughout his career, and so on. If enough athletes are studied, the factors common to producing successful outcomes can be identified. The purpose of Chapter 1 was to help the coach identify these factors.

Science can also contribute to the coaching process, but it is the same role played by the artist's tools. The scientist and the laboratory technician may be able to assist the process—but the coach must be capable of the same vision as the artist. He must "see" the athlete's career in its entirety from day one, in the same way a sculptor has a vision of his work before chisel touches stone.

A training program is guided initially by two considerations and constructed on the basis of eight fundamentals.

The two considerations are:
- The total volume of running the athlete must achieve before he or she can perform at his/her best.
- The total volume of running the athlete has already achieved.

The eight fundamentals are:
- The total volume of running the athlete will plan to achieve in the current year.
- The periodization of the year.
- The volume to be achieved in each of the major periods.
- The volume to be achieved in each of the various phases.
- The volume to achieved in each week of each phase.
- The type of workout the coach will include in each period, phase and week of the year.
- The way these workouts may be integrated into each period, phase and week of the year.
- The balance between endurance, strength and speed for a specific event.

The Total Volume Of Running The Athlete Must Achieve To Perform At His Best

Regardless of how much talent an athlete has he will not perform maximally unless he has accumulated a certain minimum volume of training.

Why are African runners (or European cyclists and swimmers from America and Australia) currently so good? Basically because they begin these activities at a very early age and by the time the athlete reaches 16 or 17 he or she has accumulated perhaps 3000 to 4000 hours of mostly aerobic training.

Run With The Best believes that these minimum volumes can be quantified (see Fig. 3-1 below).

These volumes may sound excessive, but consider an African athlete who runs 10 to 20 kilometers daily for 5 days per week for 40 weeks of a school year and supplements this with rounding up the family herds and playing games normal to school children. A mere 10 kilometers per day for only 5 days is 50km per week which is 2500km per year and 25,000km over 10 years, yet many Kenyan athletes and coaches often talk of children covering in excess of 100km per week during these years!

Studies that catalog the years individual athletes take to reach the top and equate the estimated volumes they run each year will confirm the volumes listed in the previous paragraph are probably conservative, especially if the athlete has run his miles or kilometers faster. Other anecdotal evidence, examples of which are listed below, is also readily available.

FIGURE 3-1: MINIMUM VOLUMES NECESSARY FOR MAXIMUM PERFORMANCE

800m	1,500 hours (@ 8:00/mi or 5:00/km)	12,000 miles	19,000km
1500m	2,000 hours (@ 8:00/mi or 5:00/km)	15,000 miles	24,000km
3000m S/C	3,000 hours (@ 7:30/mi or 4:39/km)	24,000 miles	39,000km
5000m	3,000 hours (@ 7:30/mi or 4:39/km)	24,000 miles	39,000km
10,000m	3,500 hours (@ 7:00/mi or 4:21/km)	30,000 miles	50,000km
Marathon	3,500 hours (@ 7:00/mi or 4:21/km)	30,000 miles	50,000km

- The relationship between their incredibly active childhoods and the ability of the African athletes to run world class times at extremely early ages has already been mentioned.
- It seems no coincidence that as American and Australian lifestyles have become steadily less active since the 1960's, no American high school athlete has broken 4 minutes for the mile since Jim Ryun, Marty Liquori and Tim Danielson in the 60's. And there are no more teenage prodigies like Gerry Lindgren or Steve Prefontaine. Equally, Australia's last world junior middle or long distance world record holders were Ron Clarke and Herb Elliott, four decades ago.
- The reason talented 400m and 800m runners are able to perform at a high level at relatively young ages is because they can reach their optimum annual volumes more quickly than longer distance runners.
- An increasing number of athletes are now producing personal bests and incredible performances in their late 20's and early to mid-30's. Some like Merlene Ottey and Carlos Lopes have recorded personal bests in their late 30's.

Had these athletes retired in their early to mid-20's, as many did years ago, their personal bests would not have been as impressive as they currently are. As most elite athletes follow a similar program throughout their careers and many have had only one or two coaches, it is reasonable to believe that the accumulated volume of work, be it mileage, weights, drills, starts, etc. is a very significant factor in an athlete's improvement.

Athletes who never achieve sufficient training volumes will never achieve their potential!

The Total Running Volume The Athlete Has Already Achieved

The first thing a *Run With The Best* program focuses on is how to get an athlete from the volume he currently has to the accumulated volume he should have. The athlete's current volume is the sum total of all he has accumulated since the ages of seven or eight. This can only be estimated, but a volume of 600 miles or 1000km per year would be reasonable for an active child of today.

For example, a 14-year-old who is just beginning his or her athletic career has probably accumulated about 5000 miles (8000km), while an athlete of the same age would have accumulated this amount of "play" mileage, plus whatever he has done in training.

A more accurate picture of the novice athlete's volume will emerge from the discussions between the athlete and coach.

Athletes who have been competing for a number of years should have a much better idea of how much running they have done.

Worksheet No. 1

The coach is asked to complete Worksheet 1 below by entering the athlete's name, training age in years (e.g., if the athlete has been training for one year enter "1" under training age) and enter an estimate of his accumulated volume to date.

The lifetime volume could be based on an estimate as simple as 30 minutes to one hour per day of continuous or largely continuous activity, e.g., playing soccer, football, basketball, tennis, etc. At an average of, say, 2:30 hours to 5 hours per week, it equals 175 hours per year. If the athlete is, say, 15 years of age and has been active since he was seven years of age it means that boy or girl has accumulated 1400 hours of training.

NOTE: There are 10 worksheets in this chapter. Extra sets of worksheets are provided in the back of the book for your convenience. These of course may be photocopied and used for other athletes or for your team as a whole.

WORKSHEET 1

Name:	Training Age: Yrs
Estimated Accumulated Lifetime Volume (Miles/Kms/Hours)	

FIGURE 3-2: OPTIMAL ANNUAL TRAINING VOLUMES

800m	1,800-2,400 miles	3,000-4,000km
1500m	2,400-3,000 miles	4,000-5,000km
3000m S/C	3,300-4,000 miles	5,500-6,500km
5000m	3,300-4,000 miles	5,500-6,500km
10,000m	4,000-5,000 miles	6,500-8,000kn
Marathon	4,000-5,000 miles	6,500-8,000kn

FIGURE 3-3: PLAN FOR A SAMPLE 15-YEAR-OLD BEGINNER

Our Athlete (age 15).
Estimated accumulated play volume of 5,000 miles (8,000km). No training volume.

Age	Volume	Annual Increment	Accumulating Volume
5-14 yrs. An average of 10 miles/16km per wk. since 5 years of age			5,000 miles / 8,000km
15 yrs	600 miles / 1,000km		5,600 miles / 9,000km
16 yrs	900 miles / 1,500km	300 miles / 500km	6,500 miles / 10,500km
17 yrs	1,350 miles / 2,200km	450 miles / 700km	7,850 miles / 12,700km
18 yrs	1,950 miles / 3,150km	600 miles / 1000km	9,800 miles / 15,850km

The Total Volume Of Running For The Current Year

Deciding on the annual volume is important for three reasons. It provides the basis for deciding how much running should be done during each period of training and, by extension, how much the athlete should aim to do each week. If the weekly volume is known it provides the coach with a means to decide how much of the workload should be assigned as aerobic, anaerobic and speed in content. The annual volume forms part of the athlete's total running base, the importance of which has already been discussed.

Run With The Best research suggests there are optimum *annual* volumes for each event (see Fig. 3-2 below).

Regardless of the athlete's event, his or her annual training plan must include an annual mileage plan.

The experienced middle or long distance runner will probably be running somewhere between 2000 and 5000 miles (3000-8000km). Beginners will have to start somewhere, and, unless the coach knows the athlete intimately, a reasonable volume to start a 14- or 15-year-old athlete with would be about 600 miles or 1000 kilometers. Based on 40 weeks this equates to 15 miles or 25km per week and can comfortably be achieved on three or four days training. Older beginners would have to start at higher mileages because they have fewer years to reach their optimum volumes.

Run With The Best suggests any volume assigned to a beginner must form part of the long-term plan to get the athlete to 12,000 miles or 19,000km without any injuries as quickly as possible. Getting there is not easy and may not happen at all if it is not planned. Study the following example and Fig. 3-3 closely.

The athlete, now nearly 19, started training at 15 with an estimated volume of 5000 miles or 8000km of play mileage already accumulated. Now in his 19th year, he has run an additional 4,800 miles or 7,850km of training mileage and totaled 9,800 miles (15,850km) or 1300 to 1400 hours. The athlete is now at the point where he will surpass the required 800m volume of 12,000 miles or 19,000km (1500 hours) in the following year!

The annual volume now can be stabilized at the required 1,800-2,400 miles (3,000-4,000km)—or 270 to 320 hours—per year if the athlete has demonstrated he has enough speed at 400m to run the middle distances, e.g., 47.0 to 49.0 (men) or 55.0 to 57.0 (women) for collegiate or national-level seniors, or 44.5-47.5 and 51.5-54.5 for aspiring internationals.

The training goal will be to target volumes at the higher end of the 800m or 1500m range (see Fig. 3-2) while maintaining 400m speed because the majority of middle distance champions and record holders of the modern era have been more competitive at 1500m than they were at 400m (see Fig. 3-4 below).

At the top end, a study of Olympic champions and world record holders shows stamina is vital to

FIGURE 3-4: PLAN FOR THE SAMPLE RUNNER AT AGE 19

Our Athlete (age 20).
He/she appears to be a 5000m runner, so the base building process continues.

Age	Volume	Annual Increment	Accumulating Volume
7-19 yrs			12,350 miles / 20,000km
19 yrs	2550 miles/4150km	600 miles/1000km	9,800 miles/15,850km
20 yrs	3150 miles / 5100km	600 miles / 1000km	15,500 miles / 25,100km
21 yrs	3650 miles / 5900km	500 miles / 800km	19,150 miles / 31,100km
22 yrs	4150 miles / 6700km	400 miles / 650km	23,300 miles / 37,700km
23 yrs	4450 miles / 7150km	300 miles / 500km	27,750 miles / 44,850km
24 yrs	4450 miles / 7150km	No increase	32,200 miles / 52,000km

surviving the necessary preliminary rounds so the athlete enters the final with a chance of winning. This is true at all levels of competition.

If the athletes's performances indicate he may be better suited to the longer distances, he would continue to increase his mileage as per Fig. 3-4. He would run 3,650 miles in his 21st year, 4,150 miles in his 22nd year, and 4,450 miles in his 23rd year. If the coach believes his athlete is best suited to the 5k/10k he would stabilize the athlete's annual volume at around 4000-4500 miles, as indicated in Fig. 3-2.

During the years the athlete was building towards his or her required accumulated volume for the 5000m (or steeplechase), the athlete should have also been racing regularly at 800m and 1500m because all distance runners need speed over 800m and 1500m and the world's best distance runners are currently able to run 1500m in 3:29-3:32.

Our athlete's best years at 5000m and 10,000m will come at or after 25, as he or she will have been on a stable volume for two to three years and the intensity would have been building to the required level.

The same is true of the marathon. The necessary base kilometers have been accumulated by the end of the athlete's 24th year and speed should be of a high standard due to the racing done over every distance from 800m to 10000m in the preceding years. Before running the marathon however the athlete should consider continuing to race seriously at 5000m and 10,000m for one to two more years while increasing annual volume to 4700 to 5000 miles (7500-8000km).

Our athlete's best years will be from 27 on. Maybe even at 37, like Carlos Lopes!

Worksheet No. 2

The coach is asked to enter the following information into Worksheet 2.
1. the athlete's training age and estimated accumulated volume (from Worksheet 1),
2. the current year, and
3. the athlete's planned volume for the coming annualized year.

Complete this exercise before moving to the next section.

The planned volume should be considered very carefully. An allowance must be made for all the weeks that the athlete will run below the annual weekly average volume. For example if the annual plan was set at 4500 miles/km the athlete must be able to average around 100 miles/km for at least 30 weeks in order to be able to run between 60 and 85 miles/km during recovery and/or weeks immediately before or after major races.

If the coach is unsure about what volumes to prescribe it is worth studying Fig. 3-8 and 3-9 later in this chapter. Both charts illustrate the range of weekly volumes required to achieved a stated annual volume target.

Worksheet No. 3

The coach is asked to complete Worksheet 3 below before moving on to the next section. Enter the athlete's total volume prior to 1998 and then list the athlete's estimated progressive target volumes for the next 3-5 years. For example, if the athlete is 15 years old and if

WORKSHEET 2

Name:	Training Age: Yrs	Year:
Estimated Accumulated Lifetime Volume (Miles/Kms/Hours)		
Planned Volume for the Current Year (Miles/Kms/Hours		

WORKSHEET 3

Year	Annual Total Mi/Km/Hr	Progressive Total Mi/Km/Hr	Year	Annual Total Mi/Km/Hr	Progressive Total Mi/Km/Hr
Pre-1998	1998		2004		
1999			2005		
2000			2006		
2001			2007		
2002			2008		
2003			2009		
			2010		

FIGURE 3-5: BASIC ANNUAL PLAN FOR AN EXPERIENCED RUNNER.

Base Period 24-30 weeks			Pre- Competition Period 8-10 weeks		Competition Period 4-12 weeks	
Phase I 8-10 wks	Phase II 8-10 wks	Phase III 8-10 wks	Phase I 4-5 wks	Phase II 4-5 wks	Phase I 4-5 wks	Phase II 4-8 wks

WORKSHEET 4

Name:						
Base Period			Pre- Competition Period		Competition Period	
No of Weeks:			No of Weeks:		No of Weeks:	
Phase I	Phase II	Phase III	Phase I	Phase II	Phase I	Phase II
Wks:	Wks:	Wks:	Wks:	Wks:	Wks:	Wks:

training began in 1998, then the coach enters, say, 8,000km in the pre-1998 row in the "Progressive Total" column and perhaps 1000 in the 1998 row, 1500 in the 1999 row, 2200 in the 2000 row, and so on.

The Periodization Of The Year

Run with the Best suggests the following basic plan as a starting point to an experienced individual's annual plan (see Fig. 3-5 next page).

The plan for the beginner may be as simple as starting a program, accumulating some volume, introducing some speed work and general body conditioning, doing a few competitions to maintain interest and basically getting the athlete into a routine.

A coach who envisages that the athlete will need to train twice or three times per day sometime in the future could even consider introducing additional activities such as swimming or cycling to begin the process of establishing the routine. Scheduling times for stretching and massage should also be considered.

Worksheet No. 4

The coach is asked to enter the number of weeks he plans to devote to training during each of the three main periods and seven main phases of the coming track & field year (Worksheet 4).

Complete this exercise before moving to the next section.

The Volume To Be Achieved In Each Of The Major Periods

It is obvious that an athlete is not going to train the same year-round and it also obvious that athletes will do more volume in the Base Training Period than in the Pre-Competition or Competition Period.

Middle distance runners will tend to do a greater percentage of their annual volume in the Base Period than will the long distance runner. For example based on the percentages in the Fig. 3-6 below the middle distance runner would probably run 63.5-65% of the volume in the Base Period and 15-16.5% in the Competition Period. The distance runner (and others, like triathletes) would probably work to a formula of 62-63.5% of volume in the Base Period and 16.5-18% in the Competition Period. Both types of athlete should do 20% of their volume in the Pre-Competition Period.

FIGURE 3-6: VOLUME PERCENTAGES BY PERIOD

Base Period	Pre-Competition Period	Competition Period
62-65%	20%	15-18%

Worksheet No. 5

The coach is asked to reenter information already provided in previous Worksheets, including the planned annual volume. Then insert the percentage of total volume planned for the Base Period, the Pre-Competition Period and the Competition Period during the coming track & field year into the appropriate box in Worksheet 5. Finally enter a hard copy of the planned volume in hours, miles or kilometers. This is very important. The coach must have an overall plan of how much work is expected of the

WORKSHEET 5

Name:	Training Age:	Yrs	Year:
Planned Annual Volume (Hours/Miles/Kms)			

Base Period	Pre-Competition Period	Competition Period
As a % of total volume	As a % of total volume	As a % of total volume
in Hours, Miles or Kilometers	In Hours, Miles or Kilometers	In Hours, Miles or Kilometers

athlete in each period.

Complete this exercise before moving to the next section.

The Volume To Be Achieved In Each Of The Various Phases

Phase I will have the lowest volume and intensity of the three base period phases because the athlete is just coming out of the post season transition. The volume will be higher in Phase II but an allowance for cross country racing must be made. Volume and intensity will be at its highest in Phase III. This practice is the same as Lydiard's positioning of his 10-week aerobic phase and is similar to the timing of the Kenyan training camps prior to their European campaigns.

Volume will decrease slightly in Phase I of the Pre-Competition Period but intensity will continue to rise. Intensity in Phase II of the Pre-Competition Period should be marginally than it was in Phase I but the both general volume and the volume of the intense workouts should decrease. The duration of the long run must be maintained.

Volume and intensity will decrease further as

FIGURE 3-7: VOLUME PERCENTAGES BY PHASE

Base Period			Pre- Competition Period		Competition Period	
Phase I	Phase II	Phase III	Phase I	Phase II	Phase I	Phase II
18-20%	21-22%	22-23%	10-11%	9-10%	7-9%	7-9%

WORKSHEET 6

Name:	Training Age:	Yrs	Year:
Planned Volume			(Hours/Miles/Kms)

Base Period	Pre-Competition Period	Competition Period
% (Hr:Mi:Km) =	% (Hr:Mi:Km) =	% (Hr:Mi:Km) =
Volume =	Volume =	Volume =

Phase I (%)	Phase II (%)	Phase III (%)	Phase I (%)	Phase II (%)	Phase I (%)	Phase II (%)

Phase I (Hr/Mi/Km)	Phase II (Hr/Mi/Km)	Phase III (Hr/Mi/Km)	Phase I (Hr/Mi/Km)	Phase II (Hr/Mi/Km)	Phase I (Hr/Mi/Km)	Phase II (Hr/Mi/Km)

the athlete enters the Competition Period because the major race should be scheduled between the fourth and sixth weeks of the Competition Period. The volume and intensity of Phase II of the Competition Period will vary significantly according to the athlete's program. Elite athletes may continue to compete if there is competition available; high school, college or club athletes may do one or two more local events or go immediately into recovery and transition (see Fig. 3-7 below—Volume Percentages by Phase).

Worksheet No. 6

The coach is asked to continue building an annual plan by reentering the information he inserted into Worksheet 5 and then to enter the volume planned for his athlete during each of the seven main phases during the coming track & field year. Enter the information as both a percentage of the annual volume and as hard copy, i.e., in hours, miles or kilometers in Worksheet 6.

With the completion of Worksheet 6. the coach and athlete will now have a very clear idea of the structure of their annualized year.

The Volume To Be Achieved In Each Week Of Each Phase

The weekly volumes are related to the phase volumes. Study the next two figures carefully. The Target 3000 chart (Fig. 3-8) summarizes the information given earlier and provides the reader with an example of how to distribute an annual volume of 3000 miles or kilometers for a middle distance runner. If the volume is 3000km (2000 miles) the athlete is probably a 400m/800m type. If the volume is 3000 miles (5000km) the athlete would be a 1500m runner.

The Target 4500 chart (Fig. 3-9) provides an example more appropriate to a distance runner. If the volume is 4500 miles the athlete is probably a 5000m or 10,000m runner. If the volume is 4500km the athlete is either a 1500m runner or a future distance runner still in the volume-building stage.

Both charts show variations in the weekly volumes. This allows for the application of the hard/easy principles and gives the athlete some control over his or her training. More or less weekly variation may be used if desired. The important thing is that the volume target for each period is achieved. Beside each weekly volume is a suggested weekly long run distance based on the principle of this run being 20-30% of the week's volume. The longer this run the less has to be done during the week.

If these charts are to be set out in hours, *Run With The Best* recommends national-class (or better) runners work to hours as follows: 400/800m runners use 7:15-8:00 per mile (4:30-5:00 per km), 800/1500m runners use 6:30-7:15 per mile (4:00-4:30 per km) and the longer distance athletes use 5:45-6:30

FIGURE 3-8: APPORTIONING THE VOLUMES FOR THE DISTANCE RUNNER—TARGET 3000

This chart illustrates one method of distributing volume and uses an annual volume of 3000 miles/kilometers as an example.

Annual Target | 3000 | **Kilometers or Miles**

Base Period 1950 Kms/Miles (60% of Time & 65% of Volume)							Pre-Competition Period 600 Kms/Miles (20% of Time & 20% of Volume)						Competition Period 450 Kms/Miles (20% of Time & 15% of Volume)					
Phase I 19% volume 570 Km/Mi			Phase II 22% Volume 660 Km/Mi			Phase III 24% Volume 720 Km/Mi			Phase I 10.5% Volume 315 Km/Mi			Phase II 9.5% Volume 285 Km/Mi			Phase I 8% Volume 240 Km/Mi			Phase II 7% Volume 210 Km/Mi		
Week No	Week's Total	Long Run	Week No	Week's Total	Long Run	Week No	Week's Total	Long Run	Week No	Week's Total	Long Run	Week No	Week's Total	Long Run	Week No	Week's Total	Long Run	Week No	Week's Total	Long Run
	Km/Mi	(+/- 10%)		Km/Mi	(+/- 10%)		Km/Mi	(+/- 10%)		Km/Mi	(+/- 10%)		Km/Mi	(+/- 10%)		Km/Mi	(+/- 10%)		Km/Mi	(+/- 10%)
1	30	7	11	45	15	21	45	10	31	45	11	36	60	14	41	60	12	46	42	9
2	45	10	12	70	15	22	70	15	32	90	17	37	45	11	42	60	14	47	42	9
3	75	17	13	60	14	23	90	17	33	75	15	38	75	14	43	45	10	48	42	9
4	45	10	14	85	16	24	70	14	34	45	11	39	60	14	44	45	10	49	42	9
5	75	15	15	70	15	25	90	17	35	60	14	40	45	11	45	30	7	50	42	9
6	60	14	16	60	14	26	70	17										51	Rest	0
7	75	15	17	90	16	27	60	14										52	Rest	0
8	60	14	18	75	15	28	75	15												
9	45	15	19	60	14	29	90	17				The peak races should be planned for between weeks 42 and 48 depending on post-major race competition commitments.					
10	60	16	20	45	14	30	60	15			
	570			**660**			**720**			**315**			**285**			**240**			**210**	

*In this example the athlete covers 65% of the annual volume in the Base Period, 20% of volume in the Pre-Competition Period and 15% of total volume in the Competition Period
*The chart is appropiate for developing athletes and elite middle distance runners.
*3000km=400/800m-type volume. 3000 mile=elite 10k/Marathon type.

28

FIGURE 3-9: APPORTIONING THE VOLUMES FOR THE DISTANCE RUNNER—TARGET 4500

This chart illustrates one method of distributing volume and uses an annual volume of 4500 miles/kilometres as an example.

Annual Target 4500 Kilometers or Miles

Base Period 2925 Kms/Miles (60% of Time & 62.2% of Volume)									Pre-Competition Period 900 Kms/Miles (20% of Time & 20% of Volume)						Competition Period 675 Kms/Miles (20% of Time & 17.8% of Volume)					
Phase I 17.5% volume 790 Km/Mi			Phase II 21.25% Volume 990 Km/Mi			Phase III 23.75% Volume 1020 Km/Mi			Phase I 10.5% Volume 460 Km/Mi			Phase II 9.5% Volume 400 Km/Mi			Phase I 9% Volume 400 Km/Mi			Phase II 8.5% Volume 400 Km/Mi		
Week No	Week's Total	Long Run	Week No	Week's Total	Long Run	Week No	Week's Total	Long Run	Week No	Week's Total	Long Run	Week No	Week's Total	Long Run	Week No	Week's Total	Long Run	Week No	Week's Total	Long Run
	Km/Mi (+/- 10%)			Km/Mi (+/- 10%)			Km/Mi (+/- 10%)			Km/Mi (+/- 10%)			Km/Mi (+/- 10%)			Km/Mi (+/- 10%)			Km/Mi (+/- 10%)	
1	45	10	11	90	23	21	60	12	31	80	17	36	100	20	41	100	20	46	80	18
2	65	15	12	110	23	22	110	22	32	110	25	37	80	17	42	90	20	47	80	18
3	85	20	13	70	20	23	120	25	33	110	23	38	100	20	43	90	15	48	80	18
4	65	15	14	110	22	24	90	20	34	70	17	39	90	20	44	70	18	49	80	18
5	90	20	15	120	23	25	120	25	35	90	20	40	70	17	45	50	15	50	80	18
6	75	18	16	90	20	26	110	22										51	Rest	0
7	100	20	17	120	22	27	90	20										52	Rest	0
8	90	20	18	120	22	28	110	22	The peak races should be planned for between weeks 42 and 48 depending on post-major race competition commitments.										
9	100	20	19	90	20	29	120	25											
10	75	18	20	70	21	30	90	20											
	790			990			1020			460			440			400			400	

*In this example the athlete covers 62.2% of the annual volume in the Base Period, 20% of volume in the Pre-Competition Period and 17.8% of total volume in the Competition Period
*4500 miles = elite 5k/10k runners.   4500 kms = elite middle distance runners.
*If the volume targeted is less than 3000 miles or 5000km the athlete would be a middle distance runner and a more appropriate breakdown might be Base Period 65%, Pre-Competition Period 20% and Competition Period 15%.

per mile (3:30-4:00 per km). The paces for other athletes may be determined by referring to Fig. 6-1 at the end of Chapter 6 (Major Aerobic Training Paces).

By developing charts such as Figs. 3-8 and 3-9, both the athlete and the coach know exactly what is expected on every week of the year and can adjust their plans in order to achieve the goal volumes.

These figures should not be adhered to if injury, illness or any other setbacks occur. However if the plan is well conceived there should not be too much variation and anything more than one minor illness and/or injury may well be a sign that the program is too demanding for the athlete.

Should a coach want to raise the annual volume from 3000 to, say, 3250 miles/km or lower it to 2750

WORKSHEET 7

Base Period			Pre-Competition Period		Competition Period	
Phase I (Miles or Kms)	Phase II (Miles or Kms)	Phase III (Miles or Kms)	Phase I (Miles or Kms)	Phase II (Miles or Kms)	Phase I (Miles or Kms)	Phase II (Miles or Kms)
Weeks 1-10	Weeks 11-20	Weeks 21-30	Weeks 31-35	Weeks 36-40	Weeks 41-45	Weeks 46-50
1.	11.	21.	31.	36.	41.	46.
2.	12.	22.	32.	37.	42.	47.
3.	13.	23.	33.	38.	43.	48.
4.	14.	24.	34.	39.	44.	49.
5.	15.	25.	35.	40.	45.	50.
6.	16.	26.	Total=	Total=	Total=	Total=
7.	17.	27.				
8.	18.	28.				
9.	19.	29.				
10.	20.	30.				
Total=	Total=	Total=				

WORKSHEET 8

Name:						
\multicolumn{3}{c}{Base Period}	\multicolumn{2}{c}{Pre-Competition Period}	\multicolumn{2}{c}{Competition Period}
Phase I	Phase II	Phase III	Phase I	Phase II	Phase I	Phase II
1.	11.	21.	31.	36.	41.	46.
2.	12.	22.	32.	37.	42.	47.
3.	13.	23.	33.	38.	43.	48.
4.	14.	24.	34.	39.	44.	49.
5.	15.	25.	35.	40.	45.	50.
6.	16.	26.				
7.	17.	27.				
8.	18.	28.				
9.	19.	29.				
10.	20.	30.				

miles/km, all that is necessary is the addition or subtraction of 5 miles/km per week. Adding or subtracting 10 miles/km per week would result in totals of 3500 miles/km or 2500 miles/km. Other target volumes can be achieved using the same method.

Finally, as mentioned earlier the "Overload/Recovery" (or Hard/Easy) principle is all too often applied only to days. It should also be applied to weeks. The coach should consider 2-3 weeks hard followed by 1-2 weeks easier or a 4-week cycle of moderate-hard-moderate-easy weeks. It can also be quite effective to schedule a high-volume week as an "easy" week and a low-volume "hard" week instead of just following the traditional strategy of maintaining or slightly decreasing volume and increasing intensity to create a "hard" week.

The advantage of running a range of mileage is that it offers the athlete the chance to recover when he or she is doing a low mileage or prepare for higher mileages when these are scheduled.

Worksheet No. 7

The coach is asked to enter the planned weekly volume for the three main periods and the seven main phases during the coming year into Worksheet 7.

Complete this exercise before moving to the next section. Be sure the total volume for each phase equals what was planned in Worksheet 6!

The athlete and coach now have a very detailed annual plan.

The next thing the athlete and/or coach must do is to determine the length of the weekly long run.

For convenience as much as anything else most athletes will run the same distance every week. The main reason for doing this is that the athlete usually runs a similar course and quite often runs as part of a group. A good guide to establishing the length of the long run is to use 20-30% of the weekly volume.

Ideally the long run, particularly during the Base Period, should be about two hours. Serious middle distance runners may do a little less on occasion provided they know they have the *capacity* to run for at least two hours if they wished to do so, while marathon runners will have to include runs of up to three hours fairly regularly.

Worksheet No. 8

The coach is asked to highlight the weeks of major races during the coming track & field year and to enter the distance of the athlete's weekly

FIGURE 3-10: TYPES OF AEROBIC AND ANAEROBIC WORKOUTS

The five types of aerobic workout are:		**The three types of anaerobic workout are:**	
Aerobic Recovery or Endurance-1	(End-1)	Anaerobic Power or Lactic Acid-1	(Lat-1)
Aerobic Conditioning or Endurance-2	(End-2)	Lactic Acid Tolerance or Lactic Acid-2	(Lat-2)
Lactate Threshold or Endurance-3	(End-3)	Speed & Power or Lactic Acid-3	(Lat-3)
Aerobic Power or Endurance-4	(End-4)		
Maximal Oxygen Uptake or Endurance-5	(End-5)		

WORKSHEET 9

Training Component	Abbreviation
Aerobic Recovery	End-1
Aerobic Conditioning	End-1
Lactate Threshold	End-3
Aerobic Power	End-4
Maximal Oxygen Uptake	End-5
Anaerobic Power	Lat-1
Lactic Acid Tolerance	Lat-2
Speed & Power	Lat-3

long run into Worksheet 8 for each week of the year.

Complete this exercise before moving to the next section.

Congratulations! You have a periodized structure for the entire year!

All that remains to be done is to decide on the daily workouts. This will require careful consideration but some general principles will apply. The workouts selected must be relevant to the period and phase of the year. For example the type of workout scheduled on any given day during Phase I of the Base Period will be different in emphasis to Phase II of the Pre-Competition Period or Phase I of the Competition Period. On the other hand while the composition of workouts might vary, the focus of a particular day may be the same year-round. For example, Monday may always have a speed focus.

The Type Of Workout For Each Period, Phase And Week Of The Year

There are eight types of workout. Five are in the aerobic zone and three in the anaerobic zones.

Each of the workouts listed in Fig. 3-10 below

FIGURE 3-11: DISTRIBUTION BY TYPE OF WORKOUT

Day		Base Period	Pre-Competition Period	Competition Period
Monday	(am) (pm)	End-1 Lat-3	End-1 End-1 including strides	End-1 End-1 including strides
Tuesday	(am) (pm)	End-2 End-3	End-1 End-4 or End-5	End-1 Lat-1 or Lat-2
Wednesday	(am) (pm)	End-1 End-2	End-1 End-2	End-1 End-1
Thursday	(am) (pm)	End-2 End-4 or Lat-1	End-1 End-5 or Lat-1	End-1 End-1 including strides
Friday	(am) (pm)	End-1 End-1	End-1 End-1	End-1 End-1
Saturday	(am) (pm)	End-1 End-5 Hills or Race	End-1 Hills, Race or Simulation	End-1 Race or Simulation
Sunday	(am)	Long Run (End-2)	Long Run (End-2)	Long Run (End-2)

has special benefits to the athlete although they are sometimes more appropriate to one period or phase than to others. Some types of workout will also be more appropriate to specific events than to others. For example, lactate threshold workouts are more appropriate to the Base Period than to the Competition Period and lactic acid tolerance workouts are best scheduled for the mid- to late weeks of the Pre-Competition Period.

The characteristics of each type of workout are summarized in Chapter 5 and more detailed descriptions, together with specific examples, may be found in Chapters 6, 7, 25, and 26.

Worksheet No. 9

The reader is asked to read on through *Run With The Best*, then, after reviewing Chapters 5, 6, 7, 25, and 26, return to this page and write in one workout he or she does under each of the aerobic and anaerobic components listed above (Worksheet 9).

Integrating These Workouts Into Each Period, Phase And Week Of The Year

Each type of workout mentioned in Fig. 3-10 is essential to an athlete's development. The number of times any particular type of workout will be used will vary according to the needs of the athlete. Athletes with excellent speed but no stamina, for example, need to concentrate on aerobic conditioning and lactate threshold training, regardless of their actual event.

The specific needs of the event must also be considered when deciding when to schedule a particular type of workout into the program because it is obvious the needs of the middle distance runner and the long distance runner are quite different, despite the similarities that may be evident in certain periods and phases (see Fig. 3-11 on previous page).

Although the example outlined in Fig. 3-11 is a general one the reader will note a continuity of focus on many days. Monday is always speed-oriented. Saturday is nearly always race-oriented. The long run is a year-round fixture on Sundays. Most morning running is recovery-oriented, except for Tuesday and Thursday in the Base Period. Friday is a recovery day, and so on.

The workouts however may vary significantly. Monday would be the best example of this. During early Base Period the athlete might be running 10 x 100m accelerations after the drills. In the late Pre-Competition Period the workout might be 2 or 3 sets of 150m - 120m - 90m, all at near-maximum speed. In the Competition Period the workout might be 4 x 200m at 400m tempo.

Worksheet No. 10

Prior to completing Worksheet 9, it was suggested that the coach should read on through Chapters 5, 6, 7, 25, and 26. If the coach has done that and completed Worksheet 9, he will now be in a position to complete Worksheet 10 by entering training components suitable to his specific needs for each of the three major periods listed. When developing the plan for Worksheet 10, the coach will have to consider the specific needs of the athlete.

WORKSHEET 10

Day		Base Period	Pre-Competition Period	Competition Period
Monday	(am) (pm)			
Tuesday	(am) (pm)			
Wednesday	(am) (pm)			
Thursday	(am) (pm)			
Friday	(am) (pm)			
Saturday	(am) (pm)			
Sunday	(am) (pm)			

Conclusion

1. It is important to emphasize that there should be no significant distinctions made between training male and female runners. Nor is there much difference in training age group athletes and elite runners. The workload should be appropriate to the caliber of the athlete, of course. However because males run faster than females of the same standard training paces must be different. For example, a 45-minute run at 85% effort is appropriate to both world class male and female 1500m runners but the distance covered will be different. The same principle applies to age-group athletes.
2. In keeping with the focus on recovery and regeneration the concept of hard - easy days should be expanded to include weeks, e.g., 2-4 weeks hard followed by 1-2 easier weeks. Secondly the athlete who is increasing his weekly and annual mileages towards the optimum volume appropriate to his event must avoid significant amounts of anaerobic training, because simultaneously increasing both volume and intensity can lead to illness and/or injury. Even more importantly, as Lydiard stated in his book, *Run To The Top*, it will lower "the runner's blood pH" and upset "his metabolism." In other words the runner's aerobic enzymes will be damaged.
3. The dangers inherent in consistently increasing both volume and intensity is the reason *Run With The Best* suggests the athlete will need from two to nine years, depending on the chosen event, to reach optimum volume and a further two to three years at optimum volume before he starts producing fast times that represent his true potential.
4. Equally, the first year at full volume should not contain a significant amount of anaerobic training. This can be increased in the second year because there will not be any increases in volume, while training in the third year can be at full intensity. If the athlete is not performing at the level consistent with the perceived potential by this time it might be advisable for the athlete and coach to reevaluate if the event chosen is the correct one.

Run With The Best believes that basic speed and the total accumulated volume of training is critical to every athlete's success. The most valuable thing coaches can do for their athletes is to nurture them through their early years so that they reach their late teens or early 20's with a solid aerobic foundation and a high level of basic speed.

CHAPTER 4
THE PERIODIZATION OF THE YEAR

This manual suggests that the training year be divided into three periods and seven phases. An example of how the annual volume is apportioned to each period and phase can be seen in Figure 3-7 in the previous chapter.

Step 1: Identify the Major Periods and Phases.

1. A Base Period (24 to 30 weeks. Divided into three 8- to 10-week Phases):
   i) Phase I: The Pre-Cross Country Base Phase
   ii) Phase II: The Cross Country-Specific Base Phase
   iii) Phase III: The Pre-Track Base Phase
2. A Pre-Competition Period (8-10 weeks. Divided into two 4- to 5-week Phases):
   iv) Phase I: The Competition Conditioning Phase
   v) Phase II: The Competition Specific Phase.
3. A Competition Period (4-12 weeks. Divided into a 4-5 and a 4- to 8-week Phase):
   vi) Phase I: The Preparation for the Major Race (4-5 weeks)
   vii) Phase II: Late Season Racing and Recovery Period (8-13 weeks). Racing continues if available and appropriate. After that, time must be devoted to regeneration.

Step 2: Plan for the Major Race.

1. Identify the date (or approximate date) of the major race for the following year.
2. Count back 4-5 weeks from that weekend. This is Competition Period: Phase I.
3. Count back another 9-10 weeks, i.e., 12-15 weeks prior to the major race. This is the Pre-Competition Period.
4. Go back a further 27-32 weeks, i.e., 40 to 47 weeks prior to the major race. This will indicate the start of the Base Period.
American coaches will note that cross country will fall into Phase II of the Base Period. (See Figure 3-7).

The period prior to the commencement of the Base Period would include two weeks rest, then three to ten weeks devoted to general recovery activity, easy running, general and specific body conditioning, aerobic running and the reintroduction of speed work.

Step 3: Assign a Specific Volume to Each Period.

1. The Base Period:
   In a single periodized year
   - devote approximately 60% of the time available for preparation, and
   - assign between 62.5% (long distance and road runners) and 65.5% (middle to long distance track runners) of the total goal volume to that period. (For example: If the goal volume for the year is 3000 kilometers/miles the coach should assign approximately 1950 km/mile to the Base Period.)
2. The Pre-Competition Period:
   In a single periodized year
   - devote 20% of the time available to pre-competition training, and
   - assign 20% of the annual volume to this period, i.e., if the annual volume is 3000 kilometers/miles, assign 600 km/miles to this period.
3. The Competition and Transition Periods:
   In a single periodized year
   - The remaining 20% of time and 17.5% of volume is allocated to these periods, i.e., 450 km/miles in the case of the runner used in our example.

The reasons for devoting the major share of the volume to the Preparation Period, in this case 1950 km/miles out of 3000 km/miles, will be obvious to all coaches.

Combining the Competition and Recovery Periods may need some explaining, however. It is done because the end of the season is never clear-cut. Some athletes finish with the nationals or the major domestic meet of their year. Others may go on to compete for weeks, even months, after what may be termed their major meet for the year. Still others will fail to complete the season. All of which may mean some athletes may still be racing, while others are either resting completely or are rebuilding themselves prior to commencing the next year's Base Period.

Step 4: Assign a Specific Volume to Each Phase.

No coach who has assigned his or her athlete an annual target of, say, 3000 km/miles is planning for that athlete to run 60 km/miles each of the 50 weeks of the year. The question then is how to distribute the mileage.

1. The Base Period (63-67% of total volume):
    i) Phase I: The Pre-Cross Country Base phase (19-20% of volume).
    ii) Phase II: The Cross Country-Specific Base Phase (20-22% of volume).
    iii) Phase III: The Pre-Track Base Phase (23-26% of volume).

The aim of Phase I is to get back into training following the end-of-season recovery period. Phase I will therefore have the lowest volume of the three Base phases.

Phase II will normally contain some cross country racing. Therefore while the volume does increase there will be weeks of lower volume. So, the increase in the volume will be relatively small.

Phase III has the largest volume because cross country racing has finished and the athlete is now gearing up for track season.

2. A Pre-Competition Period (20% of total volume):
    i) Phase I: The Competition Conditioning Phase (11-12% of volume).
    ii) Phase II: The Competition-Specific Phase (8-9% of volume).

The aim of this period is basically to maintain volume and increase intensity. However the Competition-Conditioning Phase will contain more volume than the Competition-Specific Phase.

The first two or three weeks of the Pre-Competition Period basically continues the transition from the aerobically oriented Base Period to a program with an increasing focus on anaerobic needs. Race simulation, race tactical, and surge intervals workouts would be introduced to accustom the athlete to racing conditions.

Racing would be introduced during the Pre-Competition Period because a race is the best possible form of competition-specific training. However race selection and the intensity at which the race is undertaken must be carefully controlled. There should be no confusion between the "racing to win" attitude of the Competition Period and the use of races to practice race-related skills during the Pre-Competition Period. On the other hand, the athlete must be slowly moving toward the "run to win" mentality as the Competition Period approaches.

3. A Competition and Transition Period (13-17% of total volume):
    i) Phase I: The preparation for the Major Race (7-9% of total volume):
    ii) Phase II: Late Season Racing and Transition (complete the final 6-8% of volume).

After racing has finished, the athlete should immediately take a two-week break and then move into the Transition Phase. As mentioned earlier, the length of Transition Phase will vary from athlete to athlete. For those who end with the nationals there may be up to seven weeks before the close of their track year. Two weeks break and five weeks of gradually increasing aerobic volume running would be advised for these athletes. This may also be an appropriate time for younger developing athletes to participate in other activities such as supervised ball games, swimming, cycling, etc.

At the other extreme will be numerous Northern Hemisphere athletes who will compete at their national championships and move on to another four to eight weeks of competition. Where this occurs the athlete must still take a two-week break and spend another four to six weeks in transition mode before embarking on the preparation for the following season.

In this situation the coach may have to consider a shortened periodized plan along the lines of a 24- to 27-week Base Period, a 6- to 9-week Pre-Competition Period, a normal five weeks of preparation peaking for the nationals and a 9- to 11-week period that encompasses post-nationals racing, a two-week break and the Pre-Base Training Transition Period.

Additional Considerations

• The concept of allocating the largest volume of work to the Base Period (specifically during Phase III) and the least amount of volume to the Competition Period is more important than the percentage breakdowns. For example, 10,000m runners train much the same all year round while 800m runners require significantly different volumes and intensities during the various periods.

• Since Phase I of the Base Period is preceded by the Transition Period it is important to ensure that intensity is increased gradually.

• The intensity must be at its greatest in the Pre-Competition Period.

• In order to implement a hard/easy approach, a range of weekly volumes may be employed. While Figure 3-8 shows the athlete will target an average of almost 57km/miles per week in Phase I, 66 km/mile per week in Phase II and 72km/miles per week in Phase III of the Base Period, the actual weekly volumes should vary considerably, i.e., from, say, 45 to 80km/miles to allow recovery and to prepare the athlete for higher mileages in both the immediate and long-term future.

• Another strategy that may be implemented is to

Not many athletes can boast they defeated Jim Ryun, George Young and Frank Shorter in a single race. Pictured above in the 1972 Bakersfield Classic 5000m is co-author Tony Benson (far left), along with (l to r) Jim Ryun, Jack Bacheler, Frank Shorter, Grant McLaren and Tracy Smith. Benson won in 13:36.6, with George Young (not shown) second in 13:37.6, Ryun third (13:38.2).

occasionally make the easy weeks the high volume ones by significantly reducing the intensity and to make hard weeks low-volume ones, i.e., train very hard on two or three days and include up to three days of little or no running at all. Kip Keino, the great Kenyan runner of the 1960's and early 1970's, regularly trained hard three times per day for 3-4 days and did only his policeman duties on the other days.

• Athletes may also be required to peak on two or more occasions per year. In the cases where the athlete is involved in cross country this will present few difficulties for the coach as the races simply form a part of the base training. Indoor races, which normally fall into the late Base Period or early Pre-Competition Period, and extended periods of racing after the national championships do present special challenges however. These, and other related situations requiring high school, college and international athletes to double-periodize, will be discussed in later chapters of the book.

CHAPTER 5
THE MAJOR TRAINING COMPONENTS

Once the coach has decided on the weekly volumes the next thing he or she must do is to decide what workouts will be scheduled for each week of the year. Initially there is no point in trying to decide on specific workouts. The experienced coach will be able to decide months in advance what component of the training he or she will employ on any given day.

These components are outlined in Figure 5-1 below and fully explained in Chapters 6, 7 and 8.

FIGURE 5-1: THE MAJOR COMPONENTS OF COMPETITIVE RUNNING TRAINING.

1. **AEROBIC RECOVERY RUNNING (ENDURANCE-1):**
   - 15-45 min continuous running @ 50-65% of Maximum Heart Rate (MHR).
2. **AEROBIC CONDITIONING RUNNING (ENDURANCE-2):**
   - 30 min - 3 hours of continuous running @ 65-80% MHR.
3. **LACTATE THRESHOLD RUNNING (ENDURANCE-3):**
   - 45-57 min (up to 1:45 hr for marathon runners) @ 80-85% MHR.
   - 25-45 min @ 80-87% MHR.
   - 15-35 mins of 5-10 min repetitions @ 85-92% MHR with 1-3 minutes recovery.
     This last (interval) option would normally be used only for beginners.
4. **AEROBIC POWER RUNNING (ENDURANCE-4):**
   - Continuous 15-35 min efforts done as surge intervals, fartlek or hill surge workout at a pace midway between threshold and MVO_2 pace or between 80 and 90% MHR.
   - 30 sec to 4 min reps or 200m - 1200m surges @ race goal pace with 30 sec to 2 min or 100m to 600m jog recovery. Heart rate should not exceed 90-92% MHR with recovery intervals that are normally shorter than the run interval.
5. **MAXIMAL OXYGEN UPTAKE OR MVO_2 RUNNING (ENDURANCE-5):**
   - 2-5 min reps @ 92-97% MHR with 2-5 min recovery jog.
   - 1-3 min hill reps @ 92-97% MHR with 2-8 min recovery jog.
   - 12-15 min surge intervals @ 85-97% MHR.
   - 8-12 min steady runs @ 92-97% MHR.
     MVO_2 running velocity can range from 1500m to 10k pace depending on the length of the work interval and still meet the definition of MVO_2 training.
6. **ANAEROBIC POWER RUNNING (LAT-1):**
   - 5 sec to 2 min or 50m to 800m reps @ 95-100% MHR with 10 sec to 2 min recoveries.
   - Each repetition is normally run at 800m to 1500m speed but can be as fast as 400m pace.
7. **LACTIC ACID TOLERANCE RUNNING (LAT-2):**
   - 30 second to 2 minute reps @ near maximal speed with 5 to 15 min recoveries.
   - 5 to 30 sec reps using 1-4 sets of 2 to 8 minute duration. Each rep is run at maximal or @ near maximal velocity with 30 to 60 second interval recoveries and 5 to 15 minutes between sets.
   Note: The total time for either Lat-1 or Lat-2 workouts should not exceed 6-8 minutes for high school athletes, 8-10 minutes for college athletes and 10-12 minutes for experienced athletes per week and the coach should allow 48-96hrs for recovery & 10-14 days for total adaptation.
8. **SPEED AND POWER (LAT-3):**
   - Technique drills and form run-throughs or accelerations.
   - Sprint repetitions and sprint intervals.
   - Short maximal resistance efforts.
   - 1-2% of weekly total mileage @ 80-100% of max speed.
9. **STRENGTH (AUX-1):**
   - Body, free and machine weights.
   - Resistance running.
   - Weight and circuit training.
10. **FLEXIBILITY AND RECOVERY (AUX-2):**
    - Stretching, massage, sauna, spa pool, etc.
11. **NUTRITION, HYDRATION, ETC. (AUX-3)**

A SUMMARY OF MAJOR TRAINING COMPONENTS

The major training components fall into three categories—an aerobic component, an anaerobic component and an auxiliary or support component.

THE AEROBIC COMPONENT

There are five different heart rate zones, all of which are based on percentages of the person's Maximum Heart Rate (MHR). These zones are:

The Training Zone	Abbreviation	% MHR
The Recovery Zone.	End-1	50-65% MHR
The General Conditioning Zone	End-2	65-80% MHR
The Lactate or Anaerobic Threshold Zone	End-3	80-92% MHR
Aerobic Power Zone	End-4	85-92% MHR
The Maximal Oxygen Uptake Zone	End-5	92-97% MHR

THE ANAEROBIC COMPONENT

There are three different heart rate zones, again all based on percentages of the person's Maximum Heart Rate (MHR). These zones are:

The Training Zone	Abbreviation	% MHR
Anaerobic Power Zone	Lat-1	95-100% MHR
The Lactic Acid Tolerance Zone	Lat-2	97-100% MHR
Speed and Power Zone	Lat-3	99-100% MHR

THE AUXILIARY COMPONENTS

These components are not directly related to running and therefore are not considered as training zones. They are, however, essential to optimum performance.

The Component	Abbreviation
Strength	Aux-1
Flexibility, Recovery and Regeneration	Aux-2
Nutrition and Hydration	Aux-3

CHAPTER 6
THE AEROBIC TRAINING COMPONENTS

Training cannot begin until the coach has an idea of the athlete's physical condition. The athlete's fitness or aerobic capacity, i.e., his capacity to use oxygen while exercising, can be determined by time trials and/or by measuring heart rate.

The time trial method is the easiest. All the coach must do is get the athlete to trial over 3k or 10k. The 3k time will give a very close approximation of the athlete's maximal oxygen uptake capacity and the 10k will indicate current lactate threshold capacity.

Figure 6-1 can then be used to set training paces. Beginners and juniors would normally use a 3k time trial as muscle fatigue could affect the 10k time even though the cardiovascular fitness was present.

The second method involves the use of heart rates. Initially the coach should instruct the athlete to take his heart rate every day at the same time, i.e., after resting for five minutes just prior to the afternoon session.

This *resting* heart rate (or RHR) will take a while to establish. The athlete must take his pulse daily and record it for at least a month—at which time the coach takes the lowest number recorded as the RHR.

Meanwhile the coach must establish the athlete's *maximum* heart rate (MHR). During the period that the RHR is not known and no MHR tests have been done, the MHR can be estimated by using the formula 220 minus the person's age in years = MHR. For example a 20-year old athlete may be estimated to have an MHR of 200 beats per minute (bpm).

Once the athlete starts training the coach will be able to make some estimates based on the athlete's aerobic runs and sprints. For example, if the athlete is comfortably running one hour at a heart rate (HR) around 140 bpm, his MHR is probably between 190 bpm and 200 bpm. If the athlete is also recording HR's above 175 or 180 bpm towards the end of short sprint sessions, it makes it even more likely that his MHR is up around 200 bpm.

Once estimates of the RHR and MHR have been made, use the following method of calculating the various percentages of the MHR.

- Calculate the athlete's Heart Rate Reserve (HRR): MHR minus RHR = HRR
- Calculate the athlete's percentage HRR (%HHR): HHR x % = %HHR
- Calculate the athlete's percentage of MHR (%MHR): %HHR + RHR = %MHR

Example: An athlete's MHR is 204 bpm and RHR is 50 bpm. What is 75% of his MHR?
- 204 bpm - 50 bpm = 154 bpm (HRR)
- 154 x 75% = 115.5 bpm (%HRR)
- 115.5 bpm + 50 bpm = 165.5 (%MHR)
- 165.5 bpm is 75% of the athlete's MHR of 204 bpm.

After a few months of training, which should be basically aerobic running plus a weekly speed workout, the coach could actually test the athlete to identify his or her MHR.

There are a number of ways this can be done.
1. In a laboratory. While accurate, this can be time-consuming and expensive.
2. In the general running environment. Heart rate monitors, preferably those that memorize the heart rates at regular intervals, are an essential aid to training. Have the athlete wear one during all workouts. As the athlete trains at higher intensities, especially while doing hill running, request that he keep a record every time he notes a new maximum. Each time a new MHR is recorded it should be correlated to the best known RHR and a new table of intensities developed. This method is recommended for juniors and inexperienced seniors, as most running tests are too severe. Also the coach should be concentrating on easy mileage and sprint work with beginners and juniors, not scheduling intense aerobic or anaerobic training for them.
3. Using specific running tests. As mentioned earlier, the coach could have the athlete run a race or time trial over 3k or 5k, instructing the athlete to sprint the last 200m at maximum effort.

Finally it should be said that counting the pulse is not really an alternative though it is better than doing nothing. It may be OK as far as recording the resting heart rate but it is not nearly accurate enough to base training intensities on. More importantly the athlete would have to be constantly stopping—something that should be generally avoided. After all, *a race is about a single continuous effort, not a series of interval efforts.*

Aerobic Recovery Running

There are two categories of general endurance

running: aerobic recovery running and aerobic conditioning running.

Aerobic recovery running may be described as running easily for 15 to 45 minutes at between 50-65% of maximum heart rate. These runs may either be continuous or done as fartlek, in that some relaxed striding over say 50 to 100m is included.

Basically these runs begin the aerobic conditioning process by improving general circulation, muscle capillarization and the heart's stroke volume, enhance the body's ability to recover from, and adapt to, harder training, and contribute to general running economy.

Depending on the phase of training, aerobic recovery running should incorporate 30-60% of the weekly volume. It is also preferable to run on flat ground or over mild rolling hills on grass, dirt roads, forest trails, and the like, as a pleasant environment is a great aid to mental and physical recovery.

Those athletes training more than once per day normally schedule recovery runs for the morning and they would probably do another two to four recovery runs during the week. Recovery running will also constitute a small part of the warm-up prior to harder workouts and a large part of the warm-down after such sessions.

The time of running is also closely related to recovery. All athletes will have a point in time where the run ceases to be recovery and moves into the aerobic conditioning zone. This point in time will be both general, in that it is related to the number of miles or kilometers the athlete has accumulated over his years of running, and specific to how tired he is on that particular day.

This means a junior athlete may not yet be able to exceed 20 minutes of running at 50-65% MHR before he or she moves into the aerobic conditioning zone, while a senior athlete who could normally run for 45 minutes in recovery mode could find there are days where 30 minutes is enough.

The number of days devoted to recovery running will also vary. In the Base Period the overall intensity of training is relatively low because the majority of the work is aimed at aerobic conditioning. This means only one or two days may be needed for recovery. In the Pre-Competition Period however there will be a need for more recovery days because the intensity of the workouts has increased.

Regardless of all these minor variations, however, it is a *Run With The Best* belief that *no athlete should consider a run of more than 45 minutes to be recovery*. Once the run heads towards an hour or more it has become an aerobic conditioning run and will stress the body—even if it is only a very mild stress.

Once the element of stress is introduced it means further recovery will be required. If this is not accounted for, the athlete will move into the next workout under-recovered. If this happens with any regularity it will not be long before the quality of training workouts drops and the athlete becomes susceptible to loss of form, injury and/or illness.

One final point on recovery running. If the coach has a goal of ensuring that the athlete achieve, say, one and a half hours of running on a recovery day, the obvious way to do this is two 45-minute runs or three 30-minute runs. Since 4-6 hours is sufficient to fully recover from 30 minutes of exertion at 50-65%, the athlete could easily run at 6am, 12 noon and 6pm. With two naps plus a self-massage of the legs the athlete would be fully recovered to train as planned the following day.

Aerobic Conditioning Running

Aerobic conditioning runs begin as recovery runs for the first 15 to 30 minutes. The athlete is running easily and his or her HR is gradually rising. The pace may be slightly faster than recovery running but, considering that a well conditioned athlete should be planning to run anything from one to three hours, the pace will still be easy. If the pace is not easy then the run will have to be very short or the athlete will exceed 75-80% of MHR and move into the lactate threshold zone.

In considering athletes from 800m runners to marathoners, aerobic conditioning runs may be described as runs of 30 minutes to 3 hours at 65-80% of maximum heart rate

Taken together aerobic recovery and aerobic conditioning running will constitute 65 to 80% of the athlete's total weekly volume. Improvements in tracks notwithstanding, it was probably the higher levels of accumulated running that moved the performances of the 1970's past those of the 60's.

Lydiard's athletes of the late 50's and early 60's used high volumes of mileage for about 20-24 weeks of the year. By the early 70's the Finns, under Lydiard's influence it should be noted, were running as much as 150 miles per week in the case of Viren, while others, including Juha Vaatainen, were going as high as 200 miles per week.

Aerobic conditioning running should not be considered "junk miles," because the significance of accumulated volume has already been discussed. It should also be noted we are not talking about Long Slow Distance (LSD) here. Lydiard has stressed his athletes did not deliberately run slowly. The Sunday 22-mile run through the Waiatarua Ranges was often covered in 2 hours to 2 hours 10 minutes by his athletes. The Finns of the early 1970's also ran most of their training at a strong tempo.

Lactate Threshold Running

The use of threshold running introduces faster endurance running into the athlete's program and continues to develop running economy. It also further enhances the development of muscle capillarization and the stroke volume of the heart. In addition, when done in the form of interval training, i.e., 5- to 15-minute repetitions, it improves the action of the fast oxidative glycolytic (FOG) cells—fast-twitch A muscle fibers that are powerful but do not normally use oxygen very well and thus fatigue quickly in an untrained state.

There are four major forms of threshold running, the first three involving continuous running @ 80-87% of MHR:
- 45-60 minutes for athletes whose long runs regularly exceed 90 minutes.
- 35-45 minutes for athletes whose long runs are between 60 and 90 minutes.
- 20-25 minutes for beginners, juniors and anyone who does not run beyond an hour.
- 25-35 minutes of 5-10 minute repetitions @ 87-92% of MHR.

An athlete's lactate threshold is the point where the body's ability to use oxygen to meet all its energy requirements from aerobic sources is being stretched to the limit. Any further increase in speed and/or effort raises the production of lactic acid to the point where the anaerobic system will have to come into operation. Running a threshold training session means running on the thin line between having the body operating aerobically (with oxygen) and anaerobically (without oxygen).

Sport scientists and coaches agree that there appears a direct relationship between the athlete's capabilities over 5k to 10k and his lactate threshold. In addition, the experience of both authors of *Run With The Best*, while personally preparing for competition and later as coaches, has been that *threshold training is a crucial element in transferring the benefits accrued from general conditioning training into a reservoir of strength that the athlete will need later as he or she enters the Pre-Competition Period.*

Furthermore, athletes with the cardiovascular system best able to cope with lactic acid accumulation will finish the strongest. To be able to recruit fast-twitch fibers that fatigue less quickly than normal can only be of benefit to all middle and long distance runners. The fact that the majority of all the Olympic champions and world record holders in the 800m since 1960 have been 800m/1500m types rather than 400m/800m types demonstrates the advantages of a higher threshold capacity.

A major threshold workout should be programmed at least once per week during the Base Training and Pre-Competition Period week—although the coach might consider adding a second threshold workout during the second half of the Base Period, as Lydiard did during his 10-week endurance building phase. Taken over a 12-month period, approximately 10-15 % of the athlete's volume should be devoted to this type of training. This means it may occupy 20-30% of a week's volume in some periods because it will not be used in other periods.

Advocates of the continuous form of threshold running include Lydiard who recommended a 10-miler at half-effort on Monday and a 10-miler at three-quarter effort on Friday night every week of his 10-week 100-mile-per-week "Heading For The Track" phase. And Ron Clarke says in his book, *The Unforgiving Minute*, "the long, steady exposure to stress makes it possible for the body to expend more energy in any one session."

Cerutty on the other hand preferred what he called varied pace running and the Kenyans use surges and fartlek much of the time. Their approach approximates what has been called "aerobic power running."

Aerobic Power Running

Aerobic power workouts normally last 15 to 35 minutes and may be best described as surge intervals. Steady state runs and 5k or 8 km races at this intensity are also very valuable, however, because the pace, or HR, is above threshold but marginally below MVO_2.

For example, an athlete capable of 35 min/10k and a 9:30/3k or 10:12/2-mile might run 15 - 25 min @ approximately 3:25 per km (or 5:30 per mile). Such a run would equate to around 27:30 for 5 miles or 8km and 34 minutes for 10k. The athlete is therefore practicing at a new goal pace.

The majority of aerobic power workouts however will be done as surge intervals. These consist of 20- to 35-minute efforts broken into 30 sec-4 min (or 200m to 1200m) surges @ race goal pace or 85-92% of MHR and followed immediately by 30 sec to 2 min (or 200m to 600m) recoveries that are run, not jogged, at the fastest possible pace.

For example, an athlete targeting 14 minutes for 5k could cruise 8 x 400m at goal pace (i.e., 70.0) with a 200m float. Initially the athlete may take up to 1:30 to jog the 200m recovery. With a recovery taking that long the workout would still be considered a traditional interval one. The athlete's aim however would be to reduce this substantially until the jogs are reduced to somewhere around 45 seconds for the 200m. It could be said that the change from a traditional interval workout to a cruise interval workout occurs once the athlete appears to be running as briskly as possible through the recovery rather than still jogging or running without a sense of urgency.

Three things distinguish surge intervals from traditional aerobic intervals.
- The work interval is shorter than a conventional threshold or MVO$_2$ work interval.
- The recovery jog interval is always shorter than the work interval. The exception to this occurs when the work interval is 200m or less. In this case the jog recovery interval is normally equal to the work interval.
- The recovery mode of continuous running (not jogging) is an integral part of the workout.

In cases where the coach wants to use time rather than distance he or she should make the work interval longer than the recovery interval. The exception to this is when the work intervals is 30 seconds or less. The work interval and the recovery interval can be the same in these cases.

This type of training can therefore be used in two ways.
- The coach can tell the athlete to start running at a pace that will bring him up to 85% MHR in about 6-8 minutes and then to keep running at a specified pace until the HR exceeds 87%. The time taken and the distance covered are then recorded. For example, an athlete capable of 33 minutes for 10k might be asked to run at threshold pace of approximately 3:38 per km or 5:54 per mile until the HR exceeds 87%.
- The coach may set the time and distance of the interval and ask the athlete to gradually reduce the recovery. For example, an athlete may be asked to run 5 x 800m at 5k pace with a 200m recovery. Initially the jog may be run in 90 seconds but the athlete would be encouraged to reduce this to 60 or even 45 seconds as quickly as possible.

Surge intervals can be made more difficult by using hills. An excellent workout, if the environment exists, is to have the athlete run up to 35 minutes at 85-90% MHR, alternating 3 minutes at a specified pace followed immediately by 2 min fast jog on a 5-10k (3-6 miles) continuous climb.

Races such as the 800m, 1500m, mile, 3000m and 3000m steeplechase all require high levels of aerobic power. Two former great athletes who used a specific surge interval workout regularly were Steve Prefontaine and Robert De Castella. Prefontaine alternated cruise 200's in 40-45 seconds with fast 200's in 30 seconds. De Castella ran 12 laps of cruise 200's in 40-45 seconds and fast 400's at 5k pace. While their workouts were different in structure, each took

Steve Prefontaine, a regular user of specific surge interval workouts.

14 to 15 minutes to complete.

Maximal Oxygen Uptake or MVO$_2$ Running

These workouts increase the athlete's ability to use oxygen efficiently and begin the process of introducing small amounts of acidity into the athlete's system. MVO$_2$ workouts normally total between 5k and 10k or 3 to 6 miles and consist of 2 to 5 min repetitions run at 92-97% MHR.

An athlete running at his 3k to 5k pace for approximately 5 minutes will reach approximately 97% MHR. If the athlete runs at faster speeds, i.e., 1500m, 800m or 400m pace, the time interval taken to reach 97% will drop to as low as 30 seconds. Workouts may therefore consist of repetitions, steady continuous runs, or surges. Examples of each type of workout might be:

Repetitions
- 5-10 x 600-800m or 1:30-3 min repeats with 300-800m jog or walk recoveries
- 5-8 x 1 km or 3-5 x 1 mile or 3-5 min repeats with 400m-1 mile jog or walk recoveries

Surges
- 15 minutes alternating 2 min fast and 1 min easy

Continuous runs
- 3k or 2-mile time trials (to measure the athlete's progress)

The major difference between an MVO$_2$ and an aerobic power workout is the decreased emphasis on recovery and the increased emphasis on intensity. Obviously the athlete should take the minimum recovery possible, but the concept of a fixed recovery distance to be jogged is no longer relevant.

If the athlete has time to jog 200m or 400m between repetitions, he may do it. But if jogging the distance is preventing him from getting on with another repetition, then the athlete should jog less.

Hills may also be used. For example, 10k including 13 x 400m on a 3-4° hill at 10k pace with a 400m jog-back recovery in one and a half times the work interval time.

Due to their intensity these workouts are quite stressful and recovery times must be longer than for threshold or aerobic power intervals. The total volume of work will usually be between 5 and 10k.

Summary

The five ingredients outlined in this chapter all focus on aerobic development and will constitute 85-90% of an athlete's annual training requirements. A large proportion of this work must obviously be accomplished during the 24- to 30-week Base Period and the aerobic training paces are outlined in Fig. 6-1.

FIGURE 6-1: MAJOR AEROBIC TRAINING PACES

3k Time Trial	10k Time Actual or Estimated from 3k	1k Pace Based on 10k Time	MVO$_2$ Pace Based on 10k Time	End-1 & 2 Aerobic Conditioning Pace	End-3 Lactate Threshold Pace	End-4 Aerobic Power Pace		End-5 Maximal Oxygen Uptake Pace	
mm:ss.0	Time Trial	mm:ss	*min/km*	*Per/Km*	*Per/Km*	*Per/Km*	*Per 400m*	*Per/Km*	*Per 400m*
				Continuous and Varied Pace Runs	Cont. & Rep. Runs	30" - 2' Repetition Running		2' - 6' Repetitions 12 to 25 min of Surges	
06:54.0	0:25:00	2:30.0	2:18.0	4:12.1 - 3:02.9	2:39.6 - 2:33.1	2:33.1 - 2:18.0	1:01.2 - 0:55.2	2:18.0 - 2:14.6	0:57.0 - 0:53.9
07:10.6	0:26:00	2:36.0	2:23.5	4:22.2 - 3:10.2	2:46.0 - 2:39.2	2:39.2 - 2:23.5	1:03.7 - 0:57.4	2:23.5 - 2:20.0	0:59.3 - 0:56.0
07:27.1	0:27:00	2:42.0	2:29.0	4:32.3 - 3:17.6	2:52.3 - 2:45.3	2:45.3 - 2:29.0	1:06.1 - 0:59.6	2:29.0 - 2:25.4	1:01.5 - 0:58.2
07:34.7	0:28:00	2:48.0	2:34.6	4:42.4 - 3:24.9	2:58.7 - 2:51.4	2:51.4 - 2:34.6	1:08.6 - 1:01.8	2:34.6 - 2:30.8	1:03.8 - 1:00.3
08:00.2	0:29:00	2:54.0	2:40.1	4:52.4 - 3:32.2	3:05.1 - 2:57.6	2:57.6 - 2:40.1	1:11.0 - 1:04.0	2:40.1 - 2:36.2	1:06.1 - 1:02.5
08:16.8	0:30:00	3:00.0	2:45.6	5:02.5 - 3:39.5	3:11.5 - 3:03.7	3:03.7 - 2:45.6	1:13.5 - 1:06.2	2:45.6 - 2:41.6	1:08.4 - 1:04.6
08:33.4	0:31:00	3:06.0	2:51.1	5:12.6 - 3:46.8	3:17.9 - 3:09.8	3:09.8 - 2:51.1	1:15.9 - 1:08.4	2:51.1 - 2:46.9	1:10.7 - 1:06.8
08:49.9	0:32:00	3:12.0	2:56.6	5:22.7 - 3:54.1	3:24.3 - 3:15.9	3:15.9 - 2:56.6	1:18.4 - 1:10.7	2:56.6 - 2:52.3	1:12.9 - 1:08.9
09:06.5	0:33:00	3:18.0	3:02.2	5:32.8 - 4:01.5	3:30.6 - 3:22.0	3:22.0 - 3:02.2	1:20.8 - 1:12.9	3:02.2 - 2:57.7	1:15.2 - 1:11.1
09:23.0	0:34:00	3:24.0	3:07.7	5:42.9 - 4:08.8	3:37.0 - 3:28.2	3:28.2 - 3:07.7	1:23.3 - 1:15.1	3:07.7 - 3:03.1	1:17.5 - 1:13.2
09:39.6	0:35:00	3:30.0	3:13.2	5:52.9 - 4:16.1	3:43.4 - 3:34.3	3:34.3 - 3:13.2	1:25.7 - 1:17.3	3:13.2 - 3:08.5	1:19.8 - 1:15.4
09:56.2	0:36:00	3:36.0	3:18.7	6:03.0 - 4:23.4	3:49.8 - 3:40.4	3:40.4 - 3:18.7	1:28.2 - 1:19.5	3:18.7 - 3:13.9	1:22.1 - 1:17.5
10:12.7	0:37:00	3:42.0	3:24.2	6:13.1 - 4:30.7	3:56.2 - 3:46.5	3:46.5 - 3:24.2	1:30.6 - 1:21.7	3:24.2 - 3:19.3	1:24.3 - 1:19.7
10:29.3	0:38:00	3:48.0	3:29.8	6:23.2 - 4:38.0	4:02.6 - 3:52.7	3:52.7 - 3:29.8	1:33.1 - 1:23.9	3:29.8 - 3:24.6	1:26.6 - 1:21.9
10:45.8	0:39:00	3:54.0	3:35.3	6:33.3 - 4:45.4	4:08.9 - 3:58.8	3:58.8 - 3:35.3	1:35.5 - 1:26.1	3:35.3 - 3:30.0	1:28.9 - 1:24.0
11:02.4	0:40:00	4:00.0	3:40.8	6:43.4 - 4:52.7	4:15.3 - 4:04.9	4:04.9 - 3:40.8	1:38.0 - 1:28.3	3:40.8 - 3:35.4	1:31.2 - 1:26.2
11:19.0	0:41:00	4:06.0	3:46.3	6:53.4 - 5:00.0	4:21.7 - 4:11.0	4:11.0 - 3:46.3	1:40.4 - 1:30.5	3:46.3 - 3:40.8	1:33.4 - 1:28.3
11:35.5	0:42:00	4:12.0	3:51.8	7:03.5 - 5:07.3	4:28.1 - 4:17.1	4:17.1 - 3:51.8	1:42.9 - 1:32.7	3:51.8 - 3:46.2	1:35.7 - 1:30.5
11:52.1	0:43:00	4:18.0	3:57.4	7:13.6 - 5:14.6	4:34.5 - 4:23.3	4:23.3 - 3:57.4	1:45.3 - 1:34.9	3:57.4 - 3:51.6	1:38.0 - 1:32.6
12:08.6	0:44:00	4:24.0	4:02.9	7:23.7 - 5:22.0	4:40.9 - 4:29.4	4:29.4 - 4:02.9	1:47.8 - 1:37.2	4:02.9 - 3:57.0	1:40.3 - 1:34.8
12:25.2	0:45:00	4:30.0	4:08.4	7:33.8 - 5:29.3	4:47.2 - 4:35.5	4:35.5 - 4:08.4	1:50.2 - 1:39.4	4:08.4 - 4:02.3	1:42.6 - 1:36.9
12:41.8	0:46:00	4:36.0	4:13.9	7:43.9 - 5:36.6	4:53.6 - 4:41.6	4:41.6 - 4:13.9	1:52.7 - 1:41.6	4:13.9 - 4:07.7	1:44.8 - 1:39.1
12:58.3	0:47:00	4:42.0	4:19.4	7:53.9 - 5:43.9	5:00.0 - 4:47.8	4:47.8 - 4:19.4	1:55.1 - 1:43.8	4:19.4 - 4:13.1	1:47.1 - 1:41.2
13:14.9	0:48:00	4:48.0	4:25.0	8:04.0 - 5:51.2	5:06.4 - 4:53.9	4:53.9 - 4:25.0	1:57.6 - 1:46.0	4:25.0 - 4:18.5	1:49.4 - 1:43.4
13:31.4	0:49:00	4:54.0	4:30.5	8:14.1 - 5:58.5	5:12.8 - 5:00.0	5:00.0 - 4:30.5	2:00.0 - 1:48.2	4:30.5 - 4:23.9	1:51.7 - 1:45.6

Each component is slightly more stressful than the one that preceded it and the general direction has been to move from continuous running to interval running.

The heart rate has moved from 50% MHR in recovery running to 92% MHR during the steady state and long interval running.

Speed has increased from something slower than marathon pace up to 3k pace. Where surges, fartlek, accelerations and 400m pace work have been scheduled, the pace has actually gone all the way to 400m velocity in the once-per-week speed sessions.

In other words, the athlete has been developing high levels of endurance and sprint speed. All he or she needs now is to prepare for racing by undertaking the necessary anaerobic training. The higher level of fitness an athlete can achieve through this type of training, the higher or stronger goal paces will be reached. Steve Scott knew that when he could run 50 min for 10 miles at 85% of max that he was in sub-four shape without doing intervals to aid him. He knew that when he started to add anaerobic work his mile times would drop to sub-3:50 territory.

Figure 6-1 summarizes the major aerobic paces clearly. A high school middle distance runner capable of running 10,000m in 36 minutes (or whose times over 2 miles indicate that 36 minutes is realistic) would be assigned basic aerobic running paces of between 7:00 and 8:00 minutes per mile (4:23-6:03 per km). His or her other running paces would be 5:51 to 6:06 per mile (3:40-3:49 per km) for lactate threshold running, 5:51 to 6:18 per mile (3:40-4:18 per km) for aerobic power training, and 5:13 to 5:19 per mile (3:14-3:18 per km) for MVO$_2$ training.

One speed not specifically shown here is the pace most suitable for recovery running. If the athlete is assigned a recovery run, he or she should start running at a pace that is at the slow end of their aerobic running pace. In the case of a 30-minute 10,000m runner this would be between 7:00 and 8:05 per mile or 4:20 to 5:00 per kilometer.

CHAPTER 7
THE ANAEROBIC TRAINING COMPONENTS

The working muscle relies on two anaerobic energy systems. When an athlete works at maximal or near-maximal capacity for less than 15 seconds he or she will use the alactic anaerobic system because no significant amounts of lactic acid are produced in any single effort.

If the athlete attempts to maintain maximal or near-maximal intensities beyond 15 seconds the lactic anaerobic energy system will assume the role of producing energy. If the athlete is working at maximum effort, this system will terminate generally in 45 to 60 seconds at 400m to 800m speed.

Anaerobic Power Running (Lat-1)

Anaerobic power running correlates very closely to the requirements of the 800m, 1500m, mile, 3k and steeplechase, and the primary goal of anaerobic power training is to increase the athlete's ability to hold race speeds while maintaining a smooth relaxed action.

Repetitions normally vary from 10% to 50% of the race distance and training is done at 800m to 1500m race pace. A workout would normally consist of running 200m to 800m repetitions with HR's reaching 95-100% towards the end of the last few repetitions. Since the athlete is running at 800m to 1500m pace the coach will have to manipulate the recovery time and the mode of recovery to achieve the required pace.

Recovery times could therefore vary from 20-second to 2-minute recoveries and the athlete may be required to jog a certain distance in a specified time or to wait "on the spot" for a particular time. For example, a 1500m runner targeting 4:00 may do a rhythm session of 10-30 x 200m in 31-32 seconds (i.e., 1500m/1 mile pace) with a 200m jog in 60 to 90 seconds or a race simulation session such as 1-2 sets of 3 x 400m plus 1 x 300m at 4-minute 1500m pace (i.e., 64 seconds), with 45 seconds recovery between runs and 5 to 15 minutes between sets.

A variation on the more commonly employed anaerobic power workouts is the sprint interval. The sprint interval workout is best exemplified by the 2 miles of 50-yard sprint/60-yard float recovery training Arthur Lydiard set athletes such as Peter Snell, or Ron Clarke's 10-12 laps of sprinting the straight and floating the bends. Both workouts last between 9 and 14 minutes when done by accomplished athletes who maintain a fast relaxed pace during the recovery.

Run With The Best strongly recommends the use of this type of workout because it involves the all-out power aspect of sprint training, the velocities of 400m running, the work duration of lactic acid tolerance and anaerobic power training, the continuity of effort of a 12-minute MVO_2 time trial, and the emphasis on recovery demanded by an aerobic power workout. These workouts are an integral training component in the bridging process whereby a developing athlete becomes an accomplished athlete.

Anaerobic power running develops a high tolerance to acidity and enhances the ability of the fast- and slow-twitch fibers to perform in a high lactic state. *These workouts can be used once per week by experienced athletes for up to 12 to 15 minutes per session and approximately 8-12 minutes is enough for the developing athlete.*

Regardless of experience it should be remembered that sustained high levels of lactic acid in the blood reduces the endurance capacity of the athlete by destroying the endurance enzymes. The coach, therefore, would be ill-advised to schedule another intense session within 24 to 96 hours of an anaerobic power workout. A useful general guide would be to program one of these workouts every 7 to 10 days over a 6- to 10-week period during to the Pre-Competition period.

Anaerobic power workouts can be considered as "training to race" workouts for runners at all middle and long distances.

Lactic Acid Tolerance Running (Lat-2)

Controlled lactic acid tolerance training aims to improve the buffering capacity of the blood and thus increase the athlete's ability to resist the effects, and pain, of acidosis.

If an athlete is asked to run at 100% effort, the lactic acid anaerobic energy pathway will cease to operate somewhere between 35 seconds (untrained people) and 50 seconds (trained athletes), whereas an athlete who is asked to run at 92% effort, will probably last for between 9 and 12 minutes, depending on his degree of training.

The aerobic training done by a middle or long distance runner develops a strong endurance base that enhances the capacity of the athlete to tolerate a considerable level of acidosis. However the same athlete will still lose the race to a competitor with the same endurance capacities but who can increase the force and speed of muscle contraction late in the race, because he or she possesses a higher tolerance to the accumulation of lactic acid.

It is important to remember that *lactic acid tolerance workouts, like anaerobic power workouts, must be planned carefully because overexposure to lactic acid destroys the endurance capacity of the athlete.* The muscle fibers will require 48 to 96 hours to repair themselves and for the blood chemistry to return to normal. It will also take the body 7-14 days to totally absorb this type of workout.

Speed Training (Lat-3)

Speed of movement can be thought of as the amount of power a runner possesses to enable him to move his weight over a given distance in the shortest period of time. In this section on speed it will be helpful to picture speed in a middle or long distance race as initiated by power, sustained by aerobic endurance and anaerobic tolerance, and completed with power.

Every athlete is born with different aerobic and anaerobic capacities as well as a certain percentage of fast- and slow-twitch fibers. Those who possess a greater percentage of fast-twitch fibers and higher anaerobic capacities will gravitate to the middle distances while those with more higher aerobic capacities and more slow-twitch fibers will head for the longer distances.

One of the most noticeable features of the majority of athletes is their reluctance to train their weaker area. Many 800m runners with great 400m times refuse to face the fact that their event has been dominated by the stronger 800/1500m type since 1960, while it is common to hear athletes aiming for the marathon saying they have no need of speed when a 2:08 marathon requires an athlete to run 422 x 100 in 18 seconds and 8 x 5k in 15 minutes with no recovery!

The reason that records in all events will continue to fall is that athletes with greater speed (read power) will continue to enter the sport. As they do they force other slightly slower (less powerful) athletes to enter longer events where their speed (power) also impacts on the records.

For example, if Herb Elliott with his 1:47 speed for 800m were running today he would either have had to improve to 1:43-1:44 in order to run 3:25 and so maintain his unbeaten record or he would have had to move up to 5000m where his 1500m time of 3:35 (on a dirt track) would have caused even the best of today's 5k athletes to worry!

Put simply, provided an athlete is training correctly, it is an advantage to be faster than one's opponents over shorter events. In the case of two equally strong athletes, speed would be the deciding factor, just as the stronger athlete would prevail in the case of two equally fast athletes.

While the event chosen by the athlete will determine the amount of speed work needed, it is advisable to remember that all distance runners begin, in theory, as middle distance runners. While the athlete may be running long distance races he is not a true distance runner until he has logged in excess of 18,000 to 30,000 miles or 30,000 to 50,000 kilometers— volumes usually only the Africans reach by 20 to 22 years of age.

This means that in the formative years the coach who concentrates on developing the athlete's speed as well as his aerobic endurance will be doing that athlete a great service.

There are three simple ways this can be done.
1. Incorporate sprint technique drills, acceleration runs that emphasize correct form and sprints, into the warm-up routine.
2. Schedule a 400m pace workout once per week during the Base Period.
3. Use maximal or near-maximal velocity runs like 20-30m sprints.

The five major drills used by the authors are "high knee," "butt kick," "straight leg shuffle," "stepovers" and "fast feet." The best method of doing drills is to have the middle and long distance runners join in with the sprinters. Many will resist this aspect of training but it is worth reminding those that do that running is a skill just like swimming, and like everything else, if all other things are equal the athlete with the best technique will win.

Form runs are done over distances from 50m to 400m, with the athlete concentrating solely on running in a technically correct manner. The distance chosen and the number of repetitions will depend on the maturity of the athlete.

The aim of adding sprinting to the program is to stimulate the neuromuscular system and to recruit the fast-twitch fibers. This is done by running repetitions of three to six seconds with proper technique at maximal or near-maximal speed. Again, the distances chosen and the number of repetitions will depend on the athlete's maturity, as well as the event the athlete competes in.

Power can be added to these sessions by using tethered running, short hills, running in sand or against a strong wind. Remember, however, the efforts must be limited to 3 to 6 seconds.

Secondly, the 400m pace workouts are recommended because they ensure the athlete will always be able to run fast without fear of a sudden speed-related injury, as often happens when athletes move from one period of training to another. Running once per week on competition surfaces in spiked shoes will also keep the athletes' legs a little bit track hardened—something quite different from running in cushioned shoes on hard road surfaces.

A simple but very effective workout is 10 x 100m at 400m pace with 300m jog recovery. Prior to the commencement of the new athletic year, the coach and athlete must determine what the 400m goal speed will be. For example, an athlete with a 1500m goal time of 4:00 (i.e., a junior male or elite female) would need to target a 400m time of approximately 54 seconds. Given that the second 100m is the fastest section of any 400m, the athlete would need to aim for 100m sprints in 12.8-13.2 seconds.

At the start of the Base Period the athlete will simply be doing relaxed strides that could well be as slow as 10,000m or marathon pace. Gradually the pace is increased until the athlete is running at goal 400m pace by the end of the Base Period. For the established athlete, the goal may just be to achieve the same speed level as the previous year. Other athletes, particularly developing ones, will have a new 400m goal pace every year for some time. Either way the process is the same. Set the 400m goal time and gradually increase the running speed every week over the next 20-30 weeks until the target time is achieved.

The procedure to follow which involves the least injury risk is to use accelerations. Early in the Base Period begin each run-through at about 70% of current maximum speed and gradually accelerate through to the finish. For the first three weeks do not exceed 85% speed. After that gradually work up to 95% over the next seven weeks. During the next 10 weeks begin each run-through at 80-85% and accelerate to 100%. By the end of the first 10-week period or early in the second 10-week period the athlete should have been able to run one or two 100's at 400m goal pace in every workout and by the end of the second 10-week period he or she would be running at least 4-7 at goal pace. By the end of the third 10-week period the majority of the workout should be at 400m goal pace.

The Base Period is actually the best time to develop speed because there is very little other intense running, so normally the fast-twitch muscle fibers are relatively fresh and, as experienced coaches and athletes know, relaxed striding and acceleration runs are a great way to invigorate the legs after hours of long relatively slow aerobic running.

There are also some rules to be observed in relation to the speed workouts at this time of the year. Firstly, never sprint beyond 90% in really cold weather. In fact the reason for selecting 400m pace is that it represents only about 92% of maximum speed.

Secondly, the 10,000m runner will have a different 400m goal pace to the 800m runner, so these workouts have to be done individually. Thirdly, remember to maintain a stretching routine to keep the joints loose and, finally, have regular massage to relieve tight muscles.

Another point most coaches would be aware of is that athletes in different events may want to do these workouts differently. The 800m runner won't mind plenty of recovery but the marathoner will not want to stop running. The 800m runner's workout might well be 10 x 100m with a walk-back recovery, while the marathon runner may do 10 laps alternating 100m faster and 300m slower. Other athletes may be happy with 10 x 100m with a jog-back recovery.

The type of athlete the coach is dealing with introduces a third factor into the scheduling of speed workouts. If the coach wants to emphasize leg turnover for the slower distance type runners, he or she may schedule wind- or gravity-assisted (on a slope of one degree or less) runs while the speedy athlete who needs strength may find themselves running *into* the same wind or *up* the hill!

Regardless of which environment the coach selects however, the athlete must maintain the prescribed speed for that week and not run faster in the favorable conditions or slower in the unfavorable ones.

Finally the use of maximal or near-maximal speed work in the anaerobic power and lactic acid tolerance workouts is recommended. Anaerobic power workouts like eight laps alternating 50m sprints with 50m floats or lactic acid tolerance ones such as 6-10 x 150m at a pace similar to the start of a 400m race are two useful examples. This type of workout replaces the strict 400m-oriented workouts of the Base Period.

Run With The Best takes the view that the athlete *must be encouraged to run fast all year round in order to maintain or increase speed over distances shorter than race distance.* In fact, it is essential for coaches to educate athletes in the importance of gaining greater speed and/or gaining greater rhythm at speeds they already possess.

However there are occasions when improvements over shorter distances can be counterproductive. This might sound contradictory but there are many examples of marathon runners producing 5000m and/or 10,000m personal bests just prior to major races and failing to perform up to past standards in a marathon a month or two later.

The reason for this is a directional change in the event-specific training. To get improvement on the track the marathoner may have intensified training either by changing the workouts he was doing, typically switching from lactate threshold workouts to maximal oxygen uptake ones, or by doing the normal workouts harder than usual.

On the other hand a 5000m or 10,000m performance that appears less than satisfactory at first glance just prior to a major race is often followed by an excellent result in the major race. A study of the records of Australia's three great marathon runners of the 1980's and 1990's, Robert De Castella, Lisa Ondieki and Steve Moneghetti, reveals that their best marathons have not normally come after track personal bests but rather after races that could best be described as "average" or "strong."

The speed the athlete really needs can best be described as "possessing the capacity for speed." Training over short distances suggests the 400m speed is there but the athlete has not been called on to demonstrate it in a race.

For example, Olympic 10,000m champion Haile Gebrselassie has a competitive best time for the 800 of 1:49.35 (indoors), but the times he has run at events from 1500m to 10,000m and the way he finishes his races leaves little doubt that he can run a faster 800. If his finishing speed over these longer distances is matched with his current personal best of 3:31.6 for 1500m (indoors), it is not hard to speculate that he would have the capacity to run in the 1:46-1:47 range for 800m. Further, if he were to train for the 800m it is entirely possible he would run below 1:46 for 800m and 3:30 for 1500m.

However if he were to do this, it is also very possible the introduction of additional amounts of lactic acid tolerance work would have a very detrimental effect on his 5000m and 10,000m performances. Focusing on the 800m prior to the 1988 Olympics appeared to negatively affect Said Aouita's subsequent performances in the 1500m and 5000m.

To continue the Gebrselassie example, the suggestion that he could run at least 1:47 for 800m would be followed by the proposition he could run at least 50.0 for 400m. Doing a once-per-week workout of 10 x 100m the speeds required would only be 11.5-12.0, times that would not trouble him unduly. This would provide someone as strong as he is with enough speed to run 25-26 seconds for the final 200m of a race, 38-39 seconds for the final 300m, or 52-54 seconds for the last 400m!

In summary then, the use of speed work over distances of 60-150m once per week allows the development of speed without the introduction of any lactic acid in the system. When combined with easy running before and after the fast running the total workout will provide the athlete with an ideal recovery day and prepares him for all types of faster running as the year progresses.

However there is more to developing speed than just running 100m repetitions during the Base Period. In many cases the coach will have to formulate a strategy to make many of the younger or less experienced athletes in his group much faster than they might be at present. For example, many promising middle distance runners struggle to break 54 seconds (men) or 60 seconds (women) as juniors. If these athletes hope to reach international class at some time in the future they will need to run at least 47 and 54 seconds respectively for 400m.

This means that the coach may have to devote two to three seasons weekly to speed development. In cases such as this the coach could consider replacing maximal oxygen uptake workouts, which are the most intense workouts the coach would schedule in the Base Period, and lactic acid tolerance workouts, which are the most intense workouts of the Pre-Competition Period, with sprint repetitions.

Overall, speed-focused running should equal 1-2% of the weekly volume if all the drills, form runs, run-throughs and sprints are included. This will be slightly higher for the middle distance runner than the distance runner due to the greater need for speed and the lower average weekly volumes.

One final point on speed. If an athlete is not working at 90% (about 400m-500m race pace) or higher of their 100m date speed they are not running at speed. If the aim is to avoid the production of lactic acid, keep the distances run at full speed to between 20m and 60m. This means 100m accelerations can still be used because the athlete may only be running at maximum speed for 10m-30m. If the introduction of lactic acid is required but speed is still the major emphasis, the repetitions should be limited to 200m.

Figure 7-1 summarizes the major anaerobic paces clearly. A high school middle distance runner capable of running 10,000m in 36 minutes (or whose times over 2 miles indicate that 36 minutes is realistic) would be assigned anaerobic power running paces of between 2:35 and 2:43 per 800m or 1:18-1:22 per 400m. His or her other running paces would be sub-1:02.5/400m pace for lactic acid tolerance running and sub-14.3/100m pace for speed and power development training.

It should be noted here that neither mile or kilometer pace are relevant as the time it would take to run either distance falls outside the parameters of anaerobic power training. The focus of these workouts should be efforts of 5 seconds to 2 minutes run over distances from 50m to 800m.

FIGURE 7-1: MAJOR ANAEROBIC TRAINING PACES

3k Time Trial mm:ss.0	10k Time Actual or Estimated from 3k Time Trial	800m Pace Based on 10k Time mm:ss	MVO₂ Pace Based on 10k Time *min/km*	LAT-1 Anaerobic Power Runing *per/800m*	LAT-1 *Per 400m*	LAT-2 Lactic Acid Tolerance Pace *Per 400m*	LAT-3 Power Development Pace *Per 100m*
				15" to 5' reps 2' to 12' sets		30" to 2' reps 2' - 5' sets	Maximal or Near-Maximal Efforts
06:54.0	25:00	2:00.0	1:50.4	1:53.8 - 1:47.7	0:56.9 - 0:54.0	SUB 0:52.0	SUB 11.96
07:10.6	26:00	2:04.8	1:54.8	1:58.4 - 1:52.0	0:59.2 - 0:56.2	SUB 0:54.1	SUB 12.44
07:27.1	27:00	2:09.6	1:59.2	2:02.9 - 1:56.3	1:01.5 - 0:58.3	SUB 0:56.2	SUB 12.92
07:43.7	28:00	2:14.4	2:03.6	2:07.5 - 2:00.6	1:03.7 - 1:00.5	SUB 0:58.2	SUB 13.40
08:00.2	29:00	2:19.2	2:08.1	2:12.0 - 2:04.9	1:06.0 - 1:02.6	SUB 1:00.3	SUB 13.87
08:16.8	30:00	2:24.0	2:12.5	2:16.6 - 2:09.2	1:08.3 - 1:04.8	SUB 1:02.4	SUB 14.35
08:33.4	31:00	2:28.8	2:16.9	2:21.1 - 2:13.6	1:10.6 - 1:07.0	SUB 1:04.5	SUB 14.83
08:49.9	32:00	2:33.6	2:21.3	2:25.7 - 2:17.9	1:12.8 - 1:09.1	SUB 1:06.6	SUB 15.31
09:06.5	33:00	2:38.4	2:25.7	2:30.2 - 2:22.2	1:15.1 - 1:11.3	SUB 1:08.6	SUB 15.79
09:23.0	34:00	2:43.2	2:30.1	2:34.8 - 2:26.5	1:17.4 - 1:13.4	SUB 1:10.7	SUB 16.27
09:39.6	35:00	2:48.0	2:34.6	2:39.3 - 2:30.8	1:19.7 - 1:15.6	SUB 1:12.8	SUB 16.74
09:56.2	36:00	2:52.8	2:39.0	2:43.9 - 2:35.1	1:21.9 - 1:17.8	SUB 1:14.9	SUB 17.22
10:12.7	37:00	2:57.6	2:43.4	2:48.4 - 2:39.4	1:24.2 - 1:19.9	SUB 1:17.0	SUB 17.70
10:29.3	38:00	3:02.4	2:47.8	2:53.0 - 2:43.7	1:26.5 - 1:22.1	SUB 1:19.0	SUB 18.18
10:45.8	39:00	3:07.2	2:52.2	2:57.6 - 2:48.0	1:28.8 - 1:24.2	SUB 1:21.1	SUB 18.66
11:02.4	40:00	3:12.0	2:56.6	3:02.1 - 2:52.3	1:31.1 - 1:26.4	SUB 1:23.2	SUB 19.14
11:19.0	41:00	3:16.8	3:01.1	3:06.7 - 2:56.6	1:33.3 - 1:28.6	SUB 1:25.3	SUB 19.62
11:35.5	42:00	3:21.6	3:05.5	3:11.2 - 3:00.9	1:35.6 - 1:30.7	SUB 1:27.4	SUB 20.09
11:52.1	43:00	3:26.4	3:09.9	3:15.8 - 3:05.3	1:37.9 - 1:32.9	SUB 1:29.4	SUB 20.57
12:08.6	44:00	3:31.2	3:14.3	3:20.3 - 3:09.6	1:40.2 - 1:35.0	SUB 1:31.5	SUB 21.05
12:25.2	45:00	3:36.0	3:18.7	3:24.9 - 3:13.9	1:42.4 - 1:37.2	SUB 1:33.6	SUB 21.53
12:41.8	46:00	3:40.8	3:23.1	3:29.4 - 3:18.2	1:44.7 - 1:39.4	SUB 1:35.7	SUB 22.01
12:58.3	47:00	3:45.6	3:27.6	3:34.0 - 3:22.5	1:47.0 - 1:41.5	SUB 1:37.8	SUB 22.49
13:14.9	48:00	3:50.4	3:32.0	3:38.5 - 3:26.8	1:49.3 - 1:43.7	SUB 1:39.8	SUB 22.96
13:31.4	49:00	3:55.2	3:36.4	3:43.1 - 3:31.1	1:51.5 - 1:45.9	SUB 1:41.9	SUB 23.44

CHAPTER 8
THE AUXILIARY TRAINING COMPONENTS

Strength (Aux-1)

While much as been written about the value, or otherwise, of strength training it certainly has a place in any runner's program. The methods used to gain strength however vary considerably. They include the use of calisthenics and plyometrics, free weight exercises, machine weight routines, circuit training (which usually incorporates the methods already mentioned) and all the various forms of resistance running including hills—which are probably the only form of strength training common to virtually every successful athlete.

Percy Cerutty was the one of the first coaches to stress the need for upper body strength and was most certainly the first to advocate really heavy free weights. In addition, he told his athletes to perform regular circuit body weight strength work, hike through mountainous areas with a pack, run in deep water and over loose sandy trails, as well as up steep sand dunes. Herb Elliott in his book, *The Golden Mile*, also mentions occasionally running for 30 miles or 50 kilometers while 60-mile (100-kilometer) weekends were a common feature of the Portsea regime!

Arthur Lydiard, on the other hand, did not believe a runner needed upper body strength, but he did include body weight exercises like push-ups, sit-ups, pull-ups, plyometric bounding on hills and hill running, as well as the legendary 22-mile run with its long steep uphill climbs through the Waiatarua Ranges to develop all-round stamina.

Regardless of what approach is taken to strength training however it is advisable to test and evaluate the athlete's natural strengths or weaknesses before proceeding with a serious routine. It is also true to say that the greater the athlete's natural strength the less need there is to devote time to strength training.

On the other hand it is essential to ensure that younger developing athletes are structurally strong. Males and females between the ages of 13 and 17 will benefit from a basic strength and conditioning program using a combination of body weight exercises, free weights and machines that isolate and strengthen specific muscle groups.

For older athletes of 17 years or more, a solid strengthening program is used for the larger upper and lower body muscle groups. As part of the base building process, a general conditioning program can be very helpful for many athletes who do not possess natural strength. What's most important is to develop great abdominal and lower back strength. To do this a high degree of general strength is required of all muscle groups, including those that may only be indirectly involved in running.

As mileage volumes and workout intensity increase it may become necessary to decrease volume and intensity of the strength training. Athletes have a finite amount of energy and if a choice has to be made between a weight training routine and adding the miles necessary to reach the various target volumes at each stage of the athlete's career, then the running takes priority and the athlete should revert to a body weight strength maintaince program that emphasizes the trunk and upper body.

Equally, if the choice is between the gymnasium and hills, sand dunes or mountain trails it is the running work that should take precedence. Running plyometric drills and hill bounding also should be considered because they are basic to running.

In essence a balanced program incorporating all or most of the above methods would cover the needs of most athletes in the area of strength training.

Flexibility and Recovery (Aux-2)

Injury and illness are signs of an imbalance in a program. Every athlete is born with a greater or lesser resistance to these mortal enemies of performance but a balanced program will help keep these woes to a minimum. It is not an area a coach has complete control over, however. Athletes have a tendency to ignore warning signs such as elevated heart rates and muscle tightness. They are also very likely to ignore advice about rest, sleep, hydration, nutrition, recovery, massage, stretching and so on.

Dick Brown, one-time head coach of the Nike West Track Club and coach of Mary Decker in the years she performed at her best, was fond of saying, "If you mess with Mother Nature Father Time will get you." In other words, if you ignore the warnings of the body, time off from training will be the result.

Training diaries are an invaluable aid to all coaches and athletes who really want to succeed.

Stretching

Daily stretching is a very important component of an overall program. A full stretching program must focus on all the small and large muscle groups.

Stretching before and after a workout is important but the major stretching session of the day should not be done at this time. Rather it should be done at another time.

Pool Regeneration

This refers to the use of the pool for warm-down and stretching post workouts where the athlete has availability of a pool so he can jog, swim and move around to relax. Training in the water creates hydropressure on the muscles. The waste by-products in the muscle tissue can be more readily moved out into the blood stream and processed through the athlete's system. A benefit of stretching in the water is a good way to warm down and check muscles for tightness soreness.

Ice Baths

Using a cold pool or whirlpool tube (ice bath) is another beneficial activity. The temperature of the water should be between 55-65° Fahrenheit. Have the athlete submerge the lower extremities for 10-15 minutes. The process of hydrokenitics shrinks the muscle tissue and assists in the removal of waste products left in the muscle tissue. The ice water reduces the bleeding associated with micro-tears in the muscle. Then as the muscle tissue returns to normal body temperature, new blood will flow back into the muscle tissue, completing the process of moving waste products out of muscle and into the circulatory system. Athletes should wear warm clothing, sweats preferably, after the ice bath to warm up the body.

Massage

If this can be made available to athletes on even a weekly basis it will help reduce soreness and prevent injuries. A full body massage by a trained and competent sports massage therapist is a very important process for a full and complete recovery from hard training. It is very important that the person giving the massage be trained in proper technique especially with athletes. Improper techniques can easily cause injury.

A competent masseur can massage an athlete at any time. Normally it is better before rather than after a hard workout although it should be done both before *and* after any exercises that involve chronic overuse injuries. In fact, Tim Noakes in his excellent book, *The Lore of Running,* states (page 529) that deep cross friction (or crucifixion) massage is the "only treatment that works" on chronic muscle tears.

An appropriate regimen for an athlete with no real problems may involve a sports massage 24 to 48 hours after hard workouts and 48-72 hours before important races.

Sauna

The sauna is a part of the training routine of many European athletes. Some athletes espouse the mental and physical relaxation gained from saunas, while others detest being confined in small hot boxes!

Rest

Rest is a vital component of every athlete's training. It involves getting enough sleep, having an occasional morning or afternoon off training or even taking a day completely off. It may also mean participating in activities that take the mind off athletics or scheduling a regular relaxation session into the training routine.

A period devoted to rest and recovery is also important at the end of the season. No athlete can go year after year with no break of any kind. Some may need less time off than others, some may be able to take a break while continuing to run, while some move their training venues to invigorate their training routines, but regardless of what type of athlete the coach has it is sound coaching practice to advise athletes to have at least one to two weeks per year away from running.

As has been mentioned, if the athlete does not take the rest that he or she needs then either an organic injury (sickness) or a physical injury (muscular or skeletal) will force the athlete to rest!

Hydration, Nutrition and Breathing (Aux-3)

Volumes have been written about these issues and the focus of this book is on training so detailed information on nutrition and hydration should be sought elsewhere. A few simple things, well known to all coaches, bear repeating however.

Hydration

A regular intake of water during the day is the best practice. The Australian Institute of Sport cycling program uses morning and evening weight checks to see that athletes are well hydrated. Water taken too close to training can seriously impair workouts (as it can races), but it's difficult to take too much after the workout. Two to three liters or 6-8 pints per day would be reasonable, unless temperatures are extreme.

In essence, it is really a case of saying, "Drink, drink, drink, and drink some more!"

A word of warning however. While it's basically true to say that only the most conscientious athlete is likely to overhydrate, it does happen. Too much water can leach minerals from the athlete's system and excessive amounts of fluid prior to vigorous endurance efforts can cause bowel problems during the competition.

Nutrition

An important, but often overlooked, area of nutrition involves fluid replacement after exercise. Fluid replacement both hydrates and energizes the athlete.

Recovery from hard training is enhanced if the athlete's fluid and nutritional balance is restored within two hours. The sooner the athlete recovers from a training challenge the sooner he adapts to that challenge. The faster each challenge is adapted to the sooner another challenge can be presented.

As far as it goes, the standard advice of ensuring that post-training and racing meals are taken and the athlete follow a balanced diet of fresh fruits, vegetables, grains, meats or meat substitutes, legumes and diary products is correct.

However, in this day and age, athletes and coaches should not assume that all natural foods are fresh. If they are not they will not supply the needed vitamins, minerals and trace elements necessary to ensure a productive running career, let alone a healthy life!

Therefore *Run With The Best* suggests athletes and coaches consult a nutritionist. *Run With The Best* also advises the athlete and coach to be proactive and research the kinds of athletic nutritional products that can best serve their individual needs, being sure to take into consideration daily temperature and the amount of water being consumed.

Along with all the recovery suggestions, future performance levels will undoubtedly be influenced by all the factors mentioned in the above paragraphs.

CHAPTER 9
THE TRAINING PLAN

The aim of every coach is to have his athlete achieve his peak when it counts. To achieve this aim means the coach must:
- recognize the value of each training component to a specific event,
- assess the athlete's individual strengths and weaknesses,
- know how often to include each particular component, and
- know when to insert it into the program.

Before attempting to construct the training plan in detail it is worth spending time deciding what an average week might contain on a year-round basis and adjusting the basic week in accordance with the specific needs of each major period (Fig. 9-1).

The breakdown applies virtually year round. In the Base Period the percentage of aerobic conditioning training will heavily outweigh recovery running because the overall intensity of training will be lower than in any other period, being directed more towards lactate threshold and aerobic power than towards maximal oxygen uptake and anaerobic power running.

The Base Period occupies 24-32 weeks from July 1st to mid-February for Northern Hemisphere athletes and from April 1st to mid-November for Southern Hemisphere athletes. This period will include the cross country season.

BASE PERIOD.
PHASE I: PRE-CROSS COUNTRY

July (Northern Hemisphere) and April (Southern Hemisphere)
- Build mileage slowly but steadily towards athlete's goal
- Weekly long run, preferably over hilly terrain on trails.
- Lactate threshold runs
- General conditioning and strength training 3 x week
- Stride drills, 50m & 100m accelerations.

August–September (Nothern Hemisphere) and May–June (Southern Hemisphere)
- Increase mileage by 10% or more per week above the athlete's goal for average weekly volume
- Weekly 20-30% long runs, preferably over hilly terrain on trails.
- General conditioning and strength training 3 x week
- Stride drills: 50m accelerations 2 x week; 100m accelerations 2 x week; End-3, End-4, End-5, fartlek or early season races.

FIGURE 9-1: THE BREAKDOWN OF THE AVERAGE WEEK'S TRAINING.

1. Recovery or General Conditioning Pace	= 45-55%	(of weekly mileage)
2. Lactate Threshold, Aerobic Power, MVO$_2$, Anaerobic Power	= 25-35%	(of weekly mileage)
3. One Long Run Over Trails/Parks	= 20-25%	(of weekly mileage)
4. Speed and Power	= 0.5-2.5%	(of weekly mileage)

FIGURE 9-2: A SAMPLE BREAKDOWN OF TRAINING IN THE BASE PERIOD.

1. Recovery pace	= 10-25%	(of weekly mileage)
2. General Conditioning Pace	= 35-55%	(of weekly mileage)
3. Lactate Threshold, Aerobic Power, MVO$_2$ Pace	= 15-25%	(of weekly mileage)
4. One Long Run Over Trails/Parks	= 18-22%	(of weekly mileage)
5. Speed & Power	= 0.5-1.5%	(of weekly mileage)

A Sample Training Week in August of Phase I of the Base Period
This Program is a Guide for a Developing Male or Elite Female Targeting 14:30 for 5000m

Mon: (pm) 15-20 min warm-up
45 min or 7.5 mile, or 12k @ 80-87% MHR
5-10 min recovery, form drills, 4-6 x 50m accelerations and 5-10 min cool-down

Tues: (am) 30 min or 4 miles or 6k @ 50-60% MHR
(pm) 45 min or 6 miles or 10k @ 50-65% MHR

Wed: (pm) 20 min warm-up
10-12 x 60-75 sec or 300-400m hill repeats @ 90-92% MHR with a 2-3 min recovery
This could be done as a fartlek session over a hilly course with the athlete surging the hills and running the recovery briskly.
20 min cool-down

Thur: (am) 30 min or 4 miles or 6k @ 50-60% MHR
(pm) 45 min or 6 miles or 10k @ 50-65% MHR

Fri: (am) 30 min or 4 miles or 6k @ 50-60% MHR
(pm) 15 min warm-up including form drills
8-10 x 100m accelerations working towards 400m goal pace with 300m recovery
15 min cool-down

Sat: (am) 1:45-2:15 Run or 15-20 miles or 25-32k @ 65-75% MHRs
Use natural surfaces and a hilly terrain if possible.

Sun: (am) 1:00-1:15 hr or 9 miles or 15k @ 60-65% MHR

Total Volume: 9-10 hrs or 75-80 miles or 120-130 km.

BASE PERIOD. PHASE II: CROSS COUNTRY

October (Nth Hemisphere)   July (Sth Hemisphere)
- Reduce weekly mileage to athlete's goal average.
- 20% weekly long runs: preferably over hilly terrain on trails.
- Continue weight training: 2 x week
- Anaerobic threshold runs every other week—non-race weeks
- Continue strides drills, 50m & 100m accelerations
- Weekly 10k pace running: intervals, fartlek, repeat hill sessions or hilly fartlek.
- Races or simulations or 3km or 2-mile time trials on non-race weeks.

November–Mid-December (Northern Hemisphere) August–September (Southern Hemisphere)
- Reduce mileage weekly by 10-15% prior to key cross country races.
- 20% weekly long runs, preferably over hilly terrain on trails.
- Continue weight training: 2-3 x week as needed
- Controlled End-3 or End-4 runs during weeks of races.
- Continue stride drills, 50m & 100m accelerations (pre-race day workout?)
- 10k pace intervals or race simulation of 1/2-3/4 race distance
- Weeks of important races. Don't let athlete workout go above 90% HR in workouts; hold big effort (95-100%) for races.
- Once the major seasonal race or the goal race is run, schedule two weeks recovery. Return to average weekly mileage and the 20-30% run.

A Sample Training Week in November of Phase II of the Base Period
This Program is a Guide for a Developing Male or Elite Female Targeting 14:30 for 5000m

Mon: (pm) 15 min warm-up including form drills
8-10 x 100m accelerations working towards 400m goal pace with 300m recovery
15 min cool-down

Tues: (am) 30 min or 4 miles or 6k @ 50-60% MHR
(pm) 15-20 min warm-up
20 min fartlek, e.g., 4 x 15" - 3 x 30" - 2 x 60" - 1 x 90" - 2 x 60" - 3 x 30" - 4 x 15" @ 85-92% with running recovery intervals equal to the work intervals.
5-15 min cool-down

Wed: (pm) 60-75 min or 9 miles or 15k @ 50-65% MHR

Thur: (am) 30 min or 4 miles or 6k @ 50-60% MHR
(pm) 15-20 min warm-up
20 x 200m @ 1500m race rhythm with 200m recovery jog in 60-90 sec
If racing on Saturday reduce this to 6 x 200m
15-20 min cool-down

Fri: (am) Rest or 30 min or 4 miles or 6k @ 50-60% MHR
(pm) Rest or 30 min or 4 miles or 6k @ 50-60% MHR

Sat: (am) Rest or 10-20 min jog, including striding & stretching.
(pm) 5-10k X-C race or 5-8k race simulation @ 87-92% MHR on a undulating course
If not racing the 5-8k could be done in the morning.
Sun: (am) 1:30 - 2:15 hr Run or 12-20 miles or 18-32k @ 50-65% MHR
Use natural surfaces and a hilly terrain if possible.

Total Volume: 5-10 hrs or 50-75 miles or 80-125 km.

BASE PERIOD.
PHASE III: PRE-TRACK PHASE

December–Mid-February (Northern Hemisphere)
Mid-August–October (Southern Hemisphere)
- Return to the August - September levels.
- 1-2 x 20% weekly long runs, preferably over hilly terrain on trails.
- Strong weight training: 3 x week
- Threshold runs: 45-60 mins weekly
- Stride drills, 50m & 100m accelerations 2-3 times per week.
- Introduce End-3, End-4 or End-5 workouts at least once per week.
- Weekly 3k/2miles, 3 mile/5k or 5 miles/8k time trial to test athlete's level of fitness.

A Sample Training Week in January of Phase III of the Base Period
This Program is a Guide for a Developing Male or Elite Female Targeting 14:30 for 5000m

Mon: (pm) 15 min warm-up including form drills
8-10 x 100m accelerations working towards 400m goal pace with 300m recovery
15 min cool-down
Tues: (am) 30 min or 4 miles or 6k @ 50-60% MHR
(pm) 45-60 min or 10 miles or 16k @ 80-85% MHR
Wed: (pm) 60-75 min or 9 miles or 15 km @ 50-65% MHR
Thur: (am) 30 min or 4 miles or 6k @ 50-60% MHR
(pm) 15-20 min warm-up
45 min fartlek.
This workout should include hard surges of 15" to 3' on the flat and up all gradients of hills. The work-to-rest ratio would be about 1:1. The overall impact would be about an 87% effort. The HR range might be 70-95% MHR.
5-15 min cool-down
Fri: (am) Rest or 30 min or 4 miles or 6k @ 50-60% MHR
(pm) Rest or 30 min or 4 miles or 6k @ 50-60% MHR
Sat: (am) 60-75 min or 9 miles or 15 km @ 50-65% MHR (14:30/developing male)
35-45 min or 7.5 miles or 12k @ 80-85% MHR (14:30/elite female)
(pm) Rest or 15-45 min recovery run
Sun: (am) 1:45-2:15 hr run or 15-20 miles or 20-32k @ 50-65% MHR
Use natural surfaces and a hilly terrain if possible.

Total Volume: 9-10 hr or 90-95 miles or 140-150 km.

PRE-COMPETITION PERIOD. PHASE I & II: COMPETITION CONDITIONING PHASE

Aerobic conditioning running decreases in direct proportion to the need to increase intensity during the Pre-Competition and Competition Periods. Recovery running now assumes much greater significance due to the introduction of MVO_2, anaerobic power and possibly even lactic acid tolerance workouts, if the athlete has any indoor or important pre-season races scheduled. The increased need for recovery running is especially true for the middle distance runners whose training will be more intense than the distance runners.

This period occurs 8-10 weeks from February 15th to April (including an indoor season) for Northern Hemisphere athletes, and from November 15th to mid-January (including any major pre-Christmas competition) for Southern Hemisphere athletes.

FIGURE 9-3: A SAMPLE BREAKDOWN OF TRAINING IN THE PRE-COMPETITION PERIOD

1. Recovery Pace	= 25-40%	(of weekly mileage)
2. General Conditioning Pace	= 10-25%	(of weekly mileage)
3. Lactate Threshold, Aerobic Power, MVO_2, Lactic Acid Tolerance, Lactate Production Pace	= 30-40%	(of weekly mileage)
4. One Long Run Over Trails/Parks	= 18-22%	(of weekly mileage)
5. Speed (1 session)	= 0.5-1.5%	(of weekly mileage)

Objectives and Guidelines
- Complete event-specific workouts at date and goal pace
- Develop event-specific MVO$_2$, anaerobic power and lactic acid tolerance
- Use early season races to practice tactics and strategies

Will power is used in races and some sessions must focus on this (Fig. 9-3).

Mid-February–April (Northern Hemisphere)
November–Mid-January (Southern Hemisphere)
- Reduce mileage to 10km/miles below athlete's average weekly mileage goal
- Maintain one long run consisting of 20-30% of weekly mileage total
- Continue weekly or bi-monthly in Phase I.
  2-milers to 10K runners: 45-60 min runs or 5k-10k race-specific pace simulation runs
  Milers & 800m runners: 20 min steady or 2x2 miles or 3k @ 10k pace
- Introduce event-specific End-5, Lat-1 and/or Lat-2 workouts, preferably hill running
- Treat pre-season races as goal races
- Introduce race simulation workouts
- Continue stride drills and 50m-100m accelerations once per week.

A Sample Training Week in March of Phase I of the Pre-Competition Period
This Program is a Guide for a Developing Male or Elite Female Targeting 14:30 for 5000m

Mon: (pm) 15-20 min warm-up
Form drills and 6-10 x 100m relaxed accelerations
10-20 min cool-down

Tues: (am) 30 min or 4 miles or 6k @ 50-60% MHR
(pm) 15-20 min warm-up
3 miles-2 miles-1 mile or 5k-3k-1k @ 87-97% effort
If racing on Sat run 10 x 300m @ 1500m pace with 100m jog recovery.
5-15 mins cool-down

Wed: (pm) 60-75 min or 9 miles or 15 km @ 50-65% MHR

Thur: (am) 30 min or 4 miles or 6k @ 50-60% MHR
(pm) 15-20 min warm-up
45 min fartlek.
This workout should include hard surges of 15" to 3' on the flat and up all gradients of hills. The work-to-rest ratio would be about 1:1. The overall impact would be about an 87% effort. The HR range might be 70-95% MHR.

5-15 mins cool-down

Fri: (am) Rest or 30 min or 4 miles or 6k @ 50-60% MHR
(pm) Rest or 30 min or 4 miles or 6k @ 50-60% MHR

Sat: (am) 60-75 min or 9 miles or 15 km @ 50-65% MHR (14:30/developing male)
35-45 min or 7.5 miles or 12k @ 80-85% MHR (14:30/elite female)
(pm) Rest or 15-45 min recovery run

Sun: (am) 1:45 - 2:15 hr run or 15-20 miles or 20-32k @ 50-65% MHR
Use natural surfaces and a hilly terrain if possible.

Total Volume: 9-10 hr or 90-95 miles or 140-150 km.

A Sample Training Week in April of Phase II of the Pre-Competition Period
This Program is a Guide for a Developing Male or Elite Female Targeting 14:30 for 5000m

Mon: (pm) 15-20 min warm-up
Form drills and 6-10 x 100m relaxed accelerations
10-20 min cool-down

Tues: (am) 30 min or 4 miles or 6k @ 50-60% MHR
(pm) 15-20 min warm-up
5 x 800m @ 5k pace with 200m recovery as briskly as possible
If no race on Sat. run 10 x 300m @ 1500 pace with 100m jog recovery. If racing on Sat. run 6 x 200m @ 1500m rhythm with 200m jog recovery.
5-15 mins cool-down

Wed: (pm) 60-75 min or 9 miles or 15 km @ 50-65% MHR

Thur: (am) 30 min or 4 miles or 6k @ 50-60% MHR
(pm) 15-20 min warm-up
If racing on Sat. run 6 x 200m @ 1500m rhythm with 200m jog recovery.
5-15 min cool-down

Fri: (am) Rest or 30 min or 4 miles or 6k @ 50-60% MHR
(pm) Rest or 30 min or 4 miles or 6k @ 50-60% MHR

Sat: (am) Rest or 10-20 min jog, including striding & stretching.
(pm) 800m to 3k race or 5k race simulation @ 92-95% MHR on the track
If not racing the 5k simulation could be done in the morning.

Sun: (am) 1:45 - 2:15 hr run or 15-20 miles or 20-32k @ 50-65% MHR
Use natural surfaces and a hilly terrain if possible.

Total Volume: 9-10 hr or 90-95 miles or 140-150 km.

The Competition Period

Normally the Competition Period lasts from 8 to 12 weeks between mid-March and June for Northern Hemisphere athletes and mid-January to March for Southern Hemisphere athletes. The first major competition should be scheduled within 4 to 5 weeks after the Pre-Competition Period ends. This allows the athlete to compete in peak form in the post-major race period.

In the Competition Period the bulk of the training consists of racing, a weekly aerobic run, recovery runs, race rhythm and race maintaince workouts and the occasional harder time trial if there are no races in the immediate future.

Objectives and guidelines (Fig. 9-4)
- Plan peak race performance within 3-7 weeks of the competition phase
- Plan to use the last 3-5 weeks of competition period for additional racing.

Mid-April-May-June (Nothern Hemisphere)
Mid-January-February-March (Southern Hemisphere)
- Make sure the long run and the 15-45 min recovery runs are at an easy pace and on grass or dirt
- Continue accelerations and drills on 1-2 day per week
- Complete one event-specific workout or under-distance race per week
- Reduce weight training to 1-2 days per week.
- Continue race rhythm and race simulation, and do race tactical workouts as necessary.

A Sample Training Week in May of Phase I and II of the Competition Period
This Program is a Guide for a Developing Male or Elite Female Targeting 14:30 for 5000m

Mon: (pm)   15-20 min warm-up
Form drills and 6-10 x 100m relaxed accelerations
10-20 min cool-down

Tues: (am)   30 min or 4 miles or 6k @ 50-60% MHR

(pm)   15-20 min warm-up
10-15 x 300m @ 5k pace with 100m jog recovery.
If racing on Sat. run 8-10 x 300m @ 1500m pace with 100m jog recovery.
5-15 mins cool-down

Wed: (am)   Rest or 30 min or 4 miles or 6 km easily

(pm)   45-60 min or 7-9 miles or 12-15 km easily

Thur: (am)   30 min or 4 miles or 6k @ 50-60% MHR

(pm)   15-20 min warm-up
10 laps of 100m sprint/100m float @ 90% effort
If racing on Sat. run 6 x 200m accelerations with 200m jog.
5-15 mins cool-down

Fri: (am)   Rest or 30 min or 4 miles or 6k @ 50-60% MHR

(pm)   Rest or 20-30 min or 3-4 miles or 5-6k, including 2-4 x 50m race practice starts

Sat: (am)   Rest or 10-20 min jog including striding & stretching.

(pm)   Race or 5k race simulation @ 92-95% MHR off the track
If not racing the 5k simulation could be done in the morning.

Sun: (am)   1-2 hr run or 10-18 miles or 15-30k @ 50-65% MHR
Use natural surfaces and a hilly terrain if possible.

Total Volume: 9-10 hr or 90-95 miles or 140-150 km.

PEAKING

Each athlete will probably need to race at least once prior to a major race in order to reach peak form. This will vary for each individual. The number of races outlined in Fig. 9-5 may be used as a guide.

FIGURE 9-5: THE STATISTICS OF PEAKING

The approximate number of races needed to reach peak form	
Race Distance	Races needed
800m	4
1500m/16003	3
3000m/3200m	2-3
5000m	1-2
10,000m	1

FIGURE 9-4: A SAMPLE BREAKDOWN OF TRAINING IN THE COMPETITION PERIOD.

1. Recovery Pace	= 40-50%	(of weekly mileage)
2. General Conditioning Pace	= 8-10%	(of weekly mileage)
3. Lactate Threshold, Aerobic Power, MVO$_2$, Lactic Acid Tolerance, Lactate Production Pace which includes all races.	= 18-20%	(of weekly mileage)
4. One Long Run Over Trails/Parks	= 16-22%	(of weekly mileage)
5. Speed (1 session)	= 1-2%	(of weekly mileage)

SECTION 2

TRAINING TOOLS

CHAPTER 10
PERFORMANCE INDICATORS

An essential element in producing the correct training programs is knowing the athlete's condition at all times. In this context the Bowerman concepts of "Goal Pace" and "Date Pace" are very relevant. An athlete's goal pace, i.e., the time targeted for the end of the major event of the season, will be very different from the athlete's date pace, i.e., his current capacities in, say, the early Base Period.

Obviously, time trials are the best way to establish the athlete's date pace at any given time but the coach does not want to be time trialing endlessly. It is helpful if a time trial run over one distance can be used to estimate the athlete's ability over other related distances. Some simple conversions are set out in Fig. 10-1 below. Using time trials regularly will allow the coach to set the athlete's date training pace with maximum accuracy and a minimum of interruption to training.

FIGURE 10-1: TIME TRIAL INDICATORS

Event	
400m	= (200m time x 2) + 10%
800m	= (400m time + 5.5 sec) x 2
1500m	= (800m time x 2) + 1-5 seconds
3000m	= (1500m time x 2) + 20-25 seconds
2 mile	= (1 mile time + 20 sec) x 2
3 mile	= (1 mile time x 3) + 75 sec
5000m	= (3k time x 1.70) + 5-10 seconds
10,000m	= (3k time x 3.50) + 20-30 seconds
10,000m	= (5k time x 2.10) +/- 10 seconds

The Use Of Specific Stamina Indicators

Essentially, this section of *Run With The Best* is about modelling. That means applying the information available about past and present great athletes to assist in coaching athletes for the future. The reader should note that the use of past athletes as examples is deliberate because there cannot be any further improvements to their performances. The modelling, therefore, is not theoretical and does not come from laboratory analysis. The statistical information on the performances of middle and long distance runners presented in this chapter, and throughout the book, is the result of Tony Benson's experiences and his extensive research using *Track & Field News* since 1960 and the Association of Track & Field Statisticians *International Track & Field Handbook* since 1985.

If a college coach has a male 1500m runner with a 400m PR of 51 seconds and a 1500m PR of 3:47, these are facts that can be verified. If another coach has a runner with similar speed but who has run 3:38, that too is fact. If no examples of athletes running 3:36 with a 400m PR slower than 50 seconds can be found, it is unrealistic of either of the above coaches to expect his athlete to run a 3:36 without improving his 400m time by half a second or so.

Arthur Lydiard was the first coach to draw attention to the relationship between an athlete's basic speed and his or her potential over longer distances when he made the point that most athletes have the speed to run at world record pace for almost any event but they lack the stamina to sustain the speed. Many athletes can run 200m in 25 seconds. No one has yet run four consecutive 200's in 25 seconds each, however, without recovery in between (i.e., 1:40 for 800m).

The figure that links a runner's speed and endurance can be called a "stamina indicator" (S.I.) and, is calculated by dividing one distance (the longer one) by another distance (the shorter one). For example US 800m record holder Johnny Gray has a 400m PR of 46.3 and an 800m PR of 1:42.6. His S.I. for these two events is 2.21.

If high school, college or club coaches learn the personal bests of a significant number of elite athletes, they can determine and use specific stamina indicators to inspire their athletes.

The kids may not know the names of the runners the coach uses as examples but that does not matter. What does matter is that the coach can present the squad with times they can relate to over distances they are familiar with to demonstrate what an athlete may be capable of in the future. What an athlete cannot dream he cannot envisage. Without a vision of himself at another place in time the athlete can never reach his potential.

Multi-world record holder Ron Clarke provides an instructive example for young runners. Clarke's best times were 1:53 for the 800m, 4:00.1 for the mile (equal to 3:43 for 1500m), 7:47 for 3,000m, 13:16 for 5000m and 27:37 for 10,000m. There are many high school boys who can reproduce Clarke's 800m time, so the coach of any developing runner who can run 1:53 has a model his athlete can aspire to. If Clarke could run 4:00 for the mile, 13:16 for 5000m and 27:39 for 10k, so can that athlete provided he has the will to do the daily training and the patience to let the training take effect over a number of years.

The coach could present his developing female athletes with the example of a girl whose career high 800m was only 2:05.9 yet she won an Olympic medal and ran 4:01 for 1500, 14:49 for 5000m, 30:57 for 10,000m and 2:27 for the marathon. That person was the UK's Liz McColgan (silver medal, 10K, 1988 Games).

By studying a large number of top male and female athletes the coach can develop gender-specific exemplary stamina indicators. Early on, the understanding of the relationship between 800m and the longer distances is extremely useful because youngsters perform intrinsically better at 800m before they will at any longer distance. This is the time to encourage them to believe to believe in their full potential.

If Clarke's 10k time is divided by his 800m time he demonstrates an S.I. of 14.7 and, based on the number of athletes studied over the years, this S.I. would be considered above average for a world class 5000m - 10,000m runner. A good S.I. for the college and club athlete would be between 15 and 15.5 while anyone seriously running 5k/10k who has an S.I. greater than 15.5 could be described as lacking specific stamina for the distance events.

Stamina indicators can also be used to *increase an athlete's awareness of his potential and predict future times for events.* The coach of a high school or college athlete with the potential to develop to the elite level must know what speed and strength levels the athlete needs to achieve in both the immediate and long-term future. The qualifying standards for major championships and world records of today will be different in 2000, 2004 or 2008. Any coach with a promising 16-year-old athlete has to be thinking of what the records will be in 2005 to 2010 because that is when his or her athlete will be between 25 and 29 years of age.

Studying examples of the relationships that exist today between speed and stamina in various events can be very instructive for the coach.

Haile Gebrselassie has run 3:31.76 (indoors) for 1500m. A comparison between his 1500m time and his 10k best of 26:22.75 reveals an exemplary stamina indicator of 7.47. Ron Clarke's 1500m to 10k relationship slightly betters this at 7.44. If this 7.44 indicator is applied to Gebrselassie's 1500m time it suggests a time around 26:15 for 10k is achievable.

The same principle can be applied to 5000m. Noureddine Morceli has run 3:27 for 1500m and 13:03 for 5000m. This is an S.I. of 3.87. Current 5k record holder Daniel Komen (12:39) has run 3:29 for 1500m which gives him an S.I. of 3.63. Both are behind US 5000m record holder Bob Kennedy's S.I. of 3.56 based on times of 3:38 and 12:58! A combina-

Ron Clarke

tion of Kennedy's stamina and Komen's speed makes a time of 12:30 just as realistic as 26:15 is for 10k.

Then there is the matchup of Morceli's 1500m speed and Kennedy's stamina. Can any coach get his mind around 12:15 and 25:35? Will it ever happen? Of course! When Zatopek ran 28:54 for 10,000m who would have dreamed of 26:22?

Using Stamina Indicators to Plan Training

Does information relating to stamina indicators have any relevance to planning coaching programs? Yes. Bob Kennedy has a very high S.I. Coincidently it is equal to Ron Clarke's and superior to most Africans, including both Gebrselassie and Komen. Clarke raced regularly over 800m and 1500m—something *Run With The Best* suggests all distance runners should consider. In Kennedy's situation a combination of maintaining his stamina and improving his 1500m capability by two seconds could see him run below 12:50.

The word "capability" is used advisedly. High school, college and club athletes will always have the opportunity to compete over 800m and 1500m (or 1600m) when in peak form but an elite athlete will be running his or her speciality event at this time and may not have the opportunities to race

FIGURE 10-2: EXEMPLARY STAMINA INDICATORS

Events		Elite/ International	National/ College	Developmental/ High School
400m to 800m	M	2.16 (W. Kipketer)	2.19	2.31
	W	2.13 (K. Holmes)	2.23	2.34
800m to 1500m	M	1.98 (N. Morceli)	2.00	2.07
	W	1.98 (H. Boulmerka)	2.03	2.20
800m to 1600m	M	N/A	N/A	2.23
	W	N/A	N/A	2.36
800m to 3200m	M	N/A	N/A	4.96
	W	N/A	N/A	5.18
1600m to 3200m	M	N/A	N/A	2.23
	W	N/A	N/A	2.36
1500m to 5000m	M	3.56 (B. Kennedy)	3.65	3.80
	W	3.55 (F. Ribeiro)	3.70	3.95
1500m to 10,000m	M	7.47 (H. Gebrselassie)	7.70	N/A
	W	7.63 (W. Junxia)	7.75	N/A
5000m to 10,000m	M	2.06 (P. Tergat)	2.10	N/A
	W	2.05 (L. McColgan)	2.15	N/A
10,000m to Marathon	M	4.46 (S. Lelei)	4.60	N/A
	W*	4.45 (U. Pippig)	4.65	N/A

*1984 Olympic champion Joan Benoit has the extraordinary S.I. of 4.37!

Data relating to current athletes is based on data contained in the IAAF's annual track & field handbooks.

over the shorter distances.

What about the 1500m and mile? Sebastian Coe, for example, ran 1:41.7 for 800m and 3:47 for the mile. This is a stamina indicator of 2.22. Current American record holder Steve Scott's best times were 1:45 and 3:47—a stamina indicator of 2.16, while Morceli has a stamina indicator of 2.17 based on his times of 2:13.73 for 1000m (i.e., 1:43 for 800m) and 3:44.39 for mile. A combination of Coe's speed and either Scott's or Morceli's stamina suggests a sub-3:40 mile time (and a 3:22-3:23/1500m) is definitely possible.

Finally there is the 800m. Johnny Gray's 400-800 S.I. of 2.21 has already been mentioned. Dual Olympic gold medalists Sebastian Coe and Alberto Juantorena can give the reader a clue as to the future. If we use Coe's 800m WR time of 1:41.71 and his reported 400m best of 46.5 he achieves an S.I. of 2.19 which is exactly the type of figure that could be expected from a back-to-back Olympic 1500m gold medalist. On the other hand, Alberto Juantorena's 800m World Record of 1:43.4 was achieved off a 400m time of 44.2. This is a stamina indicator of 2.34—a figure high school athletes can achieve. Because of Juantorena's 400m speed, it was good enough to set a WR in 1976.

Today there are many 400m runners with the capacity to run 800m who have already run below 45.5 400m. The 1:40 800m barrier will be broken as soon as any one of them develops their stamina to Gray's or Coe's level.

In conclusion stamina indicators should not be dismissed as being esoteric by the average coach because they have fundamental implications at the school, college and club level.

An awareness of what is occurring should alert the coach in charge of younger athletes to the importance of ensuring each of them acquires a very solid aerobic foundation and develops their speed to the highest levels possible.

An understanding of stamina indicators will also help the college coach or coach of senior athletes to pinpoint weaknesses. It is common for many senior runners to have stamina indicator levels already equal to elite internationals but few recognize the fact. These athletes continue to strive for further improvement through increased volume and/or intensity when their focus should be on attaining more speed while maintaining stamina.

CHAPTER 11
TRAINING INDICATORS

Training Pace Tables

The Training Pace Tables focus on the relationship between speed over 400m and the athlete's lactate threshold capacities. The preferred test distances are 400m and 10 miles (16km) at 85-87% effort. For athletes who are not capable of running 10k in less than 40 minutes, a run of 7.5 miles or 12k at 80-87% might be preferable.

The table is used as follows. The athlete is instructed to run 10 miles or 16k at 85% of MHR, which means he starts lower but may end as high as 87% MHR. The coach then consults Table 11-2 to assign a point score to the run. If, for example, the athlete ran 56:24 at 80-87% MHR his or her point score would be 1710.

If the coach also knows what the athlete is currently capable of running 400m in, say, 55 seconds (also 1710 points), then the coach can predict that the athlete is capable of running equivalent times over 800m, 1500m, 3k, 5k and 10k.

To score equal points for the 400m and 10-mile or 16k threshold run would be highly unusual. Still if it did occur it would tell the coach that the athlete probably needs to improve his 400m speed if he wants to improve performances over the longer distances. This diagnosis would also be true for any athlete whose 400m time was worth less points than his threshold run.

On the other hand, if the 400m time earns the athlete significantly more points than the threshold run it indicates a lack of stamina. This in turn means the coach must place more emphasis on general conditioning, threshold, aerobic power and maximal oxygen uptake to improve the 5k and 10k; on threshold, maximal oxygen uptake and anaerobic power to improve the 3k; and on threshold, anaerobic power and lactic acid tolerance to improve the 1500m and 800m.

The two scenarios outlined below are the most common a coach will encounter. The first is the athlete who can meet the various time criteria down to about 2 miles or 3000m but cannot reach the times for 1500m and below. The second scenario involves the athlete, normally a developing one, whose times from 400m to 1500m are "faster" than his times for distances from 3000m to 10k.

In the case of first scenario the coach's task is to try to increase the athlete's speed so he or she can use that speed to run faster over the longer distances. If we're dealing with a second-scenario athlete, then he/she should work on stamina, though speed must not be neglected.

Using the Tables for Training Purposes

A 10-mile or 16km threshold run may be used to test any athlete who can run 40 minutes or faster for 10,000m. When a threshold run is prescribed as a training session it should not exceed 57 minutes. A study of Fig. 11-2 shows that an athlete whose 10k PR is slower than 31:37 (1700 points or less) will exceed 57 min when running 16k/10 miles at threshold pace. If the coach then focuses on the 12km/7.5-mile column of Fig. 11-2, he will see that 7.5 miles/12km is more appropriate for an athlete who runs between 31:37 and 42:49 for 10k. If an athlete cannot run below 43 min for 10k, *Run With The Best* suggests that the coach direct his athlete to run 5 miles or 8km at threshold, and if there is any athlete in the group who cannot better 64 min for 10k, that athlete should be directed to run 4 miles (6.5k).

Figure 11-1

	Points	10 miles or 16k @ 85%MHR	10k Time	5k Time	3k Time	1500m Time	800m Time	400m Time
Scenario No 1	1710 1690 1670 1650	56:24	31:22	15:00	8:40	4:07.6	2:04.6	57.1
Scenario No 2	1770 1750 1730 1710	56:24	31:22	15:00	8:31	3:57.3	1:55.9	52.7

Some of these times, e.g., 43 minutes or 64 minutes, may sound very slow, but the coach will surely find some very fast 400m/800m types who find running 10km very difficult and nursing them along for a while will ensure they are not frightened away from running distance work.

One final point about the use of the Training Pace Tables. The coach should be aware that only the 10-mile or 16km threshold run is a valid indicator of times at 3k to 10k. The use of the 7.5-mile or 12 km is appropriate for developing middle distance runners and even elite 800m runners as a training workout but its validity extends only to 3000m at best.

If the shorter distances of 5 miles (8km) or 4 miles (6.5km) are used it should only be because the athletes are still in the developmental stages and their long runs have not yet exceeded one hour.

WORKSHEET NO. 11

The coach is asked to fill in Worksheet No. 11, entering data relating to one of his/her athletes in the appropriate spaces.
1. The athlete's best times for 400m, 800m, 1500m, 3000m, 5000m, 10,000m, and 3000m steeplechase, if applicable. (If the athlete has not run some of the longer distances, put *conservative* estimated times in the appropriate spaces.
2. The point level the athlete is currently on for each of the above events.
3. The 100m pace recommended to maintain or improve the 400m time.
4. The distance most appropriate, e. g., 10 miles/16k, 7.5 miles/12k, 5miles/8k, etc., for the athlete's threshold run.
5. The recommended time for the threshold run.

WORKSHEET 11

Event	Time	Point Level	Time for the 100m Pace Runs	Distance of the Threshold Run	Time for the Threshold Run
400m					
800m					
1500m					
3000m					
5000m					
10,000m					
3000m S/C					

Figure 11-2: Lactate Training Paces For Middle And Long Distance Runners

Value of Performance Points	Lactate Threshold Training Pace (Based on Marathon Pace) 16 km / 10 Mile	Pace Min/Mile	Pace Min/Km	Middle Distance Alternative 12 km / 7.5 Mile	Estimated 10 km Capability Time	Min/Mi	Min/Km	Estimated 3k S/C Capability Time	Min/km	Estimated 5 km Capability Time	Min/Mi	Min/Km	Estimated 2 mile and 3k (MVO2) Capabilities 2 mile Time	3k Time	400m Pace	1 Mile Time	Estimated 800m/1500m Capabilities 1500m Time	800m Time	Basic Speed 400m Time	100m Pace
2000	0:44:20	4:26	2:46	0:33:16	24:19	3:53	02:26	7:10	2:23	11:37	3:43	2:19	7:14	6:44	0:53.8	3:28.8	3:14.1	1:36.1	0:43.8	10.8
1990	0:44:45	4:29	2:48	0:33:34	24:34	3:56	02:27	7:15	2:25	11:44	3:45	2:21	7:18	6:48	0:54.4	3:30.7	3:15.8	1:36.9	0:44.2	10.9
1980	0:45:10	4:31	2:49	0:33:53	24:48	3:58	02:29	7:19	2:26	11:51	3:48	2:22	7:22	6:52	0:54.9	3:32.5	3:17.5	1:37.8	0:44.6	11.0
1970	0:45:35	4:34	2:51	0:34:12	25:03	4:00	02:30	7:24	2:28	11:58	3:50	2:24	7:27	6:56	0:55.4	3:34.4	3:19.2	1:38.7	0:45.1	11.1
1960	0:46:00	4:36	2:53	0:34:31	25:18	4:03	02:32	7:28	2:29	12:05	3:52	2:25	7:31	7:00	0:56.0	3:36.3	3:21.0	1:39.5	0:45.5	11.2
1950	0:46:25	4:39	2:54	0:34:49	25:32	4:05	02:33	7:32	2:31	12:12	3:54	2:26	7:35	7:04	0:56.5	3:38.1	3:22.7	1:40.4	0:46.0	11.3
1940	0:46:50	4:41	2:56	0:35:08	25:47	4:07	02:35	7:37	2:32	12:19	3:57	2:28	7:39	7:08	0:57.0	3:40.0	3:24.4	1:41.3	0:46.4	11.5
1930	0:47:15	4:44	2:57	0:35:27	26:01	4:10	02:36	7:41	2:34	12:27	3:59	2:29	7:43	7:12	0:57.5	3:41.9	3:26.2	1:42.1	0:46.8	11.5
1920	0:47:40	4:46	2:59	0:35:46	26:16	4:12	02:38	7:46	2:35	12:34	4:01	2:31	7:48	7:16	0:58.1	3:43.7	3:27.9	1:43.0	0:47.1	11.6
1910	0:48:05	4:49	3:00	0:36:04	26:31	4:14	02:39	7:50	2:37	12:41	4:03	2:32	7:52	7:20	0:58.6	3:45.6	3:29.6	1:43.8	0:47.5	11.7
1900	0:48:30	4:51	3:02	0:36:23	26:45	4:17	02:41	7:54	2:38	12:48	4:06	2:34	7:56	7:23	0:59.1	3:47.5	3:31.3	1:44.7	0:47.9	11.8
1890	0:48:55	4:53	3:03	0:36:42	27:00	4:19	02:42	7:59	2:40	12:55	4:08	2:35	8:00	7:27	0:59.7	3:49.3	3:33.1	1:45.6	0:48.2	11.9
1880	0:49:20	4:56	3:05	0:37:00	27:14	4:21	02:43	8:03	2:41	13:02	4:10	2:36	8:05	7:31	1:00.2	3:51.2	3:34.8	1:46.4	0:48.6	12.0
1870	0:49:45	4:58	3:07	0:37:19	27:29	4:24	02:45	8:08	2:43	13:09	4:12	2:38	8:09	7:35	1:00.7	3:53.1	3:36.5	1:47.3	0:49.0	12.1
1860	0:50:10	5:01	3:08	0:37:37	27:44	4:26	02:46	8:12	2:44	13:16	4:15	2:39	8:13	7:39	1:01.3	3:54.9	3:38.2	1:48.2	0:49.4	12.2
1850	0:50:35	5:03	3:10	0:37:56	27:58	4:29	02:48	8:16	2:45	13:23	4:17	2:41	8:17	7:43	1:01.8	3:56.8	3:40.0	1:49.0	0:49.7	12.3
1840	0:51:00	5:06	3:11	0:38:15	28:13	4:31	02:49	8:21	2:47	13:30	4:19	2:42	8:22	7:47	1:02.3	3:58.7	3:41.7	1:49.9	0:50.1	12.4
1830	0:51:25	5:08	3:13	0:38:33	28:27	4:33	02:51	8:25	2:48	13:37	4:22	2:43	8:26	7:51	1:02.8	4:00.5	3:43.4	1:50.8	0:50.5	12.5
1820	0:51:50	5:11	3:14	0:38:52	28:42	4:36	02:52	8:30	2:50	13:44	4:26	2:45	8:30	7:55	1:03.4	4:02.4	3:45.2	1:51.6	0:50.8	12.6
1810	0:52:15	5:13	3:16	0:39:10	28:57	4:38	02:54	8:34	2:51	13:52	4:28	2:46	8:34	7:59	1:03.9	4:04.3	3:46.9	1:52.5	0:51.2	12.6
1800	0:52:40	5:16	3:17	0:39:29	29:11	4:40	02:55	8:39	2:53	13:59	4:31	2:48	8:39	8:03	1:04.4	4:06.1	3:48.6	1:53.3	0:51.6	12.7
1790	0:53:05	5:18	3:19	0:39:47	29:26	4:43	02:57	8:43	2:54	14:06	4:33	2:49	8:43	8:07	1:05.0	4:08.0	3:50.3	1:54.2	0:51.9	12.8
1780	0:53:30	5:21	3:21	0:40:06	29:40	4:45	02:58	8:47	2:56	14:13	4:35	2:51	8:47	8:11	1:05.5	4:09.9	3:52.1	1:55.1	0:52.3	12.9
1770	0:53:55	5:23	3:22	0:40:25	29:55	4:47	02:59	8:52	2:57	14:20	4:37	2:52	8:51	8:15	1:06.0	4:11.7	3:53.8	1:55.9	0:52.7	13.0
1760	0:54:20	5:26	3:24	0:40:43	30:10	4:50	03:01	8:56	2:59	14:27	4:40	2:53	8:55	8:19	1:06.6	4:13.6	3:55.5	1:56.8	0:53.1	13.1
1750	0:54:45	5:28	3:25	0:41:02	30:24	4:52	03:02	9:01	3:00	14:34	4:42	2:55	9:00	8:23	1:07.1	4:15.5	3:57.3	1:57.7	0:53.4	13.2
1740	0:55:10	5:31	3:27	0:41:20	30:39	4:54	03:04	9:05	3:02	14:41	4:44	2:56	9:04	8:27	1:07.6	4:17.3	3:59.0	1:58.5	0:53.8	13.3
1730	0:55:34	5:33	3:28	0:41:39	30:53	4:57	03:05	9:09	3:03	14:48	4:47	2:58	9:08	8:31	1:08.1	4:19.2	4:00.7	1:59.4	0:54.2	13.3
1720	0:55:59	5:36	3:30	0:41:57	31:08	4:59	03:07	9:14	3:05	14:55	4:49	2:59	9:12	8:35	1:08.7	4:21.1	4:02.4	2:00.3	0:54.5	13.5
1710	0:56:24	5:38	3:32	0:42:16	31:23	5:01	03:08	9:18	3:06	15:02	4:51	3:00	9:17	8:39	1:09.2	4:22.9	4:04.2	2:01.1	0:54.9	13.6
1700	0:56:49	5:41	3:33	0:42:35	31:37	5:04	03:10	9:23	3:08	15:09	4:53	3:02	9:21	8:43	1:09.7	4:24.8	4:05.9	2:02.0	0:55.3	13.6
1690	0:57:14	5:43	3:35	0:42:53	31:52	5:06	03:11	9:27	3:09	15:17	4:56	3:03	9:25	8:47	1:10.3	4:26.7	4:07.6	2:02.9	0:55.6	13.7
1680	0:57:39	5:46	3:36	0:43:12	32:06	5:08	03:13	9:31	3:10	15:24	4:58	3:05	9:29	8:51	1:10.8	4:28.5	4:09.4	2:03.7	0:56.0	13.8

Figure 11-2: Lactate Training Paces For Middle And Long Distance Runners

Value of Performance	Lactate Threshold Training Pace (Based on Marathon Pace)			Middle Distance Alternative	Estimated 10 km Capability			Estimated 3k S/C Capability			Estimated 5 km Capability				Estimated 2 mile and 3k (MVO2) Capabilities				Estimated 800m/1500m Capabilities				Basic Speed	
Points	16 km 10 Mile	Pace Min/Mile	Pace Min/Km	12 km 7.5 Mile	Time	Min/Mi	Min/Km	Time	Min/Km	Time	Min/Mi	Min/Km	2 mile Time	3k Time	400m Pace	1 Mile Time	1500m Time	800m Time	400m Time	100m Pace
1670	0:58:04	5:48	3:38	0:43:30	32:21	5:11	03:14	9:36	3:12	15:31	5:00	3:06	9:34	8:55	1:11.3	4:30.4	4:11.1	2:04.6	0:56.4	13.9
1660	0:58:29	5:51	3:39	0:43:49	32:36	5:13	03:16	9:40	3:13	15:38	5:03	3:08	9:38	8:59	1:11.8	4:32.3	4:12.8	2:05.4	0:56.8	14.0
1650	0:58:54	5:53	3:41	0:44:07	32:50	5:15	03:17	9:45	3:15	15:45	5:05	3:09	9:42	9:03	1:12.4	4:34.1	4:14.5	2:06.3	0:57.1	14.1
1640	0:59:19	5:56	3:42	0:44:26	33:05	5:18	03:18	9:49	3:16	15:52	5:07	3:10	9:46	9:07	1:12.9	4:36.0	4:16.3	2:07.2	0:57.5	14.2
1630	0:59:44	5:58	3:44	0:44:45	33:19	5:20	03:20	9:53	3:18	15:59	5:09	3:12	9:51	9:11	1:13.4	4:37.9	4:18.0	2:08.0	0:57.9	14.3
1620	1:00:09	6:01	3:46	0:45:03	33:34	5:22	03:21	9:58	3:19	16:06	5:12	3:13	9:55	9:15	1:14.0	4:39.7	4:19.7	2:08.9	0:58.2	14.4
1610	1:00:34	6:03	3:47	0:45:22	33:49	5:25	03:23	10:02	3:21	16:13	5:14	3:15	9:59	9:19	1:14.5	4:41.6	4:21.4	2:09.8	0:58.6	14.5
1600	1:00:59	6:06	3:49	0:45:40	34:03	5:27	03:24	10:07	3:22	16:20	5:16	3:16	10:03	9:23	1:15.0	4:43.5	4:23.2	2:10.6	0:59.0	14.6
1590	1:01:24	6:08	3:50	0:45:59	34:18	5:29	03:26	10:11	3:24	16:27	5:19	3:17	10:07	9:27	1:15.6	4:45.3	4:24.9	2:11.5	0:59.3	14.7
1580	1:01:49	6:11	3:52	0:46:17	34:32	5:32	03:27	10:15	3:25	16:34	5:21	3:19	10:12	9:31	1:16.1	4:47.2	4:26.6	2:12.4	0:59.7	14.7
1570	1:02:14	6:13	3:53	0:46:36	34:47	5:34	03:29	10:20	3:27	16:42	5:23	3:20	10:16	9:35	1:16.6	4:49.1	4:28.4	2:13.2	1:00.1	14.8
1560	1:02:39	6:16	3:55	0:46:55	35:02	5:36	03:30	10:24	3:28	16:49	5:25	3:22	10:20	9:39	1:17.1	4:50.9	4:30.1	2:14.1	1:00.5	14.9
1550	1:03:04	6:18	3:56	0:47:13	35:16	5:39	03:32	10:29	3:30	16:56	5:28	3:23	10:24	9:43	1:17.7	4:52.8	4:31.8	2:14.9	1:00.8	15.0
1540	1:03:29	6:21	3:58	0:47:32	35:31	5:41	03:33	10:33	3:31	17:03	5:30	3:25	10:29	9:47	1:18.2	4:54.7	4:33.5	2:15.8	1:01.2	15.1
1530	1:03:54	6:23	4:00	0:47:50	35:45	5:43	03:35	10:38	3:33	17:10	5:32	3:26	10:33	9:51	1:18.7	4:56.5	4:35.3	2:16.7	1:01.6	15.2
1520	1:04:19	6:26	4:01	0:48:09	36:00	5:46	03:36	10:42	3:34	17:17	5:35	3:27	10:37	9:55	1:19.3	4:58.4	4:37.0	2:17.5	1:01.9	15.3
1510	1:04:44	6:28	4:03	0:48:28	36:15	5:48	03:37	10:46	3:35	17:24	5:37	3:29	10:41	9:58	1:19.8	5:00.3	4:38.7	2:18.4	1:02.3	15.4
1500	1:05:09	6:31	4:04	0:48:46	36:29	5:50	03:39	10:51	3:37	17:31	5:39	3:30	10:46	10:02	1:20.3	5:02.1	4:40.5	2:19.3	1:02.7	15.5
1490	1:05:34	6:33	4:06	0:49:05	36:44	5:53	03:40	10:55	3:38	17:38	5:41	3:32	10:50	10:06	1:20.9	5:04.0	4:42.2	2:20.1	1:03.0	15.6
1480	1:05:59	6:36	4:07	0:49:23	36:58	5:55	03:42	11:00	3:40	17:45	5:44	3:33	10:54	10:10	1:21.4	5:05.9	4:43.9	2:21.0	1:03.4	15.7
1470	1:06:24	6:38	4:09	0:49:42	37:13	5:57	03:43	11:04	3:41	17:52	5:46	3:34	10:58	10:14	1:21.9	5:07.7	4:45.6	2:21.9	1:03.8	15.7
1460	1:06:49	6:41	4:11	0:50:00	37:28	6:00	03:45	11:08	3:43	17:59	5:48	3:36	11:02	10:18	1:22.4	5:09.6	4:47.4	2:22.7	1:04.2	15.8
1450	1:07:14	6:43	4:12	0:50:19	37:42	6:02	03:46	11:13	3:44	18:07	5:51	3:37	11:07	10:22	1:23.0	5:11.5	4:49.1	2:23.6	1:04.5	15.9
1440	1:07:39	6:46	4:14	0:50:38	37:57	6:04	03:48	11:17	3:46	18:14	5:53	3:39	11:11	10:26	1:23.5	5:13.3	4:50.8	2:24.5	1:04.9	16.0
1430	1:08:04	6:48	4:15	0:50:56	38:11	6:07	03:49	11:22	3:47	18:21	5:55	3:40	11:15	10:30	1:24.0	5:15.2	4:52.6	2:25.3	1:05.3	16.1
1420	1:08:29	6:51	4:17	0:51:15	38:26	6:09	03:51	11:26	3:49	18:28	5:57	3:42	11:19	10:34	1:24.6	5:17.1	4:54.3	2:26.2	1:05.6	16.2
1410	1:08:54	6:53	4:18	0:51:33	38:41	6:11	03:52	11:30	3:50	18:35	6:00	3:43	11:24	10:38	1:25.1	5:18.9	4:56.0	2:27.0	1:06.0	16.3
1400	1:09:18	6:56	4:20	0:51:52	38:55	6:14	03:54	11:35	3:52	18:42	6:02	3:44	11:28	10:42	1:25.6	5:20.8	4:57.7	2:27.9	1:06.4	16.4
1390	1:09:43	6:58	4:21	0:52:10	39:10	6:16	03:55	11:39	3:53	18:49	6:04	3:46	11:32	10:46	1:26.2	5:22.7	4:59.5	2:28.8	1:06.7	16.5
1380	1:10:08	7:01	4:23	0:52:29	39:24	6:18	03:56	11:44	3:55	18:56	6:07	3:47	11:36	10:50	1:26.7	5:24.5	5:01.2	2:29.6	1:07.1	16.6
1370	1:10:33	7:03	4:25	0:52:48	39:39	6:21	03:58	11:48	3:56	19:03	6:09	3:49	11:41	10:54	1:27.2	5:26.4	5:02.9	2:30.5	1:07.5	16.7
1360	1:10:58	7:06	4:26	0:53:06	39:54	6:23	03:59	11:52	3:57	19:10	6:11	3:50	11:45	10:58	1:27.7	5:28.2	5:04.6	2:31.4	1:07.9	16.8

Figure 11-2: Lactate Training Paces For Middle And Long Distance Runners

Value of Performance	Lactate Threshold Training Pace (Based on Marathon Pace)			Middle Distance Alternative	Estimated 10 km Capability			Estimated 3k S/C Capability		Estimated 5 km Capability			Estimated 2 mile and 3k (MVO2) Capabilities				Estimated 800m/1500m Capabilities			Basic Speed	
Points	16 km 10 Mile	Pace Min/Mile	Pace Min/km	12 km 7.5 Mile	Time	Min/Mi	Min/Km	Time	Min/km	Time	Min/Mi	Min/Km	2 mile Time	3k Time	400m Pace	1 Mile Time	1500m Time	800m Time	400m Time	100m Pace
1350	1:11.23	7:08	4:28	0:53.25	40.08	6:25	04:01	11:57	3:59	19:17	6:13	3:51	11:49	11:02	1:28.3	5:30.1	5:06.4	2:32.2	1:08.2	16.8
1340	1:11.48	7:11	4:29	0:53.43	40.23	6:28	04:02	12:01	4:00	19:25	6:16	3:53	11:53	11:06	1:28.8	5:32.0	5:08.1	2:33.1	1:08.6	16.9
1330	1:12.13	7:13	4:31	0:54.02	40.37	6:30	04:04	12:06	4:02	19:32	6:18	3:54	11:58	11:10	1:29.3	5:33.8	5:09.8	2:34.0	1:09.0	17.0
1320	1:12.38	7:16	4:32	0:54.20	40.52	6:32	04:05	12:10	4:03	19:39	6:20	3:56	12:02	11:14	1:29.9	5:35.7	5:11.6	2:34.8	1:09.3	17.1
1310	1:13.03	7:18	4:34	0:54.39	41.07	6:35	04:07	12:14	4:05	19:46	6:23	3:57	12:06	11:18	1:30.4	5:37.6	5:13.3	2:35.7	1:09.7	17.2
1300	1:13.28	7:21	4:36	0:54.58	41.21	6:37	04:08	12:19	4:06	19:53	6:25	3:59	12:10	11:22	1:30.9	5:39.4	5:15.0	2:36.5	1:10.1	17.3
1290	1:13.53	7:23	4:37	0:55.16	41.36	6:39	04:10	12:23	4:08	20:00	6:27	4:00	12:14	11:26	1:31.5	5:41.3	5:16.7	2:37.4	1:10.4	17.4
1280	1:14.18	7:26	4:39	0:55.35	41.50	6:42	04:11	12:28	4:09	20:07	6:29	4:01	12:19	11:30	1:32.0	5:43.2	5:18.5	2:38.3	1:10.8	17.5
1270	1:14.43	7:28	4:40	0:55.53	42.05	6:44	04:13	12:32	4:11	20:14	6:32	4:03	12:23	11:34	1:32.5	5:45.0	5:20.2	2:39.1	1:11.2	17.6
1260	1:15.08	7:31	4:42	0:56.12	42.20	6:46	04:14	12:36	4:12	20:21	6:34	4:04	12:27	11:38	1:33.0	5:46.9	5:21.9	2:40.0	1:11.6	17.7
1250	1:15.33	7:33	4:43	0:56.30	42.34	6:49	04:15	12:41	4:14	20:28	6:36	4:06	12:31	11:42	1:33.6	5:48.8	5:23.7	2:40.9	1:11.9	17.8
1240	1:15.58	7:36	4:45	0:56.49	42.49	6:51	04:17	12:45	4:15	20:35	6:39	4:07	12:36	11:46	1:34.1	5:50.6	5:25.4	2:41.7	1:12.3	17.8
1230	1:16.23	7:38	4:46	0:57.08	43.03	6:53	04:18	12:50	4:17	20:42	6:41	4:08	12:40	11:50	1:34.6	5:52.5	5:27.1	2:42.6	1:12.7	17.9
1220	1:16.48	7:41	4:48	0:57.26	43.18	6:56	04:20	12:54	4:18	20:50	6:43	4:10	12:44	11:54	1:35.2	5:54.4	5:28.8	2:43.5	1:13.0	18.0
1210	1:17.13	7:43	4:50	0:57.45	43.33	6:58	04:21	12:59	4:20	20:57	6:45	4:11	12:48	11:58	1:35.7	5:56.2	5:30.6	2:44.3	1:13.4	18.1
1200	1:17.38	7:46	4:51	0:58.03	43.47	7:00	04:23	13:03	4:21	21:04	6:48	4:13	12:53	12:02	1:36.2	5:58.1	5:32.3	2:45.2	1:13.8	18.2
1190	1:18.03	7:48	4:53	0:58.22	44.02	7:03	04:24	13:07	4:22	21:11	6:50	4:14	12:57	12:06	1:36.8	6:00.0	5:34.0	2:46.1	1:14.1	18.3
1180	1:18.28	7:51	4:54	0:58.41	44.16	7:05	04:26	13:12	4:24	21:18	6:52	4:16	13:01	12:10	1:37.3	6:01.8	5:35.8	2:46.9	1:14.5	18.4
1170	1:18.53	7:53	4:56	0:58.59	44.31	7:07	04:27	13:16	4:25	21:25	6:55	4:17	13:05	12:14	1:37.8	6:03.7	5:37.5	2:47.8	1:14.9	18.5
1160	1:19.18	7:56	4:57	0:59.18	44.46	7:10	04:29	13:21	4:27	21:32	6:57	4:18	13:09	12:18	1:38.3	6:05.6	5:39.2	2:48.6	1:15.3	18.6
1150	1:19.43	7:58	4:59	0:59.36	45.00	7:12	04:30	13:25	4:28	21:39	6:59	4:20	13:14	12:22	1:38.9	6:07.4	5:40.9	2:49.5	1:15.6	18.7
1140	1:20.08	8:01	5:00	0:59.55	45.15	7:14	04:31	13:29	4:30	21:46	7:01	4:21	13:18	12:26	1:39.4	6:09.3	5:42.7	2:50.4	1:16.0	18.8
1130	1:20.33	8:03	5:02	1:00.13	45.29	7:17	04:33	13:34	4:31	21:53	7:04	4:23	13:22	12:30	1:39.9	6:11.2	5:44.4	2:51.2	1:16.4	18.9
1120	1:20.58	8:06	5:04	1:00.32	45.44	7:19	04:34	13:38	4:33	22:00	7:06	4:24	13:26	12:33	1:40.5	6:13.0	5:46.1	2:52.1	1:16.7	18.9
1110	1:21.23	8:08	5:05	1:00.51	45.59	7:21	04:36	13:43	4:34	22:07	7:08	4:25	13:31	12:37	1:41.0	6:14.9	5:47.8	2:53.0	1:17.1	19.0
1100	1:21.48	8:11	5:07	1:01.09	46.13	7:24	04:37	13:47	4:36	22:15	7:11	4:27	13:35	12:41	1:41.5	6:16.8	5:49.6	2:53.8	1:17.5	19.1
1090	1:22.13	8:13	5:08	1:01.28	46.28	7:26	04:39	13:51	4:37	22:22	7:13	4:28	13:39	12:45	1:42.1	6:18.6	5:51.3	2:54.7	1:17.8	19.2
1080	1:22.38	8:16	5:10	1:01.46	46.42	7:28	04:40	13:56	4:39	22:29	7:15	4:30	13:43	12:49	1:42.6	6:20.5	5:53.0	2:55.6	1:18.2	19.3
1070	1:23.02	8:18	5:11	1:02.05	46.57	7:31	04:42	14:00	4:40	22:36	7:17	4:31	13:48	12:53	1:43.1	6:22.4	5:54.8	2:56.4	1:18.6	19.4
1060	1:23.27	8:21	5:13	1:02.23	47.12	7:33	04:43	14:05	4:42	22:43	7:20	4:33	13:52	12:57	1:43.6	6:24.2	5:56.5	2:57.3	1:19.0	19.5
1050	1:23.52	8:23	5:15	1:02.42	47.26	7:35	04:45	14:09	4:43	22:50	7:22	4:34	13:56	13:01	1:44.2	6:26.1	5:58.2	2:58.1	1:19.3	19.6
1040	1:24.17	8:26	5:16	1:03.01	47.41	7:38	04:46	14:13	4:44	22:57	7:24	4:35	14:00	13:05	1:44.7	6:28.0	5:59.9	2:59.0	1:19.7	19.7

Figure 11-2: Lactate Training Paces For Middle And Long Distance Runners

Value of Performance Points	Lactate Threshold Training Pace (Based on Marathon Pace) 16 km 10 Mile	Pace Min/Mile	Pace Min/Km	Middle Distance Alternative 12 km 7.5 Mile	Estimated 10 km Capability Time	Min/Mi	Min/Km	Estimated 3k S/C Capability Time	Min/Km	Estimated 5 km Capability Time	Min/Mi	Min/Km	Estimated 2 mile and 3k (MVO2) Capabilities 2 mile Time	3k Time	400m Pace	Estimated 800m/1500m Capabilities 1 Mile Time	1500m Time	800m Time	Basic Speed 400m Time	100m Pace
1030	1:24:42	8.28	5.18	1:03:19	47:55	7.40	04:48	14:18	4:46	23:04	7:26	4:37	14:05	13:09	1:45.2	6:29.8	6:01.7	2:59.9	1:20.1	19.8
1020	1:25:07	8.31	5.19	1:03:38	48:10	7.42	04:49	14:22	4:47	23:11	7:29	4:38	14:09	13:13	1:45.8	6:31.7	6:03.4	3:00.7	1:20.4	19.9
1010	1:25:32	8.33	5.21	1:03:56	48:25	7.45	04:50	14:27	4:49	23:18	7:31	4:40	14:13	13:17	1:46.3	6:33.6	6:05.1	3:01.6	1:20.8	20.0
1000	1:25:57	8.36	5.22	1:04:15	48:39	7.47	04:52	14:31	4:50	23:25	7:33	4:41	14:17	13:21	1:46.8	6:35.4	6:06.9	3:02.5	1:21.2	20.0
990	1:26:22	8.38	5.24	1:04:33	48:54	7.49	04:53	14:35	4:52	23:32	7:36	4:42	14:21	13:25	1:47.4	6:37.3	6:08.6	3:03.3	1:21.5	20.1
980	1:26:47	8.41	5.25	1:04:52	49:08	7.52	04:55	14:40	4:53	23:40	7:38	4:44	14:26	13:29	1:47.9	6:39.2	6:10.3	3:04.2	1:21.9	20.2
970	1:27:12	8.43	5.27	1:05:11	49:23	7.54	04:56	14:44	4:55	23:47	7:40	4:45	14:30	13:33	1:48.4	6:41.0	6:12.0	3:05.1	1:22.3	20.3
960	1:27:37	8.46	5.29	1:05:29	49:38	7.56	04:58	14:49	4:56	23:54	7:42	4:47	14:34	13:37	1:48.9	6:42.9	6:13.8	3:05.9	1:22.7	20.4
950	1:28:02	8.48	5.30	1:05:48	49:52	7.59	04:59	14:53	4:58	24:01	7:45	4:48	14:38	13:41	1:49.5	6:44.8	6:15.5	3:06.8	1:23.0	20.5
940	1:28:27	8.51	5.32	1:06:06	50:07	8.01	05:01	14:57	4:59	24:08	7:47	4:50	14:43	13:45	1:50.0	6:46.6	6:17.2	3:07.7	1:23.4	20.6
930	1:28:52	8.53	5.33	1:06:25	50:21	8.03	05:02	15:02	5:01	24:15	7:49	4:51	14:47	13:49	1:50.5	6:48.5	6:19.0	3:08.5	1:23.8	20.7
920	1:29:17	8.56	5.35	1:06:43	50:36	8.06	05:04	15:06	5:02	24:22	7:52	4:52	14:51	13:53	1:51.1	6:50.4	6:20.7	3:09.4	1:24.1	20.8
910	1:29:42	8.58	5.36	1:07:02	50:51	8.08	05:05	15:11	5:04	24:29	7:54	4:54	14:55	13:57	1:51.6	6:52.2	6:22.4	3:10.2	1:24.5	20.9
900	1:30:07	9.01	5.38	1:07:21	51:05	8.10	05:07	15:15	5:05	24:36	7:56	4:55	15:00	14:01	1:52.1	6:54.1	6:24.1	3:11.1	1:24.9	21.0
890	1:30:32	9.03	5.39	1:07:39	51:20	8.13	05:08	15:20	5:07	24:43	7:58	4:57	15:04	14:05	1:52.7	6:56.0	6:25.9	3:12.0	1:25.2	21.0
880	1:30:57	9.06	5.41	1:07:58	51:34	8.15	05:09	15:24	5:08	24:50	8:01	4:58	15:08	14:09	1:53.2	6:57.8	6:27.6	3:12.8	1:25.6	21.1
870	1:31:22	9.08	5.43	1:08:16	51:49	8.17	05:11	15:28	5:09	24:58	8:03	5:00	15:12	14:13	1:53.7	6:59.7	6:29.3	3:13.7	1:26.0	21.2
860	1:31:47	9.11	5.44	1:08:35	52:04	8.20	05:12	15:33	5:11	25:05	8:05	5:01	15:16	14:17	1:54.2	7:01.6	6:31.0	3:14.6	1:26.4	21.3
850	1:32:12	9.13	5.46	1:08:54	52:18	8.22	05:14	15:37	5:12	25:12	8:08	5:02	15:21	14:21	1:54.8	7:03.4	6:32.8	3:15.4	1:26.7	21.4
840	1:32:37	9.16	5.47	1:09:12	52:33	8.24	05:15	15:42	5:14	25:19	8:10	5:04	15:25	14:25	1:55.3	7:05.3	6:34.5	3:16.3	1:27.1	21.5
830	1:33:02	9.18	5.49	1:09:31	52:47	8.27	05:17	15:46	5:15	25:26	8:12	5:05	15:29	14:29	1:55.8	7:07.2	6:36.2	3:17.2	1:27.5	21.6
820	1:33:27	9.21	5.50	1:09:49	53:02	8.29	05:18	15:50	5:17	25:33	8:14	5:07	15:33	14:33	1:56.4	7:09.0	6:38.0	3:18.0	1:27.8	21.7
810	1:33:52	9.23	5.52	1:10:08	53:17	8.31	05:20	15:55	5:18	25:40	8:17	5:08	15:38	14:37	1:56.9	7:10.9	6:39.7	3:18.9	1:28.2	21.8
800	1:34:17	9.26	5.54	1:10:26	53:31	8.34	05:21	15:59	5:20	25:47	8:19	5:09	15:42	14:41	1:57.4	7:12.8	6:41.4	3:19.7	1:28.6	21.9
790	1:34:42	9.28	5.55	1:10:45	53:46	8.36	05:23	16:04	5:21	25:54	8:21	5:11	15:46	14:45	1:58.0	7:14.6	6:43.1	3:20.6	1:28.9	22.0
780	1:35:07	9.31	5.57	1:11:04	54:00	8.38	05:24	16:08	5:23	26:01	8:24	5:12	15:50	14:49	1:58.5	7:16.5	6:44.9	3:21.5	1:29.3	22.1
770	1:35:32	9.33	5.58	1:11:22	54:15	8.41	05:26	16:12	5:24	26:08	8:26	5:14	15:55	14:53	1:59.0	7:18.4	6:46.6	3:22.3	1:29.7	22.1
760	1:35:57	9.36	6.00	1:11:41	54:30	8.43	05:27	16:17	5:26	26:15	8:28	5:15	15:59	14:57	1:59.5	7:20.2	6:48.3	3:23.2	1:30.1	22.2
750	1:36:22	9.38	6.01	1:11:59	54:44	8.45	05:28	16:21	5:27	26:23	8:30	5:17	16:03	15:01	2:00.1	7:22.1	6:50.1	3:24.1	1:30.4	22.3
740	1:36:46	9.41	6.03	1:12:18	54:59	8.48	05:30	16:26	5:29	26:30	8:33	5:18	16:07	15:05	2:00.6	7:24.0	6:51.8	3:24.9	1:30.8	22.4
730	1:37:11	9.43	6.04	1:12:36	55:14	8.50	05:31	16:30	5:30	26:37	8:35	5:19	16:12	15:08	2:01.1	7:25.8	6:53.5	3:25.8	1:31.2	22.5
720	1:37:36	9.46	6.06	1:12:55	55:28	8.52	05:33	16:34	5:31	26:44	8:37	5:21	16:16	15:12	2:01.7	7:27.7	6:55.2	3:26.7	1:31.5	22.6

Figure 11-2: Lactate Training Paces For Middle And Long Distance Runners

Value of Performance Points	Lactate Threshold Training Pace (Based on Marathon Pace) 16 km / 10 Mile	Pace Min/Mile	Pace Min/km	Middle Distance Alternative 12 km / 7.5 Mile	Estimated 10 km Capability Time	Min/Mi	Min/Km	Estimated 3k S/C Capability Time	Min/km	Estimated 5 km Capability Time	Min/Mi	Min/Km	Estimated 2 mile and 3k (MVO2) Capabilities 2 mile Time	3k Time	400m Pace	1 Mile Time	Estimated 800m/1500m Capabilities 1500m Time	800m Time	Basic Speed 400m Time	100m Pace
710	1:38:01	9:48	6:08	1:13:14	55:43	8:55	05:34	16:39	5:33	26:51	8:40	5:22	16:20	15:16	2:02.2	7:29.6	6:57.0	3:27.5	1:31.9	22.7
700	1:38:26	9:51	6:09	1:13:32	55:57	8:57	05:36	16:43	5:34	26:58	8:42	5:24	16:24	15:20	2:02.7	7:31.4	6:58.7	3:28.4	1:32.3	22.8
690	1:38:51	9:53	6:11	1:13:51	56:12	9:00	05:37	16:48	5:36	27:05	8:44	5:25	16:28	15:24	2:03.3	7:33.3	7:00.4	3:29.3	1:32.6	22.9
680	1:39:16	9:56	6:12	1:14:09	56:27	9:02	05:39	16:52	5:37	27:12	8:46	5:26	16:33	15:28	2:03.8	7:35.2	7:02.2	3:30.1	1:33.0	23.0
670	1:39:41	9:58	6:14	1:14:28	56:41	9:04	05:40	16:56	5:39	27:19	8:49	5:28	16:37	15:32	2:04.3	7:37.0	7:03.9	3:31.0	1:33.4	23.1
660	1:40:06	10:01	6:15	1:14:46	56:56	9:07	05:42	17:01	5:40	27:26	8:51	5:29	16:41	15:36	2:04.8	7:38.9	7:05.6	3:31.8	1:33.8	23.1
650	1:40:31	10:03	6:17	1:15:05	57:10	9:09	05:43	17:05	5:42	27:33	8:53	5:31	16:45	15:40	2:05.4	7:40.8	7:07.3	3:32.7	1:34.1	23.2
640	1:40:56	10:06	6:19	1:15:24	57:25	9:11	05:44	17:10	5:43	27:40	8:56	5:32	16:50	15:44	2:05.9	7:42.6	7:09.1	3:33.6	1:34.5	23.3
630	1:41:21	10:08	6:20	1:15:42	57:40	9:14	05:46	17:14	5:45	27:48	8:58	5:34	16:54	15:48	2:06.4	7:44.5	7:10.8	3:34.4	1:34.9	23.4
620	1:41:46	10:11	6:22	1:16:01	57:54	9:16	05:47	17:18	5:46	27:55	9:00	5:35	16:58	15:52	2:07.0	7:46.4	7:12.5	3:35.3	1:35.2	23.5
610	1:42:11	10:13	6:23	1:16:19	58:09	9:18	05:49	17:23	5:48	28:02	9:02	5:36	17:02	15:56	2:07.5	7:48.2	7:14.2	3:36.2	1:35.6	23.6
600	1:42:36	10:16	6:25	1:16:38	58:23	9:21	05:50	17:27	5:49	28:09	9:05	5:38	17:07	16:00	2:08.0	7:50.1	7:16.0	3:37.0	1:36.0	23.7
590	1:43:01	10:18	6:26	1:16:57	58:38	9:23	05:52	17:32	5:51	28:16	9:07	5:39	17:11	16:04	2:08.6	7:51.9	7:17.7	3:37.9	1:36.3	23.8
580	1:43:26	10:21	6:28	1:17:15	58:53	9:25	05:53	17:36	5:52	28:23	9:09	5:41	17:15	16:08	2:09.1	7:53.8	7:19.4	3:38.8	1:36.7	23.9
570	1:43:51	10:23	6:29	1:17:34	59:07	9:28	05:55	17:41	5:54	28:30	9:12	5:42	17:19	16:12	2:09.6	7:55.7	7:21.2	3:39.6	1:37.1	24.0
560	1:44:16	10:26	6:31	1:17:52	59:22	9:30	05:56	17:45	5:55	28:37	9:14	5:43	17:23	16:16	2:10.1	7:57.5	7:22.9	3:40.5	1:37.5	24.1
550	1:44:41	10:28	6:33	1:18:11	59:36	9:32	05:58	17:49	5:56	28:44	9:16	5:45	17:28	16:20	2:10.7	7:59.4	7:24.6	3:41.3	1:37.8	24.2
540	1:45:06	10:31	6:34	1:18:29	59:51	9:35	05:59	17:54	5:58	28:51	9:18	5:46	17:32	16:24	2:11.2	8:01.3	7:26.3	3:42.2	1:38.2	24.2
530	1:45:31	10:33	6:36	1:18:48	00:06	9:37	06:01	17:58	5:59	28:58	9:21	5:48	17:36	16:28	2:11.7	8:03.1	7:28.1	3:43.1	1:38.6	24.3
520	1:45:56	10:36	6:37	1:19:07	00:20	9:39	06:02	18:03	6:01	29:05	9:23	5:49	17:40	16:32	2:12.3	8:05.0	7:29.8	3:43.9	1:38.9	24.4
510	1:46:21	10:38	6:39	1:19:25	00:35	9:42	06:03	18:07	6:02	29:13	9:25	5:51	17:45	16:36	2:12.8	8:06.9	7:31.5	3:44.8	1:39.3	24.5
500	1:46:46	10:41	6:40	1:19:44	00:49	9:44	06:05	18:11	6:04	29:20	9:28	5:52	17:49	16:40	2:13.3	8:08.7	7:33.3	3:45.7	1:39.7	24.6
490	1:47:11	10:43	6:42	1:20:02	01:04	9:46	06:06	18:16	6:05	29:27	9:30	5:53	17:53	16:44	2:13.8	8:10.6	7:35.0	3:46.5	1:40.0	24.7
480	1:47:36	10:46	6:43	1:20:21	01:19	9:49	06:08	18:20	6:07	29:34	9:32	5:55	17:57	16:48	2:14.4	8:12.5	7:36.7	3:47.4	1:40.4	24.8
470	1:48:01	10:48	6:45	1:20:39	01:33	9:51	06:09	18:25	6:08	29:41	9:34	5:56	18:02	16:52	2:14.9	8:14.3	7:38.4	3:48.3	1:40.8	24.9
460	1:48:26	10:51	6:47	1:20:58	01:48	9:53	06:11	18:29	6:10	29:48	9:37	5:58	18:06	16:56	2:15.4	8:16.2	7:40.2	3:49.1	1:41.2	25.0
450	1:48:51	10:53	6:48	1:21:17	02:02	9:56	06:12	18:33	6:11	29:55	9:39	5:59	18:10	17:00	2:16.0	8:18.1	7:41.9	3:50.0	1:41.5	25.1
440	1:49:16	10:56	6:50	1:21:35	02:17	9:58	06:14	18:38	6:13	30:02	9:41	6:00	18:14	17:04	2:16.5	8:19.9	7:43.6	3:50.9	1:41.9	25.2
430	1:49:41	10:58	6:51	1:21:54	02:32	10:00	06:15	18:42	6:14	30:09	9:44	6:02	18:19	17:08	2:17.0	8:21.8	7:45.4	3:51.7	1:42.3	25.2
420	1:50:06	11:01	6:53	1:22:12	02:46	10:03	06:17	18:47	6:16	30:16	9:46	6:03	18:23	17:12	2:17.6	8:23.7	7:47.1	3:52.6	1:42.6	25.3
410	1:50:30	11:03	6:54	1:22:31	03:01	10:05	06:18	18:51	6:17	30:23	9:48	6:05	18:27	17:16	2:18.1	8:25.5	7:48.8	3:53.4	1:43.0	25.4
400	1:50:55	11:06	6:56	1:22:49	03:15	10:07	06:20	18:55	6:18	30:30	9:50	6:06	18:31	17:20	2:18.6	8:27.4	7:50.5	3:54.3	1:43.4	25.5
390	1:51:20	11:08	6:58	1:23:08	03:30	10:10	06:21	19:00	6:20	30:38	9:53	6:08	18:35	17:24	2:19.1	8:29.3	7:52.3	3:55.2	1:43.7	25.6
380	1:51:45	11:11	6:59	1:23:27	03:45	10:12	06:22	19:04	6:21	30:45	9:55	6:09	18:40	17:28	2:19.7	8:31.1	7:54.0	3:56.0	1:44.1	25.7
370	1:52:10	11:13	7:01	1:23:45	03:59	10:14	06:24	19:09	6:23	30:52	9:57	6:10	18:44	17:32	2:20.2	8:33.0	7:55.7	3:56.9	1:44.5	25.8
360	1:52:35	11:16	7:02	1:24:04	04:14	10:17	06:25	19:13	6:24	30:59	10:00	6:12	18:48	17:36	2:20.7	8:34.9	7:57.4	3:57.8	1:44.9	25.9

Figure 11-2: Lactate Training Paces For Middle And Long Distance Runners

Value of Performance	Lactate Threshold Training Pace (Based on Marathon Pace)			Middle Distance Alternative	Estimated 10 km Capability			Estimated 3k S/C Capability			Estimated 5 km Capability			Estimated 2 mile and 3k (MVO2) Capabilities				Estimated 800m/1500m Capabilities			Basic Speed	
Points	16 km / 10 Mile	Pace Min/Mile	Pace Min/km	12 km / 7.5 Mile	Time	Min/Mi	Min/Km	Time	Min/km	Time	Min/Mi	Min/Km	2 mile Time	3k Time	400m Pace	1 Mile Time	1500m Time	800m Time	400m Time	100m Pace
350	1:53:00	11:18	7:04	1:24:22	04:28	10:19	06:27	19:17	6:26	31:06	10:02	6:13	18:52	17:40	2:21.3	8:36.7	7:59.2	3:58.6	1:45.2	26.0
340	1:53:25	11:21	7:05	1:24:41	04:43	10:21	06:28	19:22	6:27	31:13	10:04	6:15	18:57	17:43	2:21.8	8:38.6	8:00.9	3:59.5	1:45.6	26.1
330	1:53:50	11:23	7:07	1:24:59	04:58	10:24	06:30	19:26	6:29	31:20	10:06	6:16	19:01	17:47	2:22.3	8:40.5	8:02.6	4:00.4	1:46.0	26.2
320	1:54:15	11:26	7:08	1:25:18	05:12	10:26	06:31	19:31	6:30	31:27	10:09	6:17	19:05	17:51	2:22.9	8:42.3	8:04.4	4:01.2	1:46.3	26.3
310	1:54:40	11:28	7:10	1:25:37	05:27	10:28	06:33	19:35	6:32	31:34	10:11	6:19	19:09	17:55	2:23.4	8:44.2	8:06.1	4:02.1	1:46.7	26.3
300	1:55:05	11:31	7:12	1:25:55	05:41	10:31	06:34	19:41	6:33	31:41	10:13	6:20	19:14	17:59	2:23.9	8:46.1	8:07.8	4:02.9	1:47.1	26.4
290	1:55:30	11:33	7:13	1:26:14	05:56	10:33	06:36	19:44	6:35	31:48	10:16	6:22	19:18	18:03	2:24.4	8:47.9	8:09.5	4:03.8	1:47.4	26.5
280	1:55:55	11:36	7:15	1:26:32	06:11	10:35	06:37	19:48	6:36	31:56	10:18	6:23	19:22	18:07	2:25.0	8:49.8	8:11.3	4:04.7	1:47.8	26.5
270	1:56:20	11:38	7:16	1:26:51	06:25	10:38	06:39	19:53	6:38	32:03	10:20	6:25	19:26	18:11	2:25.5	8:51.7	8:13.0	4:05.5	1:48.2	26.7
260	1:56:45	11:41	7:18	1:27:10	06:40	10:40	06:40	19:57	6:39	32:10	10:22	6:26	19:31	18:15	2:26.0	8:53.5	8:14.7	4:06.4	1:48.6	26.8
250	1:57:10	11:43	7:19	1:27:28	06:54	10:42	06:41	20:02	6:41	32:17	10:25	6:27	19:35	18:19	2:26.6	8:55.4	8:16.5	4:07.3	1:48.9	26.9
240	1:57:35	11:45	7:21	1:27:47	07:09	10:45	06:43	20:06	6:42	32:24	10:27	6:29	19:39	18:23	2:27.1	8:57.3	8:18.2	4:08.1	1:49.3	27.0
230	1:58:00	11:48	7:22	1:28:05	07:24	10:47	06:44	20:10	6:43	32:31	10:29	6:30	19:43	18:27	2:27.6	8:59.1	8:19.9	4:09.0	1:49.7	27.1
220	1:58:25	11:50	7:24	1:28:24	07:38	10:49	06:46	20:15	6:45	32:38	10:32	6:32	19:47	18:31	2:28.2	9:01.0	8:21.6	4:09.9	1:50.0	27.2
210	1:58:50	11:53	7:26	1:28:42	07:53	10:52	06:47	20:19	6:46	32:45	10:34	6:33	19:52	18:35	2:28.7	9:02.9	8:23.4	4:10.7	1:50.4	27.3
200	1:59:15	11:55	7:27	1:29:01	08:07	10:54	06:49	20:24	6:48	32:52	10:36	6:34	19:56	18:39	2:29.2	9:04.7	8:25.1	4:11.6	1:50.8	27.4
190	1:59:40	11:58	7:29	1:29:20	08:22	10:56	06:50	20:28	6:49	32:59	10:38	6:36	20:00	18:43	2:29.7	9:06.6	8:26.8	4:12.5	1:51.1	27.4
180	2:00:05	12:00	7:30	1:29:38	08:37	10:59	06:52	20:32	6:51	33:06	10:41	6:37	20:04	18:47	2:30.3	9:08.5	8:28.6	4:13.3	1:51.5	27.5
170	2:00:30	12:03	7:32	1:29:57	08:51	11:01	06:53	20:37	6:52	33:13	10:43	6:39	20:09	18:51	2:30.8	9:10.3	8:30.3	4:14.2	1:51.9	27.6
160	2:00:55	12:05	7:33	1:30:15	09:06	11:03	06:55	20:41	6:54	33:21	10:45	6:40	20:13	18:55	2:31.3	9:12.2	8:32.0	4:15.0	1:52.3	27.7
150	2:01:20	12:08	7:35	1:30:34	09:20	11:06	06:56	20:46	6:55	33:28	10:48	6:42	20:17	18:59	2:31.9	9:14.1	8:33.7	4:15.9	1:52.6	27.8
140	2:01:45	12:10	7:37	1:30:52	09:35	11:08	06:57	20:50	6:57	33:35	10:50	6:43	20:21	19:03	2:32.4	9:15.9	8:35.5	4:16.8	1:53.0	27.9
130	2:02:10	12:13	7:38	1:31:11	09:50	11:10	06:59	20:54	6:58	33:42	10:52	6:44	20:26	19:07	2:32.9	9:17.8	8:37.2	4:17.6	1:53.4	28.0
120	2:02:35	12:15	7:40	1:31:30	10:04	11:13	07:00	20:59	6:59	33:49	10:54	6:46	20:30	19:11	2:33.5	9:19.7	8:38.9	4:18.5	1:53.7	28.1
110	2:03:00	12:18	7:41	1:31:48	10:19	11:15	07:02	21:03	7:01	33:56	10:57	6:47	20:34	19:15	2:34.0	9:21.5	8:40.6	4:19.4	1:54.1	28.2
100	2:03:25	12:20	7:43	1:32:07	10:33	11:17	07:03	21:08	7:02	34:03	10:59	6:49	20:38	19:19	2:34.5	9:23.4	8:42.4	4:20.2	1:54.5	28.3
90	2:03:49	12:23	7:44	1:32:25	10:48	11:20	07:05	21:12	7:03	34:10	11:01	6:50	20:42	19:23	2:35.0	9:25.3	8:44.1	4:21.1	1:54.8	28.4
80	2:04:14	12:25	7:46	1:32:44	11:03	11:22	07:06	21:16	7:04	34:17	11:04	6:51	20:47	19:27	2:35.6	9:27.1	8:45.8	4:22.0	1:55.2	28.5
70	2:04:39	12:28	7:47	1:33:02	11:17	11:24	07:07	21:21	7:05	34:24	11:06	6:53	20:51	19:31	2:36.1	9:29.0	8:47.6	4:22.8	1:55.6	28.6
60	2:05:04	12:30	7:49	1:33:21	11:32	11:27	07:09	21:25	7:07	34:31	11:08	6:54	20:55	19:35	2:36.6	9:30.9	8:49.3	4:23.7	1:56.0	28.7
50	2:05:29	12:33	7:51	1:33:40	11:46	11:29	07:10	21:30	7:08	34:38	11:10	6:56	20:59	19:39	2:37.2	9:32.7	8:51.0	4:24.5	1:56.3	28.8
40	2:05:54	12:35	7:52	1:33:58	12:01	11:31	07:12	21:34	7:10	34:46	11:13	6:57	21:04	19:43	2:37.7	9:34.6	8:52.7	4:25.4	1:56.7	28.8
30	2:06:19	12:38	7:54	1:34:17	12:16	11:34	07:13	21:38	7:11	34:53	11:15	6:59	21:08	19:47	2:38.2	9:36.5	8:54.5	4:26.3	1:57.1	28.9
20	2:06:44	12:40	7:55	1:34:35	12:30	11:36	07:14	21:43	7:13	35:00	11:17	7:00	21:12	19:51	2:38.8	9:38.3	8:56.2	4:27.1	1:57.4	29.0
10	2:07:09	12:43	7:57	1:34:54	12:45	11:38	07:16	21:47	7:14	35:07	11:20	7:01	21:16	19:55	2:39.3	9:40.2	8:57.9	4:28.0	1:57.8	29.1
0	2:07:34	12:45	7:58	1:35:12	12:59	11:41	07:17	21:52	7:15	35:14	11:22	7:03	21:21	19:59	2:39.8	9:42.1	8:59.7	4:28.9	1:58.2	29.2

CHAPTER 12
THE LONG RUN
SPEED THROUGH ENDURANCE

The Value of the Weekly Long Run

The weekly long run merits a special mention because it is a part of virtually every middle and long distance runner's program. Those who do not do one, usually 400m/800m types, normally do not convert their 800m speed to 1500m as well as those who do.

The shortest period that could be considered a long run is probably an hour. The most effective long runs are probably about 22% of the weekly volume. For example, an athlete targeting 100 miles per week would run 22 miles for his long run.

The greatest benefits come from a run of two hours, though marathon runners would need to run for three hours or 50km (whichever comes first), occasionally. Any fun runner or jogger can run for an hour, so it's hard to argue that an elite middle or long distance runner would get much from just an hour.

Run more quickly a one-hour run becomes a threshold run and delivers quite different benefits. However, without the leg strength to run steadily for 1:30-2 hr a threshold run of an hour is going to put a lot of pressure on the muscular and skeletal system. *Run With The Best* believes that developing athletes, 10,000m runners, and marathoners should achieve a full long run 40-45 weeks per year. A full long run may be defined as a run that equals 20-24% of a middle distance runner's weekly volume and 18-22% of a distance runner's weekly volume.

A major advantage of developing the capacity to do a long run is that it takes the pressure off achieving the weekly volume. For example, a middle distance runner aiming at a total of 75 miles or 120km per week (fairly common targets) would target 15-18 miles or 24 to 30km for the weekly long run. This may not seem like a two-hour run, but think again! As most middle distance runners do not run below 30 minutes for 10k (and those who do are more the 1500m/5000m type who would run 20-22 miles or 30-35km anyway), most 800/1500m runners should be running between 1:30hr to 2hrs if they maintain a 70% effort (Fig. 12-1).

At slower aerobic conditioning paces (Fig. 6-1) all the 15-mile or 24km runs become 1:30hr or more and will exceed a two-hour run for any athlete who runs 10k slower than 33 minutes. If the distance of the run is extended to 18 miles or 30km, even a 28-minute 10k runner will be running for two hours or more unless he runs at the high end of his aerobic conditioning pace.

Some may say it does not matter if the athlete runs a little less per week. They are incorrect because if the athlete runs less per week, then he or she runs less per year. This means he takes longer to reach his optimum volumes. This means his career at its peak is shorter!

Others say "make it up at other times in the week." This puts greater stress on the athlete to add mileage to his or her warm-up or cool-down or to add extra volume into recovery runs which then destroys the delicate balance that exists between rest and recovery.

Other Benefits

The athlete gets other benefits from long continuous running. These runs improve the ability to use fat as a fuel source and enhance all the following physiological adaptations:
- capillarization of the muscle fibers,
- the number of mitochondria in the cells,
- the enzyme activity within the mitochondria,

FIGURE 12-1

10k Best km	Minutes per mile	Minutes per km	Time 15 mile or 24km @ End-2 Pace	Time 18 mile or 30km @ End-2 Pace
28:00	5:30-6:30	3:24-4:04	1:22hr-1:38hr	1:39hr2:01hr
29:00	5:42-6:45	3:32-4:12	1:25hr-1:41hr	1:43hr2:06hr
30:00	5:54-7:02	3:40-4:22	1:28hr-1:46hr	1:47hr2:12hr
31:00	6:08-7:24	3:47-4:35	1:32hr-1:51hr	1:51hr2:16hr

Co-author Irv Ray won this 1983 Russian River trail marathon in 2:36:22.

- myoglobin in the muscle cells, as well as
- the muscle's ability to store glycogen.

The net effect of all this is that more fuel is available to the body and the fuel that is available can be used more effectively.

Endurance running also trains the fast-twitch fibers so they have greater aerobic capacity than normal. The counter-proposition that long running slows an athlete down is only valid if the athlete's program does not contain any work that recruits fast-twitch fibers.

Peter Snell, for example, ran a marathon in 2:40 only 10 weeks prior to setting his world 800m record of 1:44.3 on a 350m grass track in 1963. More importantly, Snell was running with the leaders up to 20 miles before he decided it might be prudent not to overextend himself.

It wasn't always this way for Snell. Legend has it that the first time he attempted Lydiard's famous 22-mile Sunday run he had to stop outside a small store two miles from the finish. He told another member of the group to tell Mr. Lydiard that he needed to be picked up when the athlete returned to the finish. Mr. Lydiard reportedly collected the future Olympic champion on this occasion but placed himself outside the store for the next two weeks to ensure there were no repeats of this behavior!

Herb Elliott's strength was perhaps even more impressive. By 18 years of age he had run the 35 miles from Portsea to Frankston. Later, due to the demands of his studies and work, he often followed a weekly routine that comprised rest days on Monday and Friday, easy to steady 10-mile runs on Tuesday and Thursday, a very fast 2.5- to 5-mile run on Wednesday and a 60-mile (100 km) weekend at Portsea. The 60-mile weekend was composed of long steady-to-fast continuous runs, intense 30-meter sandhill repetitions, hard 800m and mile repetitions around sandy trails adjacent to Cerutty's camp, plus weight lifting, swimming in the rugged Portsea surf (Elliott was a very strong open water swimmer and he once had to use his surf swimming ability to rescue his coach!) and, along with all the other athletes in residence, wood cutting, whenever Percy needed more firewood!

Finally, long easy running (with great stress on the word *easy*) strengthens all the ligaments, tendons, muscles and bones of the body. This reduces the likely occurrence of muscular and skeletal injury during the harder periods of training.

It is good to remember that many endurance athletes, such as swimmers and cyclists, have great cardiovascular efficiency and strength. It does not help them run at the same level as they swim or ride (despite the fact many use running at various times to increase their stamina), because they lack specific running economy—something that can only be developed gradually over years of running.

While *Run With The Best* is not aware of any elite runner turning to swimming with any success there are many documented examples of average to good runners becoming outstanding cyclists. Australia's Kathy Watt, the Barcelona Olympic road race champion, was really no more than a good club runner for many years before turning to cycling due to injury. In Australia the same is true of the triathlon. Most triathletes come from run or swim/run backgrounds, because of the efficiency requirements of these two quite different sports but take to cycling very quickly. World champion triathletes Miles Stewart, Jackie Gallagher and Emma Carney are three excellent examples.

CHAPTER 13
SURGE INTERVALS
WHERE THRESHOLD MEETS MVO₂

Interval workouts are a commonly used form of training and they have many advantages.
1. The athlete is enabled to run many times the race distance at racing velocities because he can take a period of recovery after each repetition of fast running.
2. Speed is developed through the athlete running for very short periods at maximal effort and taking a full recovery before running the next repetition.
3. Increases in the athlete's ability to tolerate lactic acid will occur if the athlete uses a regimen of near-maximal intensity running followed by near-complete recoveries.
4. The aerobic capacities will improve provided moderate intensities and short recoveries are used.

A traditional interval training session has five characteristics. They are:
- the distance of each repetition,
- the number of repetitions to be done,
- the intensity or pace of the repetitions,
- the time allocated to recovery, and
- the mode of recovery.

Run With The Best suggests that this form of training is much better suited to improving the anaerobic qualities of an athlete than the aerobic ones and that when an interval training session is set the coach should specify three or four of the workout's characteristics and leave either one or two to the athlete.

The disadvantage of traditional interval training as far as the development of the *aerobic* capacities are concerned is that the more recovery the athlete takes between each effort the less specific the training is to racing; a race has no recovery periods. For example, a workout of 4 x 400m with 1 minute walk recovery will be less intense than 4 x 400m with a 200m recovery jog in 1 minute or a race, e.g., four consecutive 400's with no recovery at all!

The intensity of the recovery is therefore critical to race specificity and is a product of:
- the time period allocated for recovery,
- the mode of recovery, and
- the distance allocated for recovery.

Surge intervals have several distinctive characteristics.
1. They are concerned with rhythm and tempo therefore even the recoveries are more of a run than a jog, i.e., the impression is the athlete has kept running and has not slowed to a jog.
2. They are concerned with the quality of the recovery. When the workout focuses on time, e.g., 20 min of 1 minute at 5k pace with 1 minute recovery, the emphasis is on running further during the recovery but not so fast that the athlete cannot repeat the next minute at 5k pace. When the workout focuses on distance, for instance, 12 laps of 400m at 5k pace with a 200m float recovery, the emphasis is on running the recovery faster but not so fast the next 400m cannot be run at 5k pace.
3. They take it for granted the race speed isn't a problem. An athlete aiming at 14:30, say, would be able to run 2:20 for 800m easily, so endurance, not speed, it the important factor.
4. The surge distance is usually 2-4 times the recovery distance—for example, 12 laps of 400m fast followed by 200m float. Steve Prefontaine's workout of 200m in 30 seconds followed by 200m in 40 seconds is the best of the equal distance variations.
5. They may employ either threshold, MVO₂ or lactic acid tolerance pace surges with recovery times less than the surge time, e.g., 1-2 minute surges would be followed by 30-60 second recoveries.

The following example, based on a 5000m runner aiming to run 14:30, can be used to highlight the differences between traditional and surge intervals.

Traditional interval session:
6 x 800m in 2:20 seconds with 3 minutes recovery early in the season with the aim of reducing the recovery to, say, 1 minute as competition approaches.

A surge interval session:
5 x 800m at 2:20 pace with a 200m recovery float in 1 minute 30 seconds. As the athlete gets fitter the focus is to lower the recovery time to 60 seconds.

Both workouts total three miles or 4.8k but the surge workout is far more specific to 5000m than the 6 x 800m. If an athlete were to average 2:20 per 800m and 60 seconds per 200m on recovery, the workout time would be 15 minutes 40 seconds, whereas the athlete who completes the six 800m runs in 2:20 with the one-minute rest totals 19 minutes.

To complete the workout in 15:40 using the traditional method the athlete would have to run 6 x 800m in 2:20 with 20-24 seconds recovery. So while the surge workout would be operating as an MVO_2 session, the traditional session would take the athlete deep into the lactic acid tolerance zone.

Surge workouts also focus on an end result rather than a series of intermittent results. That end result will be either a final time or a total distance. The 4.8k (3 miles) of 800m surge/200m float has a final time as the most important indicator. If this workout were converted to time, for instance, 15 minutes of 2:00 at 5k pace with a 1:00 float, the aim would be to improve the total distance run by running the recovery more quickly. This focus on the finish gives a greater race quality to the workout.

Finally, surge intervals give a very accurate indication of the athlete's current condition. When done regularly by the athlete, it becomes easy to differentiate what is a good effort on a day when the athlete is tired as well a good effort on a good day. In this respect they have a time trial quality without the pressure, because no one in full training is going to be continually producing personal records!

Examples of Surge Intervals for Base Building, Cross Country and 5k and 10k on the Track:

12km Workout: 35 minutes of 6 x 5:00 @ 10k pace/effort with 1:00 float recovery.
7-Mile Workout: 3 miles - 2 miles - 1 mile with @ 85-87% MHR with 800m float recovery.
10km Workout: 7 x 1k @ 87-92% MHR with 500m float recovery;
   5 x 1 mile (1600m) @ 10k goal pace with 400m float recovery.
6-Mile Workout: 28 minutes of 6 x 3:00 @ 5k pace/effort with 2:00 float recovery.
8km Workouts: 3 x 2k @ 87-92% MHR with 1k float recovery;
   20 x 200m @ 1 mile/1500m goal pace with 200m float recovery.
5-Mile Workout: 23 minutes of running 30.0-45.0-60.0-1:30-2:00-1:30-60.0.45.0-30.0 sec @ 3-5k pace with equidistant float recoveries, i.e., 30.0 recovery float after 30.0 fast, 45.0 float after 45.0 fast, 60.0 float after 60.0 fast, etc.
5km Workout: 12 minutes of 2:00, 4:00, 30.0, @ 85-92% and 2:30 @ 95-100% to finish. Run a 1:00 float recovery after each fast run.
3 Mile Workout: 12 laps of 400m @ 5k pace/effort with 200m float recovery. Note: The athlete begins this session with the 200m float.

Examples of Surge Intervals for Middle Distance Events.

1500m: 600m (race pace), 200m float, 400m (RP), 100m float, 200m (RP)
   The aim is to float @ 20.0 per 100m or about 5.0 slower than race pace*
800m: 300m (race pace), 100m float, 200m (RP), 100m float, 100m (RP)
   The aim is to float @ 20.0 per 100m or about 5.0 slower than race pace*

*The coach may allow 5-10 seconds longer for recovery and do 2-4 sets of these workouts.

CHAPTER 14
SPRINT INTERVALS
WHERE MVO$_2$ MEETS LACTIC ACID TOLERANCE

This type of workout was first promoted by Arthur Lydiard, who used two miles or 3,200m of 40m sprint/60m float (see *Run To The Top*, page 57) to prepare his athletes for racing. Ron Clarke adapted this idea into his training by running three miles (4,800m) of "straights," alternating 100-yd. sprints on the straight with 120-yd. floats around the bend.

It is important to emphasize these sprints were all-out efforts. Clarke, for example, often had Pam Kilborn, an Olympic 100m hurdler, and Judy Pollock, an Olympic 400m sprinter, positioned at the top of each straight. As he circled the track Pam and Judy took turns racing Clarke down the straight.

These are similar to surge intervals in that there is an hard effort followed by a run or float recovery. There are, however, a number of differences.

- The hard effort is a sprint, that is, the athlete must accelerate to top speed as explosively as possible, then relax but maintain high speed for the rest of the interval. The athlete must be at top speed within 20-30 meters.
- The float interval, as Lydiard says, is really only a "cessation of driving" until the athlete starts accelerating into the next sprint.
- The sprint distance and the recovery distance are about equal, so the recovery time is greater than the work time. The standard workout of this type is normally a 50m sprint followed by a 50m float or 100m sprint/100m float. However, Lydiard's approach of shorter sprints and longer recovery distances, e.g., 40m sprint/60m float or 80m sprint/120m float, probably promotes a smoother transition from one speed to the next.

The basis for these workout is three miles (4.8km) for the 80m or 100m sprints and two miles (3.2km) for the 40m or 50m sprints. However, workouts can be done in any of the following ways.

12 continuous laps of 120m float/80m sprint
- 2-3 x 4-6 laps of 120m float/80m sprint with 400m jog recovery
- 3-4 x 3-4 laps of 120m float/80m sprint with 400m jog recovery.

8 continuous laps of 60m float/40m sprint
- 2-3 x 3-4 laps of 60m float/40m sprint with 400m jog recovery
- 3-6 x 1-2 laps of 60m float/40m sprint with 400m jog recovery.

Sprint/float sets, for example,
- 2-4 x 400m of 40m sprint/60m float
- 2-4 x 800m of 40m sprint/60m float
- 1-2 x 1600m or 1 mile of 40m sprint/60m float.

Finally, these workouts can also be used for testing, e.g., 1500m of 100m sprint/100m float or 800m of 50m float/50m sprint. Monitor the sprint times and record the total time to calculate the average recovery times.

Sprint intervals can be used at any time of the year provided the athlete has sufficient leg speed to avoid the risk of injury. They are perhaps best done in the Pre-Competition Phase and also prior to cross country racing.

CHAPTER 15
WILL POWER
WHERE THE WILL TO PREPARE MEETS THE WILL TO WIN

Most of the year an athlete's training follows a predictable course. Periodization and monitoring ensures the quantity and quality are within the athlete's capabilities. This as it should be. However, it also presents a problem because it is mostly testing the athlete physically and it means there is also a place for occasional workouts that test the limits of an athlete's mind and spirit.

Will power workouts have two major benefits. Firstly, they boost the athlete's confidence, and secondly, provided enough recovery time is given, the overcompensation the body makes to the workout may allow the athlete to move to a higher training level.

Herb Elliott is reported to have said that *most athletes think they have reached their limits when they are no more than 70% exhausted. Most coaches know that this applies to the majority of their athletes.*

What Elliott was actually saying is that an athlete must be able to extract the very best from himself in a race situation, and to that end he must have experienced the feeling in training. In other words, the athlete must have the "will to prepare" during training in order to have the "will to win" in races.

The will power session therefore relies on the athlete having will power in the first place. Initially this will be shown by following the training schedule, getting to training venues, being able to train alone when necessary, and all the other things coaches know indicate the athlete has the right attitude to succeed. Any athlete without these attributes will not have the will power to do a true will power workout.

Will power sessions normally follow a similar format to a regular training session, but there is a "twist." For example, Percy Cerutty regularly prescribed sessions on the famed Portsea sandhills and athletes were expected to do an optimum number that ensured a good workout, but at the same time left them with enough energy to perform the other running and strength sessions scheduled for that day.

Occasionally however it was expected the athlete would continue on until their quadriceps were shaking so badly it was impossible to complete another repetition. These workouts were extremely demanding and the athletes themselves were the only ones who truly knew if they were totally spent or had quit before total exhaustion.

There used to be one mirror in the camp bunkhouse at Portsea and its function had nothing to do with shaving. Athlete's were told to look into the mirror and see if a man looked back (women were a rarity at Cerutty's camp—there were no Olympic women's distance races in that era). A man only looked back if the athlete could truly say he had meet every training challenge that day.

Percy believed that the difference between success and failure in important competition is so small that even the slightest weakness would predispose the athlete to losing, because the athlete best able to accept and control pain would perform the best.

Great performances will always be about accepting steadily increasing levels of discomfort and pain as a race progresses. At the extremes an athlete may either refuse to slow down because of the pain or significantly reduce his efforts as the pain increases.

Herb Elliott's undefeated record at the mile and 1500m shows what his response to pain was, and only a few competitors will respond in the same way. The vast majority of athletes will fall somewhere between this level of resolve and capitulation.

A word of warning must be inserted here however. *Will power sessions are the toughest workouts an athlete can do; therefore they must be used sparingly, and not at all during the last 8 weeks prior to the major race.* And they must be used with discretion, as each athlete will respond differently.

Those athletes who naturally possess great will power will push hard in all their workouts, and the coach will only suggest will power workouts when a specific outcome is desired.

Then there will be those athletes on the team who have a real reluctance to push themselves, so the coach must be careful not to destroy the athlete's confidence and enjoyment of the sport by setting challenges that are too difficult.

This is particularly true where team points are involved. Most teams will have only a small percentage of athletes with true will power. The majority will only possess moderate amounts and the rest may have little or none at all. To excel in team competition the whole squad must be ready and eager to compete. Trying to make the whole team into individual champions may mean some will drop out or perform badly due to the pressure.

In this respect a coach's attitude will influence the amount of will power an athlete will bring to bear during practice. The greater the team perceives that the coach expects success the more will power and determination they will apply to their workouts.

The more will power the athlete uses in day-to-day training the greater the psychological drain on the nervous system. The greater the stress on the nervous system the higher the heart rate at any given pace and therefore the more likely the athlete is to move from one zone into a higher one. An athlete who does this too often, however, will not perform well on a regular basis.

Will power sessions can be as varied as the coach's imagination. In the case of a beginner it might be asking him to run on a soft surface and increase his long run from 30 minutes to 60 or 90 minutes. The senior athlete may be asked to run three hours or do a 30-mile run, as Cerutty asked of Elliott occasionally, instead of his normal 2-hour run. The opposite of these aerobically oriented sessions would be Cerutty's sandhill workout referred to earlier.

Rhythm workouts are also easily converted to will power workouts. One such example (which is perhaps better done off the track but can be viewed as a track example) is 24 x 400m at 5000m goal pace with a 75-second out-and-back 100m jog recovery. One change to this session would be to run the first 12 with 75 seconds recovery, the next 6 with 60 seconds recovery and as many as possible of the last 6 with 45 seconds recovery. A second option on a workout like this is to run as many repetitions as possible at 5000m goal pace.

One final point. To be able to bring will power into play, an athlete must be physically capable of meeting the challenge, so a workout such as 8 x 300m at 400m pace with 3 minutes recovery would be inappropriate.

Some Further Examples

- Put on a 20-40lb (8-16kg) backpack and walk for 4-6 hours through hilly country during the transition phase.
- Run for the same time as a normal long run but do it in a tougher environment, for instance, through hills, on sand or cross country surfaces, into a headwind, up a long hill, etc.
- Run repetitions in similar tougher circumstances.
- Run 800m repeats @ 10k pace with a 400m jog in 3:00 for as long as possible
- Run the maximum number of 400m reps @ 1500m pace with 4:00 between reps.
- Run the maximum number of 300m reps at 800m pace with up to 15 minutes recovery.
- Run 1 minute repetitions @ a selected pace (e.g., 3-5k) or effort (87-92%) for as long as possible using the following recovery plan. Begin with a 90-second or 2:00 slow jog recovery and reduce the recovery by 5 seconds after each repetition.
- Race simulation sessions, for example,
  4 x 200m @ 800m goal pace with 20 seconds recovery
  5 x 300m @ 1500m goal pace with 20 seconds recovery.

Remember, the important thing about will power sessions is that the athlete terminates the workout. Once the workout begins the coach becomes an observer. It is the athlete who must decide when he or she can no longer maintain the pace, the recovery or the combination of both.

EXAMPLES OF HOW REGULAR WORKOUTS MAY BE TURNED INTO WILL POWER SESSIONS

1. The Sunday 2-hour long run.	Tell the athlete to run for 3 hours.
2. 13 x 400m hill @ 10k pace with a jog-back recovery in a time 1 minute slower than 10k pace.	Tell the athlete to run as many repetitions as possible @ 10k pace with a jog-back recovery 1 minute slower than 10k pace.
3. 8 x 300m @ 800m pace with a 200m jog in 90 seconds.	Tell the athlete to run 8 repetitions with the minimum possible recovery times.
4. 6 x 1k @ 5k pace with a 400m recovery jog.	The same workout, but break each kilometer into 400m @ 5k pace, 200m @ 3k pace and 400m @ 5k pace.
5. Run 20 minutes on the track, including 2 x 50m sprint every lap.	The same workout but run 1 x 50m sprint and one sprint of anything from 75m to 250m while still completing the same number of laps.

CHAPTER 16
RACE PRACTICE WORKOUTS
PUTTING IT ALL TOGETHER

The difference between a trained runner and someone who is merely extremely fit is that the runner uses his fitness to perform a specific task—to race successfully. Race practice workouts are designed to weld all the various forms of training together so the athlete is able to race successfully.

They are also particularly valuable in the last 7 to 10 days prior to a major race. Generally the only mistake that can be made this close to a race is to overdo things. A carefully selected race practice workout will allow the athlete to do enough to feel relaxed but not so much that he leaves his best performances on the training track.

There are four types of race practice workouts:
1. Race Rhythm Workouts.
2. Race Simulation Workouts.
3. Race Tactical Workouts.
4. Race Maintenance Workouts.

1. Race Rhythm Workouts

These workouts contain significant amounts of race pace running. As these workouts aim to develop rhythm, the intensity of the efforts should be moderate, the distances run should be relatively short—5-25% of the race distance—and recovery should be generous.

For the longer distance athletes it becomes increasingly important that the recovery is not so slow it breaks the rhythm of workout. This means these workouts will be similar to surge interval training. The middle distance male and female runner can afford to jog quite slowly during the recovery because the pace they race at is high—83-91% of their basic 400m speed. They have to remain efficient for only a short time, i.e., 1 minute 40 seconds to 4 minutes 10 seconds. However it is worth remembering efficiency and rhythm will be slightly more important to females than male because their times for 800m and 1500m are slightly slower.

Conversely, the long distance runners race at lower speeds, normally 70-80% of their basic 400m speed. This speed, however, has to be maintained for periods of 12 minutes to 2 hours 30 minutes. For this reason it is advisable for them to keep their recovery speeds as high as 70-75% of their race pace to sustain rhythm. A 2:22 marathon runner, for example, would probably be very comfortable running 400m recoveries in 1:45 to 1:55 while a 2:08 runner would find 1:36 to 1:42 per 400m relatively easy.

This means the coach should set longer recovery distances for the long distance runners than the middle distance athletes when both athletes are at a similar standard in the particular event the scheduled workout is focusing on.

Let's say a coach has a good miler who runs a 4:08 and a very good 5000m runner who can run 1500m in 3:50. The coach prefers the athletes to train together whenever possible and wants them to do a workout of 30 x 200m in 32 seconds with a 2-minute recovery. His problem, due to both athletes being equally capable of running repeat 200's in 32 seconds, is how to make the workout as strenuous for the 5000m runner as it is for the miler. His solution might be to specify that, while both athletes will get a 2-minute recovery, the 5000m runner must jog 250m (perhaps using lane 8) while the miler jogs 200m.

Three final points about race rhythm workouts:
- The athlete must not be straining. If he is, then one of three things is wrong. The goal pace is too fast, the recoveries are too short, or the number of repetitions is too great.
- While the athlete will be working at about lactate threshold, the training zone could best be described as event-specific aerobic power workouts.
- These sessions should be done year round. They are ideal as recovery sessions or as a replacement for a true lactate threshold session in a week prior to a competition.
- These workouts should not be done in excessively windy conditions or on hills beyond 3-4 degrees, because the athlete will not be able to maintain both race pace and race rhythm. Where conditions are more difficult than normal the athlete will just have to schedule extra recovery.
- Because race rhythm workouts are extensive rather than intensive, a reasonable amount of running may be scheduled. The following may

be used as guides:

800m	1-2 miles or 2-3km
1500m	2-4 miles or 3-6 km
3k steeple & 5k	3-6 miles or 5-10km
10k & Marathon	3-10 miles or 5-15km

Examples of race-specific workouts. (All are run at race goal pace):

800m	20-30 x 80-120m with 120-160m jog recovery.
1500m	15-30 x 200-300m with 100-200m jog recovery.
3000m Steeple	10-20 x 400-800m over 4 barriers with 400-800m jog recovery.
5000m	20-30 x 200-400m with 100-200m jog recovery.
10,000m	10-30 x 400-800m with 200-400m jog recovery.
Marathon	5k-4k-3k-2k-1k with a relaxed 500m-1km jog recovery, or 3 miles-2x2 miles-3x1 mile with a relaxed 400-800m recovery jog.

2. Race Simulation Workouts

The intention of these workouts is to duplicate the physical stresses associated with racing but to place controls on the amount of mental stress the athlete will experience.

Like race rhythm sessions these workouts focus on race pace but there are major differences associated with recovery mode and total volume.

The recovery is a fixed time, usually so short it has to be done on the spot, with the next repetition starting at the place where the previous one finished. Or it can be a fixed distance, normally 100-400m, though it can be longer, with the athlete aiming to run it in the quickest time possible.

The total volume of either the entire workout or a set is closely related to race distance. One example might be a 1500m runner doing 5 x 300m with 20 seconds recovery. The target pace would be the athlete's goal pace and the recovery is done "on the spot" because the time period is extremely short.

A second example could be a 5000m runner doing 12 laps, alternating a 400m at race goal pace with a 200m "float" recovery and a fast 200m to finish. The aim of this workout would be to maintain race goal pace while striving to cover the 200m recovery at the fastest possible pace.

In regard to total volume there is also no real reason why a middle distance runner could not do 2-3 sets of work if the distance of each set was 800m or two sets if the distance was 1500m, provided they were given enough rest prior to beginning the next set. On the other hand it's highly unlikely the athlete could do a second set of 12 laps!

The relationship between race simulation workouts and current race fitness will be individual to each athlete but some broad correlations do exist. For example the total time for the five 300's should be within 3-6 seconds of the athlete's current 1500m capability. The time for the 12 laps of 400m surges will be very similar to the athlete's current 5000m form.

Basically there are three types of simulations. The first is the **time trial.** It is commonly done in one of three ways.

- Over 50-75% of the race distance at 95-100% intensity. The objective is the best possible time.
- Over 60-85% of race distance at race pace. The objective is to reach a given point having run hard but with the feeling that there is something in reserve for the remaining distance.
- Over 85-100% of the full racing distance at 85-90% intensity. The objective is to get the feel for the race distance but to have something in reserve to improve the time in a race. It is often not even important to time these runs.

The second is the **fixed-time race simulation.** The workout breaks the race distance into a series of repetition runs with a short recovery interval between each run. As mentioned above, the athlete recovers "on the spot" and starts the next repetition at the point where the previous one finished.

The aim of the workout is to take the specified recovery times and to target improvements in the repetition times. For example an 800m runner doing 4 x 200m with 20 seconds recovery must meet the 20-second recovery time or the coach terminates the workout. The aim is to achieve the best possible 800m time by adding the four 200m times together.

This type of session is probably more appropriate to middle distance runners because of the power component involved in stopping and then accelerating back up to race pace.

The third type of workout is the **fixed-distance race simulation.** The workout breaks the race distance into a series of surge intervals with a shorter recovery distance to be run between each fast run. The athlete recovers "on the move" as he or she floats to the start of the next repetition.

The aim of the workout is to run each repetition at race pace and to target improvements in the recovery times. For example, an athlete running a 12-lap workout will run the 400m repetitions at race goal pace and attempt to run the 200m float as quickly as possible. The time the athlete runs the 12 laps in will approximate his current 5000m fitness.

Examples of Race Simulation Workouts (all are run at or very close to race pace):

800m	600m TT @ 95-100%.
	600m TT @ race pace, decelerating gradually over the next 50m.
	800m TT @ 90% or 1-2 seconds per 100m slower than goal pace.
	4 x 200m with 20 seconds "on the spot" recovery between each 200m 800m run: 300m (Race Pace), 100m float, 200m (RP), 100m float, 100m (RP) (Floats are normally 5-6 sec per 100m slower than the race pace runs).
1500m	1200m TT @ 95-100%.
	1200m TT @ race pace, decelerating gradually over the next 50m.
	1500m TT @ 90% or 1-2 seconds per 100m slower than goal pace.
	5 x 300m with 20 seconds "on the spot" recovery between each 300m.
	3 x 500m with 40 seconds "on the spot" recovery between each 500m.
	600m (Race Pace), 200m float, 400m (RP), 100m float, 200m (RP) (Floats are normally 5-6 sec per 100m slower than the race pace runs).
	3 x 400m + 1 x 300m with 30-45 seconds recovery.
3000m Steeple	2 x (3 x 1000m over 4 barriers) with 30.0 between reps & 3:00 between sets.
	6 x 800m over 4 barriers @ race pace with 200m recovery jog between reps.
5000m	12 laps alternating 200m floats and 400m @ race pace. (Start with the float.) Normally this type of workout would be last done 7-10 days before races.

3. Race Tactical Workouts

These workouts are designed to prepare the athlete to either initiate or respond to any tactic likely to be encountered in a race.

Basically there are three major race tactics:

1. A very fast start. One competitor attempts to break clear of the field and then hopefully be able to relax and maintain the advantage to the finish. This tactic is not *usually* successful though there are several examples of successful (and sometimes surprising) front running in major track & field competitions. And sometimes no one in the chasing pack wants to be the "rabbit" and lead the pack to catch the leader, only to be outsprinted anyway.

2. The sprint finish. An athlete with a strong sprint but is able maintain contact with the rest of the pack and have enough power to kick clear at the end.

3. The mid-race surge. An athlete waits until some point in the race where he feels he can accelerate suddenly and surge for long enough to establish a lead sufficient to reach the finish ahead of the pursuing pack. This is a favored Kenyan tactic.

Race tactical workouts should work on all three of the above-mentioned race tactics. The main criterion needed to plan a session is imagination

Examples of Race Tactical Workouts:

800m	800m reps of 200m easy, 400m @ race pace or faster, 100m float, 100m sprint.
	400m easy, 400m all out.
	300m @ 2-3 sec faster than race pace, 150m float, 200m sprint, 100m float.
1500m	1500m of:
	800m @ race pace, 200m float, 300m hard, 200m float.
	600m easy, 400m fast, 200m easy, 300m sprint.
3000m Steeple	6-10 laps over barriers surging from the water jump to the finish line.
5k/10k	15-25 laps, alternating laps of 70.0, 60.0, 70.0 and 80.0 seconds.
	15-25 laps including 2-3 x 1200m @ 3k pace.
	15-25 laps finishing every laps with a sprint of between 50m and 200m.
Marathon	15-23k, alternating 1-7k @ half marathon pace with 1-3k @ marathon pace.

4. Race Maintaince Workouts

Once the athlete reaches the Competition Phase the biggest challenge facing the coach is deciding on the minimum amount of training needed to make sure the athlete achieves peak performance on the day it counts. The word "minimum" is used deliberately. There is no point in having the athlete do more training than is necessary in the Competition Period.

Early in the Competition Period the coach may continue to use regular workouts but either increase the recovery or decrease the volume. A workout that is normally 10 x 300m with 100m jog could become 10 x 300m with 200m jog or 10 x 200m with 100m jog.

Later the coach may consider using "cutdowns." These are workouts where each repetition is run progressively faster. For example 6 x 300m might be run as 50.0-48.0-46.0-44.0-42.0-40.0 by a 4-minute miler or 1500m runner with a target of 3:45.

Basically the competition period is about decreased overall volume (though the weekly long run should be maintained whenever possible), decreased numbers of repetitions, and increased intensity. However the majority of the increased intensity is going to come as a result of racing.

Examples of Race Maintaince Workouts:

- 1-2 x 4 laps of striding the straights and jogging the bends.
- 6-10 x 100m accelerations.
- 5-10 x 200m rhythm runs.
- Easy to moderate fartlek involving 15-second to 5-minute surges.
- Cutdowns, e.g., 2-4 x 400m or 3-5 x 300m or 4-6 x 200m.

Summary

One of the core concepts behind the *Run With The Best* approach to training is belief that *the key to using race practice workouts effectively is to select workouts that have a dual or triple purpose and can be used year round.* Some examples:

6-10 x 100m accelerations

In the early part of the year this workout can be used to practice race pace. Later the warm-up run-throughs can be done at race pace while the workout itself will improve the athlete's 400m.

12 laps, alternating 200m float and 400m @ 5-10k pace.

Surge intervals are basically an aerobic power workout. In addition they will enhance an athlete's lactate threshold and MVO$_2$ capacities, develop will power as the athlete pushes harder at running the recovery float as quickly as possible, and they will acquaint the athlete with three of the four race practice workouts. Since the workout is run at race rhythm, it simulates racing conditions and the surges remind the athlete of race tactics.

1-3 sets of 4 x 200m @ 800-1500m pace with 20-30 seconds recovery and 4-5 minutes between sets.

This workout could replace a traditional interval workout like 10-15 x 200m @ 800-1500m pace with 1:30 -2 minutes recovery. Both workouts would be run at similar speeds and include similar recoveries. The traditional workout would incorporate 30 seconds of recovery between each rep (9-13 reps), e.g., 9 x 60 to 90 seconds. Using 3 sets of 4 x 200m would mean 3 to 4 minutes with 30 seconds of recovery within the sets, e.g., 3 x 60-90 seconds plus either a 4- or a 5-minute recovery between the sets.

This last workout will retain its MVO$_2$ characteristics, contribute to lactic acid tolerance development, act as a race simulation workout and demand will power to adhere to the short recoveries.

Since no coach can ever hope to use every type of workout he or she has ever read or heard about, the secret to good coaching lies in using workouts that are multi-faceted, that is, workouts that are 100% beneficial to the athlete in a number of ways rather than just one.

The coach must also be aware of the dangers of incorrect workout selection. The 12 laps of 200m/400m will not have much benefit to a miler or 1500m runner because, while it will develop the athlete's aerobic power and MVO$_2$, his or her will power is being activated unnecessarily and the workout has virtually no 1500m race practice value. Changing it to 8 x 400m at 1500m pace with slow 200m jog would be more relevant.

If the coach wanted to stay with a workout involving about 5k he or she might consider 10 x 300m at 1500m pace with 200m jog, 13 x 200m at 1500m pace with a brisk 200m jog (perhaps only 15-30 seconds slower than the race pace 200m), or 12 laps of 80-100m at 400-800m pace followed by 100-120m jog recovery.

Finally, surge interval and sprint interval workouts are very valuable as race tactical workouts. Surge intervals develop the ability to change pace quickly which will be needed to either establish a break or to cover one attempted by someone else. Sprint intervals will improve finishing power.

CHAPTER 17
THE HALLMARKS OF THE GREAT ATHLETE
"SO RUN AND TRAIN IN SUCH A WAY THAT YOU MAY WIN THE PRIZE!"

Every athlete dreams of being a champion. Only a few athletes will achieve true success, however. In the majority of cases the athletes willing to commit themselves the most lack genetic attributes and those with an abundance of talent lack commitment! The athlete who is willing to commit to pursuing his goal will succeed in optimizing his ability. This is true success. It can only happen if the training plan is correct, but unfortunately many committed athletes do not follow optimum training schedules.

WINNERS
YOU are a winner if YOU fulfill your God-given potential.
YOUR coach is a winner if he or she helps YOU fulfill YOUR God-given potential

---

However, to paraphrase the quote from the Bible "it is easier for a camel to get through the eye of a needle than it is for a highly talented athlete to achieve his potential." Talented athletes are often too accustomed to getting success without giving full commitment, so when that full commitment is required they are unable to give it.

Indeed, for those who are reasonably talented it is relatively easy to become a national- or even a world-class runner *precisely because most of their equally or more talented competitors are often not willing to do all that is necessary to maximize their potential.* It is much easier for coaches to produce age-group or collegiate champions than national or international representatives, because at these less competitive levels, natural talent will still be able to overcome commitment.

Later as talent evens out and the willingness to work hard becomes a more important factor, it is not unusual for the athlete who has enjoyed early success to fail to progress significantly and eventually drop out of the sport.

When Herb Elliott said most athletes only train to 70% of their limit he was alluding to the inability of most athletes to really push themselves. Percy Cerutty described it a different way when he divided athletes into two categories, "willers"—those can make a 100% effort until the task is achieved—and "wishers"—those with equal potential and similar goals but who do not have the necessary dedication, perseverance or intelligence to be successful.

Winners are athletes who commit themselves unreservedly to the task of achieving their goals. They will eliminate those activities in their lives that can be described as distractions. This does not mean they have to become hermits. To train properly does not require more than 10-15 hours per week. This leaves plenty of time for work, family, friends and other activities.

It *does* mean, however, that late nights and activities that require significant energy output on a regular basis have to be eliminated.

Winners will
- demonstrate a high degree of balance in their lives, though this does not mean they will be ideal parents, friends, or employees because they will still have an undercurrent of focus that means they will never lose sight of the goal.
- possess a lot of common sense.
- be intellectually honest, because an athlete who cannot recognize his own strengths and weaknesses or who cannot honestly examine his own performances in training and competition can never get the best out of himself.

Coaching winners is a relatively easy task. Winners have enough common sense and intelligence to set realistic, tangible goals and they commit themselves to achieving them. The coach is like the coxswain on a rowing shell. The athletes have made sure that the boat is afloat and pointed in the right direction, so all that is required of the coach is a few slight corrections to the rudder. The athletes' endeavors guarantee that everyone arrives at the destination.

Losers are a much more complicated type of athlete. They come in all shapes and sizes.
- Some don't really want to work hard at all while others are willing to work hard but will not modify their lifestyles.
- There are those who are willing to work hard on some aspects of the training but shy away from

other essential aspects of correct preparation.
- Others train really well but have real difficulty competing without reservation.
- Still others will manufacture injuries or illnesses just prior to competition to provide an excuse for failing to perform. Others will train harder than instructed just prior to a race for the same reason.
- Finally, there are those who profess to want success but will not train for the event they might achieve it in. Every coach knows the 200m runner who should be running 400m, the 800m runner who should look to 1500m, the 1500m or 5000m runner who should try the steeplechase, and so on.

Coaching losers is also a very time-consuming task that will test the patience of any coach. If he is approached to coach such an athlete there are a number of strategies.
- The first is to reject the athlete as soon as the weakness becomes apparent—a not uncommon approach where coaches work for success-seeking institutions.
- A second is to employ a "make or break" approach in which the athlete is subjected to a very rigorous routine and he or she makes the decision about continuing or not. Again, this is a not uncommon approach in an institutional setting and it most certainly is the approach taken by the elite units of most of the world's Armed Forces, e.g., Australia's Special Air Forces or the U.S. Navy Seals. Getting selected to the Kenyan team also has this "survival of the fittest" aspect.
- The third option is to try and work through the athlete's problems. This involves time and patience and the coach must try to balance the amount of time and energy he or she is putting into this athlete with the needs of all the members of the squad.

The path that the coach chooses will be dictated by the type of coach he or she is and a coach working for an institution will probably behave differently from a club coach, as the institutional coach has probably recruited the athlete, whereas the club coach has usually been approached by the athlete.

In the former case there is an understanding that the scholarship benefits being offered to the athlete carry the responsibility that the athlete will perform, providing the coaching is correct. The initial interview will be critical to the future success of the scholarship holder. For example, it is not likely that an 800m runner who is skeptical of the value of endurance training will succeed with a Lydiard-style coach, unless the coach is willing to be patient and adopt a strong educative role.

The club coach does not usually recruit athletes, though he or she may attempt to encourage athletes to join their squad. More often athletes approach the coach for assistance, and this generally leads to a more relaxed relationship between athlete and coach. The squad may be made up of every type of athlete, from novice to Olympian—each with his or her own set of goals. The athlete's goals will be the coach's goals and neither will be encumbered with the goals of an organization or school interested only in winning team competitions or producing international medalists.

Again, the initial interview is important, but it is not crucial. Room exists for a little trial and error because the relationship can easily be terminated if either party is dissatisfied. If the athlete has come to the coach because he is aware of how the coach operates, the program is much less likely to come as a surprise.

If the coach follows the Lydiard approach, i.e., gradually strengthening the athlete over a number of years, the athlete is bound to improve. The steady development of stamina and speed will result in faster times, regardless of whether the athlete is highly motivated or not. Some athletes may never be able to get more than 90% out of themselves, but still all that greater strength, stamina, and speed will result in improved performances.

Those few who do rise above the rest, however, are those who have an expectation that they *will* succeed and the personal traits to transform that expectation into reality.

Let us compare the "Champ" and the "Chump," two characters made famous by Bud Winter in his excellent book, *So You Want To Be Sprinter*.

Worksheet No. 12

The "Champ" is characterized by many things. So is the "Chump!" Some of these characteristics are listed in the two assessment sheets below. The athlete is invited to complete the sheets. A rating of "5" in the boxes of the "Champ" sheet means the athlete believes he or she possesses the quality very strongly and is capable of living the quality in his or her daily training. A "1" means the opposite!

The "Chump" also has certain characteristics. Hopefully the athlete will be writing only "1" in these boxes!

There is no pass or fail. Any number less than "5" in the "Champ" sheet is simply an area to be worked on. Coaches are encouraged to add more characteristics of their own!

WORKSHEET 12: THE CHAMP AND THE CHUMP

Write "5" in the box if you (or an athlete you coach) *always* behaves like this regularly.
Write "4," "3," or "2," if you *often or sometimes* behave like this.
Write "1" in the box if you (or an athlete you coach) *never* behaves like this.

The Champ has the WILL TO SUCCEED. He/She:
- Recognizes the importance of patiently following a goal-oriented long-term training plan. ☐
- Calls on hidden reserves during training and competition. ☐
- Eases back on training when physical or mental signs indicate the need to. ☐
- Identifies which type of pain is a warning sign to be heeded and which is a challenge to be overcome. ☐
- Seeks the best advice and travels to the optimum training venues regardless of any inconvenience ☐
- Resists the temptation to train "behind the coach's back" or to change any element of the program without discussing it with the coach. ☐
- Takes the opportunity to train with groups when the workout is appropriate. ☐
- Respects every competitor but idolizes none. ☐
- Exhibits moderate behavior and always appears unhurried. ☐
- Is a good listener who seeks knowledge and has the ability to differentiate between those who have genuine knowledge and those who are merely full of ideas and theories. ☐
- Does not "sponge" off people, is loyal to those who help him/her and acknowledges it freely. ☐
- Has a daily relaxation routine, e.g., yoga, tai chi, etc., in place, and possesses the ability to relax before, during and after competition. ☐
- Accepts pre-race nerves but keeps anxiety and worry to a minimum. ☐
- Focuses totally on personal goals and is not distracted by what others are doing or saying. ☐
- Confronts limitations and works to overcome them. ☐
- Keeps detailed personal training records. ☐
- Avoids compromising on sleep, nutrition, hydration and the safety aspects of training. ☐
- Understands that training is useless unless the body is given the correct amount of time to regenerate. ☐
- Focuses positively and aggressively on competition. ☐
- Never concedes defeat until the competition is over, and even then only concedes that the defeat is a temporary one which will be rectified at the next competition or the competition after that! ☐
- Shows poise and courage in a crisis. ☐
- Trains and practices drills in all the conditions likely to be encountered in a race. ☐

The "CHUMP" has the WILL TO FAIL. He/She:
- fails to prepare him- or herself and/or their equipment properly for competition. ☐
- trains excessively prior to competition and/or fails to allow enough post-race recovery time. ☐
- does not develop an established pre-competition routine and/or puts training ahead of racing. ☐
- gets injured or ill regularly, especially just prior to competition. ☐
- jumps from one training regimen or group to another and/or indiscriminately copies the others. ☐
- eases off because "it's impossible to catch them" or because "I can't win/place." ☐
- expects times to "just come" or come easily because "I've been doing the training." ☐
- ignores rest, nutrition, massage, stretching, relaxation, e.g. yoga, tai chi, etc., detailed record keeping, and so on. ☐
- never trains or practices drills unless the conditions are perfect. ☐
- believes breathing, drafting, transitions and pack running skills come automatically. ☐
- thinks any "hard" session is a good session without reference to specificity or physiology. ☐

CHAPTER 18
RUNNING AND BREATHING TECHNIQUES
GETTING THE MOST FROM YOUR TRAINING

Run With The Best believes that the better an athlete's technique the faster he or she will run. Technique will never replace training, but other things being equal the athlete with superior technique will always win.

Breathing

There are two aspects to technique. The first is breathing and it is not uncommon to hear coaches and athletes say breathing is not something that has to be practiced because it comes naturally to everyone. Arthur Lydiard was one such person.

The opposing view was presented by Percy Cerutty. He believed that most athletes do not breathe effectively and that the 3:30 mile would be possible when a correctly trained, highly talented athlete mastered the proper breathing (and running) techniques.

Full Exhalation

Which opinion is correct? At first glance it would appear that those who believe that breathing comes naturally are correct because it is not the capacity of the lungs to accommodate air that limits performance. The truth is otherwise. The athlete must breathe correctly because poor technique, which is normally characterized by shallow exhalation, limits the ability of the blood to convey oxygen to the working muscles.

Through training the athlete hopes to achieve three things. The first is to steadily improve the cardiovascular system so it operates aerobically for longer than it did previously. He or she then aims to train the muscles to operate more effectively than they normally would in a semi-aerobic state. Finally the athlete trains so he or she can continue operating anaerobically for longer than is possible in an untrained or semi-trained state.

The effectiveness of the athlete's training will be diminished however if anything limits the amount of air entering the lungs and this will occur if the athlete's breathing is too shallow.

Shallow breathing leaves a residue of carbon dioxide in the lungs and this limits the amount of air that can enter the lungs on the subsequent inhalation. This means the athlete enters an anaerobic state earlier than necessary and, regardless of how well he or she is trained, fails to achieve the results he is capable of.

Cerutty constantly told the Portsea athletes that correct breathing relies on rhythm. He would point to the need for rhythm in swimming because, unless a swimmer can breathe underwater, he can only breathe to a certain rhythm. Cerutty stressed that to fully aerate the lungs the athlete must focus on breathing to a rhythm and *fully exhaling* all the air from the lungs.

Breathing And Stride Patterns

Like swimming, there are two major rhythms that can be adopted. The first is similar to the bi-lateral breathing pattern a swimmer uses when he breathes every third stroke and alternates the side he breathes on.

The second method is the one more commonly seen in competitive swimming. The athlete breathes every second stroke and breathes to the same side for perhaps ten to twenty strokes before stroking three times and breathing to the opposite side for a short period of time.

The bi-lateral rhythm is best suited to slower endurance paces because the body encounters more resistance in the frontal position between the second and third strokes, and the intake of air is 50% slower.

Running is similar. During aerobic conditioning running, the athlete should focus on breathing to a three-stride rhythm. This means that the athlete exhales over three strides and inhales during the next three strides. If this is done rhythmically, the athlete will feel very relaxed as he or she flows over the ground.

If the athlete is running at a recovery pace he or she will have to modify the three-stride pattern slightly because the intensity level is so low. This low level of intensity means that the body needs so little oxygen that there is no need to fully inhale and exhale every six strides. As this does result in the accumulation of residual carbon dioxide in the lower lungs, the athlete will need to exhale slowly and completely every few minutes. The long slow exhalation should take place over four strides.

The runner will also need to modify the pattern when running at lactate threshold pace. At this pace the demand for oxygen has increased significantly. The breathing routine remains a six-stride pattern but the exhalation should be more complete. To complete a full exhalation may now take between three and three and a half strides and the inhalation may take two and a half strides to three strides.

An athlete who has slipped into a five-stride breathing routine, i.e., three strides to exhale and two stride to inhale, has moved from pure threshold to the zone between threshold and maximal oxygen uptake.

As the breathing pattern moves to a four-stride routine the athlete's exertion has reached maximal oxygen uptake intensity. Left unregulated this pattern will quickly become two strides to exhale and one to inhale and then degenerate into a two-stride routine—one stride exhalation, one stride inhalation.

Once the breathing pattern has assumed the three-stride routine the infamous "wall" is just around the corner.

By learning to regulate his or her breathing the athlete can delay the movement from one intensity zone to the next. Delaying the movement from one intensity zone to the next means the heart rate stays lower. If the athlete then acquires the capability to do this at race speeds he is able to run faster at lower heart rates for longer periods of time. This, obviously, means the athlete records faster times.

Regulating Breathing Rhythms

The secret to regulating the breathing is simply being aware of what breathing pattern is being used. If the athlete is running a 10k race, for example, he or she must adhere to a six-stride routine at race pace for as long as possible. Every time the athlete becomes aware he has slipped into a five-stride routine (which means the heart rate is rising), he must fully exhale, focus on reducing the heart rate by eliminating any unnecessary tension in his running, and resume the six-stride routine.

Naturally as the race progresses he or she will be able to stay on a six-stride routine for ever shorter periods of time. But if the same principle is applied from the six-stride routine all the way through to the three-stride routine, the athlete will have delayed the onset of lactic acid significantly and will have left all his or her equally well trained opponents (and many better trained ones, as well) far behind.

Movement

The second aspect of technique is the technique of movement. Lydiard and Cerutty agreed on the importance of correct movement but differed on how to achieve it.

Lydiard saw proper technique as the result of doing the correct training. The long steady runs developed an efficient style, the hill bounding emphasized the appropriate arm and leg action, and the speed work developed proper form.

Cerutty says in his book, *Middle Distance Running*, a runner who is strong but "poor in technique, one who hits the ground heavily, or in other ways gives evidence of poor technique" may "have the chagrin of finding that at 25 years he is not running any faster than at 21 years—a quite common experience, let it be noted."

Cerutty also believed an athlete could only run really fast if his running was free and uninhibited. He identified four types of movement on foot—walking, ambling, trotting and galloping—and believed that an athlete who could not run slowly for hours with virtually no effort (shades of the Africans running to school) would never be able to run fast. He detested what he called the military posture and had no time for coaches who wanted their athletes to run in an even beat, metronomic way. Cerutty believed this form of running (trotting as he called it) was not natural in nature, that the trot was inferior to the gallop and most runners used it because they lacked raw animal power and the ability to breathe correctly.

Run With The Best favors the Cerutty approach. The way to achieve this "off-beat" gait is to allow the expansion of the abdomen and the chest as the athlete inhales to cause the entire body to rise ever so slightly and to accentuate the downward thrust of the lead arm (probably the right) as the exhalation occurs.

The "trotters" lead with the legs and the arms and this does little more than balance the body. There are no "trotters" who are great sprinters because a powerful arm drive is essential to fast running. Newton's First Law of Motion ("to every action there is an equal and opposite reaction") comes into play here. The downward thrust of the arms and legs causes the hips to rise and the athlete to "run taller" with a slightly longer stride—an action that requires more than normal power to maintain.

Naturally the longer the distance the less vigorous the arm drive needs to be however. As with everything, all things being equal, the athlete trained to be able to mobilize power from his or her arms when needed (as all strong-finishing athletes can), will beat opponents who do not have this ability.

Again Cerutty pointed to the action of an animal's lead leg and the part played by the forelegs of the animal as it drove forward, reached ahead to full extension, gathered into a power position and drove forward again. He stressed the rhythm of this series of movements, how each movement varied from the next by an infinitesimally small time period.

He pointed to the weight lifters who apply the greatest force of movement as they exhale and asked his runners to do the same. Apply the force while exhaling by driving the arms down. By driving the arms down the legs will also drive down. The reaction to this downward movement is to cause the body to be lifted so the athlete runs tall.

Relax while inhaling so muscle tension around the lungs does not impede the natural flow of air into the lungs. During these two to three strides the athlete is literally recovering at high speed and gathering him or herself for the next power phase.

The thing that distinguishes the great athlete is the ability to remain relaxed while running at high speeds. One reason this is possible is that by driving and relaxing rhythmically the blood has an easier time moving into and out of the muscle fibers during the relaxation phase. This means a greater volume of blood will reach the muscle fibers. The greater the volume of blood reaching the muscles the better the delivery of oxygen and nutrients to the muscles and the more efficiently waste products will be removed.

Mastering a proper, power-laden running technique is difficult because, like swimming, mastering proper running technique requires many hours of practice.

The basis for this type of running is to concentrate on applying a millisecond of downward force as the lead arm, normally the right, is pulled backwards. The downward drive of the leg then causes the body to rise and so the foot tends to land more directly under the body. This means the foot spends less time on the ground than in the traditionally recommended front-of-the-body heel landing.

Heel landings rob the athlete of many advantages. The first is the use of the muscles in the feet to absorb the shock. Nobody running barefoot, regardless of speed, will land on his heel. Nobody who is told to jog on the spot will jog on his heels. Sprinters do not land on their heels. The only reason anyone lands on his heels is because he has shoes which, in theory, absorb the shock of this unnatural way of running.

The second advantage the athlete loses is the use of the calf muscles. These muscles both assist with shock absorption and provide propulsive power. Heel landings mean the athlete simply (and slowly) rolls over his or her foot then up onto the toes before pushing very slightly forward. Almost all the propulsive force comes as the athlete pulls his body forward over the foot while it is on the ground.

Before going any further however it is critical the athlete does not try to land on his toes or on the ball of the foot. The landing position is decided by the athlete's arm and leg action. Today's distance runners who are capable of 13 minutes for 5000m or 27 minutes for 10,000m have to have the speed of the very best 800m and 1500m runners of 30 to 40 years ago. Therefore they have to run with a technique similar to those runners. Since few athletes capable of 1:46 to 1:48 for 800m and 3:34 to 3:38 run on their heels it means the distance runners of today must run like middle distance runners of the 1950's and 1960's.

Generally speaking, the faster the runner the higher he carries himself because he not only has a higher stride frequency, he strikes the ground with more force. This also increases stride frequency and it is this type of runner who will possess the most powerful kick at the end of the race. Conversely, the slower the runner the lower the hips, and naturally the body in general, the further ahead of the body the foot will hit the ground. The further ahead of the body the foot hits the ground the more the foot lands on the heel.

In Cerutty's words, the foot of the runner with correct technique, for example Sebastian Coe, tends to "slither" onto the ground. In order to improve his or her technique, all the slower, heel landing athlete has to do is to concentrate on pushing down on the thigh for a millisecond every time he takes a step during easy runs and practice his drills regularly. The "high knee," the "stepovers," and the "fast feet" drills all require a strong push down to execute them properly and keep the body high.

The straight leg shuffle, like hill bounding, requires a strong springing action so the landing is on the ball of the foot. Naturally a vigorous arm action is also important and other forms of power training contribute to the runner's capacity to improve technique.

The experience of *Run With The Best* at camps and clinics in Australia and the USA is that the less experienced runners improve out of proportion to the amount of training they have done. Improvements in the order of four minutes over 10k or 2 minutes in the 5k within 2 or 3 months were common for many of those athletes who normally race at around 4 to 5 minutes per kilometer or 6:30 to 8 minutes per mile.

Faster athletes obviously improve less but the improvements are even more significant to performance.

CHAPTER 19
TRAINING FOR THE FUTURE
SO YOU WILL NOT BE LEFT BEHIND

Scoring Tables of Athletics, commonly called "The Hungarian Tables" because it was produced by a group of Hungarian track & field statisticians, provides the most widely accepted means of comparing a performance in one event with a performance in another event. Its point tables show us, for instance, that a 26:27.85 mark in the men's 10k is an intrinsically "better" mark than a 1:41.11 men's 800meter time or a 2:20.47 time in the women's marathon. These times are all current world bests, and the Hungarian Tables give us a handy way to compare these present-day records (see Figure 19-1).

Even a cursory examination of Figure 19-1 suggests the women's 5000m is in need of revision, and that the very best women are capable of performing within 10% of the best male runners. The average elite female (#20 on the world list) however appears to perform at about 87% of the average elite male (#20 on the world list in his corresponding event).

Coaching for the future involves two main things: ensuring that all the basic elements of a good training program (recovery runs, long runs, speed and power work, hills, intervals, repetitions, etc.) are present, and using resources such as the Hungarian Tables, Stamina Indicators, and Performance Indicators to break new ground. Once an athlete has accomplished the required basic volume and has sufficient speed, the coach migh consider training his athletes more like Kenyans or triathletes train.

Professional triathletes regularly train between 25 and 40 hours per week, using a three-a-day routine. Weekly volumes of 7-10 hours running (65-90 miles or 105-150km), 12-20 hours of cycling and 8-15 hours of swimming are not uncommon.

If even motivated *age-group* triathletes in full-time work can train 12-15 hours a week, surely it is not beyond track & field athletes who want to compete with the best in the world to raise their workloads from an average of 6-10 hours (middle distance runners) and 8-13 hours (long distance runners) by an additional 1-2 hours.

Training three (or more) times a day is not really new. It happened at Cerutty's camp. And quick lunchtime runs by Australian runners were not unusual in the 1960's. Former world 10k record holder David Bedford was famous for the intensity of his three-times-a-day schedule and the Finns of the 1970's also used this approach.

Cerutty once said, "The athlete of today who would achieve the highest honours is a dedicated athlete who trains hard all year round. He has few rest days, and will feel that any day he is unable to train is a day wasted in his life. He will do some running every day—even if only in his street clothes when going somewhere."

All athletes today have to be fast over 400m. A 26:30 10,000m requires 3:31-3:33 1500m speed. This requires 1:45-1:47 800m speed which demands at least the capability to run 48-50 seconds for 400m.

The same is true for the women. Wang Junxia has run 3:50 for 1500m and 29:30 for 10,000m. This means she could have easily broken 1:58 for 800m and was probably capable of 53-55 seconds for 400m.

To achieve optimal results athletes must ensure they maintain the correct balance between aerobic recovery and aerobic conditioning training (easy training) and lactate threshold, aerobic power, maxi-

FIGURE 19-1: COMPARING RECORDS IN THE MIDDLE AND LONG DISTANCE EVENTS.
(World Records as of June 1, 1998)

Event	Men's WR	Hungarian Tables Pts.	Women's WR	Hungarian Tables Pts.	Pct. of Men's Record
800m	1:41.11	1282	1:53.28	1266	89.25%
1500m	3:27.37	1268	3:50.46	1290	89.98%
3000m	7:20.67	1319	8:06.11	1318	90.65%
5000m	12:39.74	1339	14:28.09p	1270	87.52%
10,000m	26:22.75p	1333	29:31.78	1306	89.33%
Marathon	2:06:50	1241	2:20:47p	1277	90.09%

p = pending record, as of 6/1/98.

mal oxygen uptake, anaerobic power, lactic acid tolerance and speed (hard training). Since a training ratio of 65-70% easy to moderate and 30-35% moderate to hard is manageable for most elite athletes any increase in intense training means an increase in total volume.

No athlete, except perhaps a marathon runner, can view his or her event in isolation from other events. To improve an athlete's 400m time the coach must improve the 200m time. To improve the 200m time an athlete's standing 60m and flying 30m times may have to improve. To improve these, the coach may have to introduce circuit training, hopping and bounding (on slight slopes only), calisthenics, running drills, and so on.

A male athlete aspiring to run 1:40 for 800m and 3:23 for 1500m would need the threshold capability to run 10 miles or 16km in around 50 minutes. He would also need the maximal oxygen uptake capacity to run 3000m in 7:40-7:50 and 5000m in 13:20-13:40. To achieve these standards, he would have to develop a substantial aerobic base.

In the case of the female athlete who aims at 1:50 and/or 3:47, the same is true. Improving the athlete's 400m time would be achieved in the same way as for the men. The athlete would need to develop the ability to run 54-55 minutes for 10 miles or 16km at 80-87% MHR, which means she would have the capability of running 8:30-8:35 for 3000m and 14:40-14:50 for 5000m.

The best middle and long distance athletes of today are already both strong and fast. The athletes

---

RUNNERS' WORK RATE SLAMMED
1968 800m Olympic gold medalist Ralph Doubell hit out at the current crop of Australian middle distance runners for not doing enough work. He said "both Herb (Elliott) and I feel the results over the last few years don't match what we achieved many years back and that the runners are not doing the hard yards." *The Australian* (newspaper), May 21, 1998.

---

of the future are going to be stronger and faster. The male 800m runner targeting 1:40 should follow Cerutty's advice (offered in 1960) and "practice on the assumption that he will join two sub-50-second 440's (400's) together in one supreme effort—by developing the stamina to run fast, long" (Cerutty, *Middle Distance Running*, p. 136). The female targeting 1:50 should practice to join two sub-55-second 400's together.

Athletes of both sexes will need to be running volumes similar to middle/long distance athletes of the 1970's and 1980's if they are to achieve the threshold and maximal oxygen uptake capacities listed above. Taken in isolation, a superior 400m time will not guarantee a superior 800m time.

Implicit in the *Run With The Best* philosophy is the belief that there should not be too much difference in the training methods applied to all middle distance and long distance runners. Both Lydiard and Cerutty believed that the conditioning phase of all these runners should be similar. The differences only begin to emerge during the Pre-Competition and Competition Periods. Even then the differences may not be too clear.

Efim Shurvetsky, the Australian national multi-event coach and a former head coach of the USSR's regional Olympic training camp at Odessa, commented to co-author Tony Benson that he found it very hard to tell who were the 800m runners and who were the 10k runners after watching the Kenyans training together in Atlanta during the 1996 Olympics. In the end, he said it all came down to which athletes had the fastest 400m times. Those with the best 400 times were the middle distance runners. The others were the long distance runners!

The simplest way to develop an annual training schedule which accords with the example of a 1500m program below is to use a multi-tier approach to training similar to Peter Coe's "Five-Tier" system.*

Day	Training Focus
Monday	Aerobic Recovery + Speed (Alternate 200 and 400m Training) + Auxiliary Training
Tuesday	Aerobic Conditioning + Stamina (Alternate 5k and 10k Training)
Wednesday	Aerobic Recovery + Aerobic Conditioning + Auxiliary Training
Thursday	Aerobic Recovery + Specific Event (Alternate 800m and 1500m Training)
Friday	Aerobic Recovery + Aerobic Conditioning + Auxiliary Training
Saturday	Power Training (Various Types of Hill Workouts or XC Races) + Aerobic Recovery
Sunday	Significant Aerobic Conditioning (Marathon Training) + Aerobic Recovery or Rest.

The same principles of Monday (speed), Tuesday (over-distance), Wednesday (consolidation), Thursday (event-specific), Friday (recovery), Saturday (power) and Sunday (endurance) may be applied to a 5000m program. When finished it would appear as follows:

---

* XII International Track & Field Congress, Aix Les Bains, France, March 1990.

Day	Training Focus
Monday	Aerobic Recovery + Speed (Alternate 400 and 800m Training) + Auxiliary Training
Tuesday	Aerobic Conditioning + Stamina (Alternate 10k and Half-Marathon Training)
Wednesday	Aerobic Recovery + Aerobic Conditioning + Auxiliary Training
Thursday	Aerobic Recovery + Specific Event (Alternate 1500m and 5000m Training)
Friday	Aerobic Recovery + Aerobic Conditioning + Auxiliary Training
Saturday	Power Training (Various Types of Hill Workouts or XC Races) + Aerobic Recovery
Sunday	Significant Aerobic Conditioning (Marathon training) + Aerobic Recovery or Rest.

The multi-tiered system of training is particularly suited to training up to three times per day as would happen in a training camp situation. The following weekly schedule (Fig. 19-2) is an example of how it would work using a two-week "hard" and one-week "easy" approach.

The reader will note that the number of sessions varies from 16 per week in weeks one and two to 10 sessions in week 3. This is a total of 42 sessions for the three-week cycle or an average of 14 sessions per week. Secondly, this program is written in distance but it could also be written in time. Thirdly, the program specifies effort (e.g., 55-65% effort) not heart rate because it is assumed not every athlete has access to a heart rate monitor with feedback and memory facilities.*

In conclusion, it is imperative the athlete and coach are working to a plan which accounts for short-, medium- and long-term improvements in their chosen event. The athlete or coach who aims at achieving what is considered a present-day elite performance level in three, five, or ten years time will find the world has moved on by the time he or she reaches the target.

> "Two years later, right on schedule, I broke the mark that had been the world record when I set my goal. But by then the game had changed and suddenly I am 14 seconds back." Bob Kennedy's words after running 12:58.21 for 5000m. *Track & Field News*, August 1997.

Bob Kennedy: "Suddenly I am 14 seconds back."

*The coach who is concerned about the possibility of injury in relation to increased training is asked to read the last paragraph of Chapter 20 and all of Chapter 22 thoroughly.

FIGURE 19-2: THREE-WEEK SCHEDULE USING TWO-WEEK HARD AND ONE-WEEK EASY APPROACH.

Day of Week	Week 1	Week 2	Week 3
Monday			
(6 am)	5-8k at 55-75% effort. Stretching.	5-8k at 55-75% effort. Stretching.	7-12k at 55-75% effort. Stretching.
(10 am)	5-8k including drills and 6 x 150m at 400m pace. Stretching.	5-8 k including drills and 2-3 sets of 120m-90m-60m at 200m pace. Stretching.	
(4 pm)	5-8k at 55-75% effort. General circuit training, Stretching.	5-8k at 55-75% effort. General circuit training, Stretching.	Pre-Competition warm-up. Stretching.
Tuesday			
(6 am)	5-8k at 55-75% effort incl. 100m strides. Stretching.	5-8k at 55-75% effort incl. 100m strides. Stretching.	5-8k Pre-Competition-type jog. Stretching.
(10 am)	12-16k at 85-92% MHR on a flat or undulating course. Stretching.	15-24k @ 85-92% MHR on a flat or undulating course. Stretching.	400 or 800m Time Trial. Stretching.
(4 pm)	5-8k including 10-20 x 70-100m power sprinting on a 10-15-degree hill at sprint pace. Stretching.	5-8k including 5-10 x 100m-200m hill running on a 2-4-degree hill at 800m pace. Stretching.	5-8k at 55-75% effort. Stretching.
Wednesday			
(10 am)	10-16k at 65-80% effort. Preferably on an undulating to hilly course. Stretching.	10-16k at 65-80% effort. Preferably on an undulating to hilly course. Stretching.	10-15k including 6 x 100m accelerations. Stretching.
(4 pm)	5-8k at 55-75% effort. Power circuit training. Stretching.	5-8k at 55-75% effort. Power circuit training. Stretching.	Stretching.
Thursday			
(6 am)	10-12k including 20 min of hard fartlek, surging and sprinting over hills.	10-12k including 6 x 500-800m on a 2-4-degree uphill at 5k-10k pace.	5-8k aerobic recovery run. Stretching.
(10 am)	5-8k at 55-75% effort. Stretching.	5-8k at 55-75% effort. Stretching.	10-15k including a 3k or 5k Time Trial.
(4 pm)	5-8k including 4-6 x 400m at 1500m pace with 400m jog recovery. Stretching.	5-8k including 2k-3k of 50-100m sprint with 50-100m float. Stretching.	
Friday			
(10 am)	5-8k at 65-80% effort. Endurance circuit training. Stretching.	5-8k at 65-80% effort. Endurance circuit training. Stretching.	Rest day.
(4 pm)	3-5k aerobic recovery run.	3-5k aerobic recovery run.	
Saturday			
(8 am)	27-37 km at marathon pace on flat ground or at marathon effort through hills.	27-37 km at marathon pace on flat ground or at marathon effort through hills.	Ultra-long run, e.g., 5k longer than normal at 65-80% effort.
(3 pm)	4-7k including 10-20 x 80-150m hill of 3-5 degrees at 400-800m pace. Stretching.	4-7k including 4-6 x 300-500m hill of 2-4 degrees at 1500m-3k pace. Stretching.	4-7k including 7-10 x 50-70m hill of 10-15 degrees at maximum maximum effort with full recovery.
Sunday			
(10 am)	15-25k at 65-80% effort. Finish with calisthenics and stretching.	15-25k at 65-80% effort. Finish with calisthenics and stretching.	Rest day.
(4pm)	Rest.	Rest.	

FIGURE 19-3: THE IMPROVEMENT IN WORLD RECORDS, 1971-1996 (Men), 1975-1996 (Women)

Event	Men 1971	Men 1996	Diff.	%Imp.	Women '75	Women '96	Diff.	%Imp.
800m	1:44.3	1:41.73	2.57	2.5%	1:57.5	1:53.28	4.32	3.7%
1500m	3:33.1	3:27.37	5.73	2.7%	4:01.4	3:50.46	10.94	4.5%
3000m	7:39.6	7:20.67	18.93	4.1%	8:46.6	8:06.11	40.49	7.7%
5000m	13:13.0	12:44.39	29.21	3.7%	15:53.6	14:36.45	77.15	8.2%
10,000m	27:30.8	26:38.08	52.72	3.2%	34:01.4	29:31.78	4:29.62	13.2%
Marathon	2:08:34	2:06:50	1:44.0	1.4%	2:38:19	2:21:06	17:13.0	10.9%

CHAPTER 20
JUNIOR ATHLETES
PLAN TO PERFORM AS ELITE SENIORS

In his book, *Middle Distance Running*, Percy Cerutty made the following comments about junior athletes.

(1) All youths should be encouraged to test themselves both to strength development (barbells, sandhills, and the like) and to running distances. It is not abnormal for a lad as young as ten years of age to run 20 miles in a nonstop effort. On the other hand, few lads that age will be found mature enough in either their mentality, their innate ability, or physical strength to hold themselves to such a task. But the boy who can do it, should do it—but never be forced to do it, just encouraged.

(2) No youth, or anyone for that matter, should be set tasks and be expected to perform them under rigid conditions. By rigid direction I mean being told they have to do it. Each should be allowed to travel at their own speed in their upward climb to success.

Arthur Lydiard also states in his book, *Run To The Top*, that "I can always remember the words of Gunder Hägg's coach [Gosta Holmer]: 'If you can get a boy in his teens and encourage him to train and not race until he has matured, then you have laid the foundations of an Olympic champion.' I believe that sums the whole thing up. Encourage the boy, don't force him. Let him play at athletics and with athletes."

Lydiard also states that "I have seen boys 8 to 15 years of age run to the club rooms on Saturday, play chasing around the hall for half an hour, run up to 3 miles (of cross country running) in packs, change back at the rooms and then run around for another half an hour waiting for afternoon tea (and) they were still going afterwards" (page 115).

Both statements are very much at odds with what happens in countries with high-profile youth distance running programs, but they summarize perfectly what happens in many African countries where the kids are running and walking constantly. And they compete infrequently in competitions that are rarely defined by age. And they regularly run out from their houses to try and run with their heroes as groups of elite athletes pass through the villages.

Run With The Best has stated in Chapter 3 that junior athletes will never reach their potential as senior athletes unless they accumulate a sufficient base. Ideally this base will be accumulated in an encouraging social environment. The volume of base required may be considered as similar for all athletes contesting similar events.

There are many examples of individual athletes emerging earlier than the rest of a group following virtually identical programs under the supervision of well respected coaches. That these athletes perform better off the same base as their squad mates is merely an indication of superior talent, earlier maturation, and/or will power, not the sign of a superior program.

The *Run With The Best* research suggesting minimum accumulated volumes deserves restating here.

800m	12,000 miles	20,000km
1500m	18,000 miles	30,000km
3000m Steeplechase	25,000 miles	40,000km
10,000m	30,000 miles	50,000km
Marathon	30,000 miles	50,000km

The first priority of any coach must be to develop a plan to get his or her athlete to the 12,000-mile or 20,000km level. Again Lydiard's comments are interesting. "How far and fast a child runs in training should be left to his own feelings. But there is no reason why a boy of fourteen should not run ten, fifteen or even twenty miles, so long as he is allowed to do it of his own free will."

Priority No 1. Build your athlete's aerobic base

The challenge for the coach is therefore to encourage the athlete to run regularly and not to inhibit him when it comes to running long distances or testing himself in any other way athletically. The second priority is to develop the athlete's speed to the maximum.

Just before this book went to the printer Haile Gebrselassie ran 10,000m in 26:22.75. Prior to this he ran 3:32 (indoors) for 1500m and 8:01 for 2 miles. To do these times requires great speed over 400m and 200m because, even with his great stamina he would still need at least a 1:46-1:47 capability at 800m. Equally, any female with ambitions of approaching

Wang Junxia's women's 10,000m world record would need to be running 1:59 or faster for 800m. If the 10,000m runners are currently capable of perhaps 48-49 seconds for 400m (men) and 54-55 seconds (women) how much more speed is required for the 800m and 1500m runners?

In fact, any male athlete with aspirations to be an Olympic finalist at 800m should be planning on having the speed to run 45.5 seconds (for the 400m/800m type) or below 47 seconds (for the 800m/1500m type). The females would need to be under 51 seconds (400m/800m) type or less than 53.5 seconds (800m/1500m type).

Priority No 2. Maximize your athlete's speed capabilities

The major reason so few Western distance athletes are succeeding centers on coaching philosophy. The coaches who believe in endurance running are often afraid of speed because at some stage or another speed work has been perceived to have caused an injury to their athletes.

Equally, many coaches who recognize the importance of speed are afraid of endurance because they think slow running is detrimental to speed development and/or they perceive long endurance running has been the cause of injury to their athletes.

If either situation was really true then there should be massive injury problems with the African athletes today, none of Gerschler's athletes in the 1930's, 40's or 50's should have done well, Iglói's, Cerutty's, Lydiard's and Bowerman's athletes of the late 1950's to early 1970's should not have succeeded.

Yet succeed the Africans do and the athletes of the late 1930's to early 1970's could lay claims to times of 1:44-1:46 for 800m, 3:35-3:38 for 1500m, 13:35-13:45 for 5000m and so on. These are times many 1990's coaches would like to achieve!

For juniors the key to the program must be variety and challenge. If they are not enjoying what they are doing they will drift away to other sports. The ideal program would challenge the youngster to run long distances, to develop his strength using weights and resistance running, and to build his speed. The coach should regularly schedule fartlek sessions so the athlete can run through a whole range of speed from 100m to marathon paces.

How can a coach schedule longer distance paces for their 14-15 year old athletes? Simple. Use imagination. A 400m time plus 10 seconds multiplied by two can be the 800m pace. Twice the 800m pace can be the 1500m pace. Multiply the projected 1500m time by 2.1-2.2 will do as a 3k pace and the projected 1500m time multiplied by 3.6-3.7 will be good enough for the 5k pace. To get a 10k and a marathon pace simply multiply the projected 5k by 2.1-2.2 for the 10k and 9.5 to 10 for the marathon pace.

Accuracy isn't especially important but the variety of paces is. Mark out two or three courses in parkland or around the streets and mark various points along the route. Have the athlete sprint short distances (60-100m), run fast and relaxed over others (100m-200m), stride out over longer distances (200-400m) and cruise over longer distances (400m-2k). To ensure that the tempo is what has been scheduled give the athlete various times to achieve, for example, "Aim for 65 seconds between this tree and that driveway. I don't want it any faster." Or "Be sure to take the full 5 minutes to jog from the driveway to next intersection."

Running hill surge fartlek is also excellent training. Make out a course suitable to the athlete's age and stage of development and get him to run the course surging up the hills and jogging slowly between each hill.

These sessions must be done in such a way that the athlete experiences the range of speeds desired by the coach but has averaged about 75% MHR for the whole workout and has not spent any significant period of time at heart rates in excess of 85% MHR. This type of work could be done two to three times weekly.

The key to basic endurance is a steady running. Two or three times (or more) per week the athlete should run steadily for up to 1:30 hours and even two-hour runs done slowly will not cause problems for a properly conditioned youngster (after all, plenty of sports require in excess of two hours to play). In fact, the coach should model the long runs on soccer, tennis or football-like intensity. The opportunities to walk are removed but so are the hard dashes required to get to the ball.

The final component is speed. One day per week, two if doing less fartlek, should be devoted to smooth fast relaxed running interspersed with some full speed sprints over 20-50m. Activities like 100m runs at 400m speed, 150-200m runs at 800m speed, short steep hill sprints, and the like, would all be appropriate provided the athlete was given very generous recoveries between efforts and the overall volume of the session was not more than 1-3% of the weekly running volume.

The most important competitions for a junior are sprints and cross country. Their true potential in middle and long distance races is so far away, any results are irrelevant. Let them run these for fun if they want to. With their superior endurance, and the not inconsiderable anaerobic benefits they will gain from their alactic sprint training, they may well defeat most of the lactic anaerobically trained competitors anyway.

The basic program for a junior is simple. The

following is an example.

Monday:	Speed and Power
Tuesday:	Endurance Fartlek
Wednesday:	Aerobic Endurance
Thursday:	Speed and Rhythm Fartlek
Friday:	Aerobic Endurance or Rest
Saturday:	Track or Cross Country Competition or Competition Simulation
Sunday:	Long Aerobic Run

Additional components would include body conditioning work, a flexibility program and a regeneration routine.

Finally the athlete would not need to start training twice daily until he is training in excess of eight hours per week. Some may like to include a 15-30-minute morning run in their program just to loosen up, however. Such an approach has the additional benefit of accumulating the required base mileage faster so long as it is not introduced too quickly and causes injury—and loss of opportunity to accumulate the base volume and increase speed!!

From *In The Long Run*, Steve Moneghetti's biography, by Peter Howley

"In the winter of 1977, the Year 9 boys of St. Patrick's College competed in their annual 6km class lap of Lake Wendouree...

"When the next class commenced, English teacher Tony Benson scanned the results with some interest. Benson himself was a champion runner representing Australia at the 1972 Munich Olympic Games... The fastest result of the day caught his eye—a time of 24 minutes 35 seconds—placed opposite the name of S. Moneghetti. Impressed by the time for that age group, Benson spoke to Steve and offered to design a training programme for him if he was keen to pursue running as a sport. He [Benson] recalls talking to Steve. 'He joined a group of promising young kids I was coaching. I thought he had a great deal of potential. He was a skinny little boy with arms and legs going everywhere but able to cover the ground very well. He was very determined.'

"Steve started training with Tony Benson. The programme was based on three philosophies: Percy Cerutty for hard training, Arthur Lydiard for the long running and the Kenyans, who never get upset after a bad run or training session. He ran over a hill course, did lap work on the oval for interval-type training over 200 metres and undertook a long run. In the beginning he was doing about 50-60 kilometres a week. Benson takes up the story... 'To my mind the amount of kilometres per week was the most important thing, to build it up so that when he was 19 he would be doing about 110-120 kilometres per week...'

"The training programme had to be fitted in with Steve's other commitments but his running did improve. The influence of Benson had a significant impact on the young runner's thinking and the dream of being an Olympian became all the more tangible. 'This person was someone who had been to the Olympics and he was now advising me. I imagined that my training programme was the sort of programme he had followed to get to the Olympics. For me it was a concrete step towards the Olympics.'"

Steve Moneghetti has been one of the world's premier marathoners since the '80s. He has a complete set of Commonwealth Games medals: gold, Victoria 1994; silver, Auckland 1990; bronze, Edinburgh 1986, and has won at Berlin and Tokyo. His best of 2:08.16 came at Berlin in 1990 (age 29). He has represented Australia at three Olympic Games, 1988 (5th), 1992 (48th), and 1996 (7th). He took the marathon bronze medal at the 1997 World Championships in Athens (age 36).

CHAPTER 21
AGE-GROUP AND RECREATIONAL ATHLETES
CREATE YOUR PERSONAL PROGRAM

The *Run With The Best* program is designed to cater for every person, regardless of age, sex, innate ability, or goals. The way the program works is outlined in Chapter 3.

Assume for example a 30-year-old ex-basketballer named Martina Smith decides to take up running with the idea of completing some 5k and 10k races in six months time. *The Run With The Best* approach would be as follows.

Step 1. The Consultation

The athlete would be advised to have a thorough medical examination and an attempt would be made to estimate how much running the person had done to this point. In the case of a basketballer the total volume might be considerable, though its specificity in relation 5k or 10k running would be very low. The athlete indicates she played basketball for recreation only and ran approximately 20k (12 miles) per week. In the course of the discussion Martina indicates she prefers to work in kilometers rather than miles or hours.

Name: Martina Smith	Training Age: 1 Yr
Estimated Accumulated Lifetime Volume (Km)	15,000km (Av 1000km per Yr—20km per wk)

Step 2. Establishing the Plan

The starting date can be any time but this example will assume it is December 29, 1997. The running volume is planned to increase by 1000km (600 miles) per year because the muscular and skeletal systems would be quite strong and the athlete has indicated strongly that she wishes to be competitive in 3 years(Fig. 21-1).

Step 3. Establishing the Annual Volume for the First Year

The athlete now establishes her first long-term goal.

Name: Martina Smith	Training Age: 1 Yr	Year: 1998
Planned Volume	2000km—an average of 40km/wk	

Step 4. Periodizing the Year

Martina's goal is a 10k race on September 6th, 1998, which allows 36 weeks of training if she begins on December 29, 1997. As the goal race is a 10k there is less need for an extensive Pre-Competition Period, so the plan will involve 30 weeks of base

FIGURE 21-1: ANNUAL TRAINING PROGRESSION (VOLUME).

Year	Total Km	Cumulative Total Km	Year	Total Km	Cumulative Total Km
1984	1000	2,000 (1000-1983)	1996	1000	14,000
1985	1000	3,000	1997	1000	15,000 (30)
1986	1000	4,000	1998	2000	17,000 (31)
1987	1000	5,000	1999	3000	20,000 (32)
1988	1000	6,000	2000	4000	24,000 (33)
1989	1000	7,000	2001	4000	28,000 (34)
1990	1000	8,000	2002	4000	32,000 (35)
1991	1000	9,000	2003	4000	36,000 (36)
1992	1000	10,000	2004	4000	40,000 (37)
1993	1000	11,000	2005	4000	44,000 (38)
1994	1000	12,000	2006	4000	48,000 (39)
1995	1000	13,000	2007	4000	52,000 (40)

FIGURE 21-2: GENERAL TRAINING PLAN (DURATIONS).

Name: Martina Smith						
Base Period Dec 29th 1997 - July 26th			Pre-Competition Period July 27th - Aug 23rd		Competition Period Aug 24th - Dec 27th	
No of Weeks: 30 weeks			No of Weeks: 4 weeks		No of Weeks: 18 weeks	
Phase I	Phase II	Phase III	Phase I	Phase II	Phase I	Phase II
Wks: 10	Wks: 10	Wks: 10	Wks: 2	Wks: 2	Wks: 2	Wks: 16

training, 4 weeks of competition-specific (or pre-competition) training and 2 weeks of taper (or Competition Period-type training). The year, however, comprises 52 weeks so Martina will not be running 2000km in 36 weeks. It will look as above (Fig. 21-2) and while Phase II of the Competition Period may contain a further 2-4 weeks of racing it must also include at least 2 weeks of complete rest and all other weeks should be composed of easy aerobic running because one major peak is enough for any athlete in his or her first year of competition.

The reader will note this example of a periodized year looks quite different from the one given for a track athlete in Chapter 3. The reader will also note both examples are based on exactly the same principles.

Step 5. Develop an Annual Plan

The athlete has a goal of achieving 2000km for the year. This means an average of 40km per week. However the Base Period should contain more volume than the later periods so the plan must reflect this.

The next thing the athlete must do is decide how much volume to assign to each phase of each period

FIGURE 21-3: THE COMPLETE ANNUAL PLAN (VOLUMES).

Name: Martina Smith						
Base Period Dec 29th 1997 - Jul 26th			Pre-Competition Period Jul 27th - Aug 23rd		Competition Period Aug 24th - Dec 27th	
1250km in 30 wks. Av = 41-42km per week			80km in 2 weeks. Av = 40 km/wk		530km in 16 weeks. Av = 38-39 km/wk. Include two weeks of complete rest.	
Phase I	Phase II	Phase III	Phase I	Phase II	Phase I	Phase II
340km 10wks Av. 34 km/wk	420km 10wks Av. 42 km/wk	490km 10wks Av. 47 km/wk	80km 2wks Av. 40 km/wk	80km 2wks Av. 40 km/wk	60km 2wks Av. 30 km/wk	530km 14wks Av. 38 km/wk
Weeks 1-10	Weeks 11-20	Weeks 21-30	Weeks 31-32	Weeks 33-34	Weeks 35-36	Weeks 37-52
1. 25k 2. 30k 3. 25k 4. 40k 5. 35k 6. 25k 7. 40k 8. 35k 9. 30k 10. 40k	11. 40k 12. 40k 13. 40k 14. 50k 15. 40k 3-5k Road or XC Race 16. 40k 17. 40k 18. 50k 19. 40k 20. 40k 5-8k Road or XC Race	21. 50k 22. 50k 23. 50k 24. 50k 25. 50k 26. 50k 27. 50k 28. 50k 29. 40k 5-8kRoad or XC Race 30. 50k	31. 40k 32. 40k A 5k Race	33. 40k 34. 40k A 5k Race	35. 35k 36. 25k The Race	During these weeks the athlete could run 2-3 more races. The athlete should then take 2 weeks rest, then begin preparing for 1999 by running 38-42k per week.

and to each week of each phase.

Finally, the athlete must attempt to identify a race schedule to assist in the preparation for the goal race.

When all these things have been done the athlete has a complete annual plan in terms of volume and a race schedule (Fig. 21-3).

Step 6. The Long Run

Ideally the long run will be 20-30% of the weekly volume. Therefore it will be:
- 6-10k in a 30k week
- 8-13k in a 40k week, and
- 10-16k in a 50k week.

Step 7. Planning the Weekly Training Program

This is something that will be individual to each athlete but a sample week from each major period of a *Run With The Best* year is outlined in Fig. 21-4.

FIGURE 21-4: A SAMPLE WEEK FROM EACH PERIOD.

Day	Base Period: A 50k Week	Pre-Competition Period: A 40k Week	Competition Period: A 30k Week
Monday	5k including 10 x 100m @ 400m Pace	3k including 2 x 400m of 50m sprint/50m jog	3k including 6-8 x 100m relaxed accelerations
Tuesday	10k @ 80-85% MHR	11k including 2 x 3k @ 10k pace. Use an uphill road of 1-2 degrees if possible. Jog-back recovery	5k or 20 min surge session
Wednesday	5k @ 65-80% MHR	Rest	Rest
Thursday	5k @ 85-90% MHR	6k including 10 x 200m @ 800m pace with a 200m recovery jog	5k including 4-6 x 200m @ 800m pace
Friday	Rest	Rest	Rest
Saturday	10k including a hilly XC race or 6k TT over a hilly course	8k including a 3k or 5k race or a 5k or 20 min surge session	3k, 5k or 10k race
Sunday	15k @ 65-80% MHR	12k @ 65-80% MHR	6-9k @ 60-75% MHR

CHAPTER 22
REHABILITATION EXERCISING
THE PRICE OF SUB-OPTIMAL TRAINING

Injuries are a frustrating part of an athlete's career. Hopefully the athletes reading this book will take notice of the number of times recovery and regeneration are emphasized and be astute enough to know when to reduce volume and/or intensity before minor irritations become major problems.

To deal satisfactorily with rehabilitation the athlete must remain positive and be aware of the following things.

The body must be given a chance to focus on repairing the injury. Just as the body goes into digestion mode once a person has eaten, so must it go into repair mode when an athlete is injured. When injury occurs, we must stress that the athlete should not immediately seek to continue training using methods other than running. An injured animal retreats to a safe, comfortable haven to let nature run its course.

The athlete should therefore relax (worrying is pointless!), seek out the best treatment, and view the period as one of regeneration. In the same way that exercising vigorously after eating will distract the body from the digestive process, so too will training-focused exercise (as distinct from relaxation-focused exercise) distract the body from regeneration. It is acknowledged that interrupting the digestive routine will cause poor digestion but never mentioned that interrupting the rehabilitation routine may cause poor healing.

The daily routine must be maintained. Do not lie in bed any longer than normal or go to bed significantly later than your normal routine. When training was scheduled, go for a walk, swim in a pool, or ride a bike. Alternatively, view the scheduled visit to the sports medicine clinic as a replacement activity.

The exercise routine should begin once it is possible to walk energetically without any sensation of pain.

At this point the athlete can start to focus again on continuing to accumulate training hours. Walking is not equal to running as a cardiovascular conditioner but it is infinitely superior to doing nothing at all because it does begin the process of conditioning the ligaments, tendons, muscles and bones preparatory to running. Begin by walking on flat ground then gradually increase the effort by moving to undulating and then hilly courses. On the steep hills stride out vigorously to increase the workout intensity and to stretch out the muscles that have shortened. If no pain exists, walk on steep hills to shorten the stride so the body weight forces the heel down and causes the achilles tendon to be fully extended. The cardiovascular and circulatory intensity can be increased further by wearing a weighted vest or backpack.

The next stage begins when the athlete can "sloth jog"* for one minute. The target now is to alternate a one-minute jog with a four-minute walk for an hour, i.e., to jog 12 minutes in one hour. Once he achieves this level, the athlete aims to eventually reverse the ratio until he or she can jog for four minutes and walk for one minute, i.e., jog for 48 minutes in the hour. Remember, the walk should be vigorous and the stride as long as possible while the jog should be relaxed and the stride very short.

Once the athlete can run for 48 minutes out of the 60 minutes, it is time to replace the walking with faster running. The athlete should now jog 8-10 minute per km (13-16 minutes per mile) around a loop that takes about three to four minutes to complete. On arriving back at the starting point after the jog, he or she runs 2 x 100m with 30 seconds recovery. Start very conservatively, say 27-30 seconds per 100m (or 45-50-minute 10k pace) on the first day. Repeat this routine for 60 to 90 minutes. If no pain is experienced after this workout, run for 45 to 60 minutes at a slightly increased pace, say 6-7 minutes per km (9-12 minutes per mile), and attempt 10 x 100m in 24-27 seconds (40-45-minute 10k pace).

The athlete is advised to continue this routine until he or she can run an hour to an hour and a half at his normal long run endurance pace and do his 100m run-throughs at their normal 800m pace. For example, 4:30 per km (7:00 per mile) if she usually runs about 26-27km (17 miles) during the normal 2-hour long run and 15-16 seconds for the 100m run-throughs if she is capable of 2:06 to 2:12 for 800m

---

*A "sloth jog" can be described as taking 2 strides per meter or 3 strides per 2 meters at the most.

Steve Scott jogs with Jason Pyrah on the Azusa Pacific track.

when fully fit.

At this point the athlete would be ready to resume normal training, initially at a lower speeds for the higher intensity workouts, but at normal speeds for all training up to 92% MHR. One way to raise intensity while keeping the speed low is to find a very hilly circuit. Anything from 400m to 5k is ideal. Run slowly for 20 minutes or more around the course. It will recondition the body and provide a good stimulus for the cardiovascular system.

Summary

When injury strikes don't get mad at your body for "letting you down." Remember, intelligence is a function of the brain. You have to develop the capacity to avoid injury. Once you have an injury, however, try to relax and enjoy yourself. Those "sloth" jogs are really quite pleasant if you just focus on time and face the fact that regardless of whether you run fast or slow an hour is still 60 minutes of running.

CHAPTER 23
THE *RUN WITH THE BEST* AMERICAN PROGRAM
A DUAL PEAK SEASON

The American high school (ages 13-18) and college (ages 19-24) sports systems have a nine-month competition year that begins in September and runs through to the end of May or early June. It contains two very separate championships—one for cross country and another for track and field. It may even contain three championship seasons, if indoor track is part of the program.

The reason for defining the competition year as nine months is because the rules governing both systems forbid coaches from having contact with their athletes during the summer vacation months of June, July and August.

The regular cross country season begins September - October with league or conference championships starting the first week of November. These are followed by regional or state championships with the national championships scheduled on the last week of November or the first week of December.

Track then follows with an indoor season scheduled from January to March (though schools in the mid-west and north east parts of America focus on this more than schools in the south or west) and an outdoor season running from April through to the middle or end of June. Most league or conference championships start on the first week of May and these are followed by district, regional, state and national championships.

Cross country races are normally run over 8k-

FIGURE 23-1: ANNUAL TRAINING PLAN FOR 14-19-YEAR OLD AMERICAN HIGH SCHOOL ATHLETES (VOLUMES FOR EACH PHASE).

Ref:bookch5.doc Developed by Irv Ray and Tony Benson

	BASE PERIOD 24-30 weeks							PRE-COMPETITION 8-10 wks		COMPETITION 8-10 wks	
	PHASE I 8-10 wks		PHASE II 8-10 wks		PHASE III 8-10 wks		PHASE I 4-5 wks	PHASE II 4-5 wks	PHASE I 4-5 wks	PHASE II 4-5 wks
June Transition	July 4 Weeks	August 5 Weeks	September 4 Weeks	October 4 Weeks	November 4 Weeks	December 5 Weeks	January 4 Weeks	February 4 Weeks	March 5 Weeks	April 4 Weeks	May 5 Weeks
20-45 mi per week	250 mi Average 50 mi/wk	300 mi Average 60 mi/wk	240 mi Average 60 mi/wk	220 mi Average 55 mi/wk	200 mi Average 50 mi/wk	275 mi Average 55 mi/wk	240 mi Average 60 mi/wk	200 mi Average 50 mi/wk	200 mi Average 50 mi/wk	160 mi Average 40 mi/wk	150 mi Average 30 mi/wk
0-35 mi per week	160 mi Average 40 mi/wk	250 mi Average 50 mi/wk	200 mi Average 50 mi/wk	150 mi Average 45 mi/wk	160 mi Average 40 mi/wk	225 mi Average 45 mi/wk	200 mi Average 50 mi/wk	160 mi Average 40 mi/wk	200 mi Average 40 mi/wk	120 mi Average 30 mi/wk	100 mi Average 20 mi/wk
0-25 mi per week	120 mi Average 30 mi/wk	200 mi Average 40 mi/wk	60 mi Average 40 mi/wk	140 mi Average 35 mi/wk	120 mi Average 30 mi/wk	175 mi Average 35 mi/wk	160 mi Average 40 mi/wk	120 mi Average 30 mi/wk	150 mi Average 30 mi/wk	80 mi Average 20 mi/wk	100 mi Average 20 mi/wk

FIGURE 23-2: ANNUAL PLAN FOR 14-19-YEAR-OLD AMERICAN HIGH SCHOOL ATHLETES (TYPES OF TRAINING).

June	July	August	September	October	November	December	January	February	March	April	May
Transition	4 Weeks	5 Weeks	4 Weeks	4 Weeks	4 Weeks	5 Weeks	4 Weeks	4 Weeks	5 Weeks	4 Weeks	5 Weeks

[Cross Country Period] [Indoor Track] { Outdoor Track }

| Recovery Running —— |
| Aerobic Conditioning Running ———————————— |
| Lactate Threshold ——————————————————— |
| Aerobic Economy Running ——————— |
| MVO_2 ————————————— |
| Lactic Acid Tolerance ———————— |
| Lactate Production Running ——— |
| Speed & Power Running ——————————————— |
| Intensive & Extensive Hill ——————— |
| X-C Races - |
| Goal Pace Running ————— |
| ———— Base Training ———— | --Pre-Competition-- | -Competition ↑
                                                                              | Race Rhythm ↑
                                                                              | Race Simulation ↑
                                                                              | Race Tactical ↑
                                                                              | Race Maintaince ↑
| Strength, Flexibility & Recovery ————————————————————————————————————— ↑
| Nutrition & Hydration ——— ↑

102

FIGURE 23-3: ANNUALIZED TRAINING PLAN FOR 19-24-YEAR-OLD AMERICAN COLLEGIATE ATHLETES

Ref:bookch5.doc   Developed by Irv Ray and Tony Benson

	BASE PERIOD 24-30 weeks							PRE-COMPETITION 8-10 wks		COMPETITION 8-10 wks	
	PHASE I 8-10 wks		PHASE II 8-10 wks		PHASE III 8-10 wks		PHASE I 4-5 wks	PHASE II 4-5 wks	PHASE I 4-5 wks	PHASE II 4-5 wks
June Transition	July 4 Weeks	August 5 Weeks	September 4 Weeks	October 4 Weeks	November 4 Weeks	December 5 Weeks	January 4 Weeks	February 4 Weeks	March 5 Weeks	April 4 Weeks	May 5 Weeks
JUNIOR-SENIOR (1500m-5000m) Annual Total 3,600 miles. Av = 75mi/wk												
30-55 mi per week	300 mi Average 75mi/wk	400 mi Average 80mi/wk	340 mi Average 85mi/wk	300 mi Average 75mi/wk	260 mi Average 65mi/wk	425 mi Average 85mi/wk	360 mi Average 90mi/wk	300 mi Average 75mi/wk	300 mi Average 75mi/wk	260 mi Average 65mi/wk	275 mi Average 55mi/wk
SOPHOMORE-JUNIOR (1500m-5000m). Annual Total 3200 miles. Av = 65mi/wk												
30-55 mi per week	260 mi Average 65mi/wk	375 mi Average 75mi/wk	300 mi Average 75mi/wk	260 mi Average 65mi/wk	240 mi Average 60mi/wk	375 mi Average 75mi/wk	340 mi Average 85mi/wk	300 mi Average 75mi/wk	325 mi Average 65mi/wk	220 mi Average 55mi/wk	225 mi Average 45mi/wk
FRESHMAN-SOPHOMORE (1500m-5000m) Annual Total 2800 miles. Av = 55mi/wk												
20-50 mi per week	220 mi Average 55mi/wk	325 mi Average 65mi/wk	260 mi Average 65mi/wk	260 mi Average 65mi/wk	220 mi Average 55mi/wk	325 mi Average 65mi/wk	130 mi Average 75mi/wk	260 mi Average 65mi/wk	275 mi Average 55mi/wk	180 mi Average 45mi/wk	175 mi Average 35mi/wk

10k for the college men (5k for women), while the high school athletes usually race over 3 miles or 5km. The track program at the college level encompasses all the Olympic distances including the 3000m steeplechase, 5000m and 10,000m. High school track races are limited to the 800m, the 1500m (or 1600m) and the 3000m (or 3200m) for both boys and girls.

The challenge facing the American coach is to prepare his or her athletes for two or three peaks over a 8-9 month competitive season—a challenge made more difficult by the rule that forbids contact during what should be the base training months of July and August and the number of times the athlete will be expected to compete.

At high school level for example it is not uncommon for athletes in Sun Belt states of age 13-18 to compete 10-16 times in cross country during the 12-week season and 10-16 times during the track season. So 20-30 competitions per year are possible, adding up to 80 to 120 competitions over four years in high school!

The American college system is similar. Athletes will compete in 6-10 major cross country competitions, a further 6-10 times during indoor track season, and an additional 10-16 times in major outdoor track meets. This totals 22 to 36 major races per year, 88 to 144 competitions in four years of college and a grand total of 160 to 250 competitions over eight years of schooling.

This high number of competitions (and the even higher number of actual races when doubling and tripling are factored in), when combined with a heavy reliance on anaerobic training methods may be one of the major reasons why only a small percentage of American athletes ever make it to national or international level.

CHAPTER 24
SAMPLE TRAINING PROGRAMS

International-Class Athletes

Steve Scott. 38 years of age.
Target: sub-3:39/1500m, sub-3:55/mile and 7:51/3000m
Date of Peaking: Mid-June to August
Coach: Irv Ray

Steve is the current American record holder in the mile. His training during this period was intrinsically different from when he was running 3:31-3:32 for 1500m and 3:47-3:49 for the mile. The reason for this was that Steve recognized he was a chronic "overtrainer." In order to solve this problem he approached Irv Ray for guidance and direction. Irv explained to Steve that he was continually destroying his endurance capacity by training too hard in the Pre-Competition Track Period in the mistaken belief that the harder he trained the closer he would be able to stay to his previous best performances.

Using the *Run With The Best* philosophy, Irv directed Steve to focus on aerobic endurance and 400m speed and to significantly reduce the more intense forms of anaerobic training.

The results were noteworthy. In December of 1993 Steve finished 10th at the U.S. National Cross Country Championships—his best finish ever in this event. Things were progressing extremely well and all the performance indicators pointed towards a 1500m time around 3:34 and a mile of approximately 3:53.

In May of 1994 Steve was diagnosed as having testicular cancer. He underwent major surgery and cancer treatment which ended his 1993-94 program. Fortunately he made a full recovery and is once again training towards becoming a sub-four-minute miler at age 42.

Base Period 1993-94. Phase I. (10 Weeks)

Mon: (am)
    (pm) 45-75 min incl. 7.5 miles/12km @ 85% MHR
Tues: (am)
    (pm) 10 miles/16km @ 70-75% MHR
Wed: (am)
    (pm) 10 miles/16km @ 70-75% MHR over hilly trails
Thur: (am)
    (pm) 10 miles/16km @ 60-65% MHR
Fri: (am) 5 miles/8km @ 60-65% MHR
    (pm) Drills, 8-10 x 100m accelerations to 400m pace, i.e., 11.8-12.2
Sat: (am) 15-17 miles/24-27km @ 70-75% MHR between 5,000 and 7,500 feet.
    (pm)
Sun: (am) 7-10 miles/11-16km @ 50-65% MHR
Weekly Volume: 8-9 hrs of running including warm-up and cool-down, or 80-85 miles/130-140km.

Base Period 1993-94. Phase II. (10 Weeks)

Mon: (am) 5 miles/8km @ 60-65% MHR (usually 6:10-6:30 per mile)
    (pm) 10 miles/16km @ 80-85% MHR
Tues: (am) 5 miles/8km @ 60-65% MHR
    (pm) 6-9 miles/10-15km @ 70-75% MHR, followed by 50m sprint drills, accelerations, etc.
Wed: (am) 5 miles/8km @ 60-65% MHR
    (pm) 10 miles/16km incl. 6-9 x 3 min @ 90-93% MHR with 2 min recovery to 60-65% MHR
Thur: (am) 5 miles/8km @ 60-65% MHR
    (pm) 6-9 miles/10-15km @ 70-75% MHR
Fri: (am) 5 miles/8km @ 60-65% MHR
    (pm) Drills, 8-10 x 100m accelerations to 400m pace or 3200m of 50m sprint/50m float
Sat: (am) 17-19 miles/27-30km @ 70-75% MHR between 5,000 and 7,500 feet
    (pm)
Sun: (am) 6-9 miles/10-15km @ 70-75% MHR
Weekly Volume: 9-10 hrs of running including warm-up and cool-down, or 85-90 miles/135-150km.

Base Period 1993-94. Phase IIIa. (8 Weeks)

Mileage Phase.

Mon: (am) 5 miles/8km @ 60-65% MHR
    (pm) 10 miles/16km @ 80-85% MHR (now 49-50 min)
Tues: (am) 5 miles/8km @ 60-65% MHR
    (pm) 10 miles/16km @ 70-75% MHR, followed by 50m sprint drills, accelerations, etc.

Wed: (am) 5 miles/8km @ 60-65% MHR
(pm) 10 miles/16km incl. either 30-45 min of fartlek or 5 x 1 mile with 400m jog recovery
Thur: (am) 5 miles/8km @ 60-65% MHR
(pm) 10 miles/16km @ 70-75% MHR
Fri: (am) 5 miles/8km @ 60-65% MHR
(pm) Drills, 10 x 100m + 5 x 200m @ 48-second 400m pace
Sat: (am) 17-19 miles/27-30km @ 70-75% MHR in mountains. Last 20 min @ 80% MHR
(pm)
Sun: (am) 7-9 miles/11-15km @ 50-65% MHR
Weekly Volume: 9-11 hrs of running incl. warm-up, strides & cool-down. 90-105 miles/145-170km.

Base Period 1993-94. Phase IIIb. (4 Weeks)

Hill Phase.

Mon: (am) 3-5 miles/5-8km @ 60-65% MHR
(pm) 10-12 miles/15-18km incl. 6-9 x 3 min hill surges with 2 min jog recovery.
Tues: (am) 3-5 miles/5-8km @ 60-65% MHR
(pm) 9 miles/15km @ 60-65% MHR.
Wed: (am) 3-5 miles/5-8km @ 60-65% MHR
(pm) 12 miles/18km incl. 16-20 x 300m steep (20%) hill bounding.
Thur: (am) 3-5 miles/5-8km @ 60-65% MHR
(pm) 9 miles/15km @ 60-65% MHR
Fri: (am) 3-5 miles/5-8km @ 60-65% MHR
(pm) Drills, 10 x 100m + 5 x 200m @ 48-second 400m pace
Sat: (am) 15-17 miles/24-27km @ 70-75% MHR in mountains.
(pm)
Sun: (am) 7-9 miles/11-15km @ 50-65% MHR
Weekly Volume: 9-10 hrs of running incl. warm-up, strides & cool-down. 80-90 miles/130-145km.

Pre-Competition Period 1993-94. Phase I. (4 Weeks)

Mon: (am) 3-5 miles/5-8km @ 60-65% MHR
(pm) 45-60 min incl. 6-7.5 miles/10-12km @ 75-80% MHR
Tues: (am) 3-5 miles/5-8km @ 60-65% MHR
(pm) 20 x 200m @ mile goal pace (28.5-29.0) with 200m jog recovery in 75-90 sec
Wed: (am) 3-5 miles/5-8km @ 60-65% MHR
(pm) 6 miles/10km @ 65% MHR
Thur: (am) 3-5 miles/5-8km @ 60-65% MHR
(pm) 6-8 x 200-300m hill repeats @ 1500m rhythm or 800m TT + 100m fast
Fri: (am) 3-5 miles/5-8km @ 60-65% MHR
(pm) 3-5 miles/5-8km @ 60-65% MHR
Sat: (am) 8-10 x 400m @ 58.7 with 100m jog in 60.0, OR

(pm) Invitational Race. 800m or 1500m + 3 x 800m @ 3200m goal pace
Sun: (am) 11-13 miles/17-21km @ 60-70% MHR
Weekly Volume: 8-9 hrs of running incl. warm-up, strides & cool-down. 75-85 miles/120-135km

Pre-Competition Period 1993-94. Phase II. (4 Weeks)

Mon: (am) 3-5 miles/5-8km @ 60-65% MHR
(pm) 6 miles/10km @ 65-75% MHR and 50m drills + 4-6 x 50-100m accelerations
Tues: (am) 3-5 miles/5-8km @ 60-65% MHR
(pm) 800m - 1 mile of sprint 50m/float 50m
Wed: (am) 3-5 miles/5-8km @ 60-65% MHR
(pm) 6 miles/10km @ 65% MHR
Thur: (am) 3-5 miles/5-8km @ 60-65% MHR
(pm) 3-4 x 200m @ 800m race rhythm pace (26-27 sec) with 200m recovery jog in 2 min
Fri: (am) 4-6 miles/7-10km @ 60-65% MHR
(pm)
Sat: (am) 2 x 3 x 400m + 1 x 300m @ 58-59/400m with 45.0 between reps & 10 min between sets
(pm)
Sun: (am) 11-13 miles/17-21km @ 60-70% MHR
Weekly Volume: 7-8 hrs of running incl. warm-up, strides & cool-down. 65-75 miles/105-120km.

Competition Period 1993-94. Phase I. Buildup to the USA National Championships. (4 Weeks)

Mon: (am)
(pm) 6-8 miles/10-13km @ 65-75% MHR and 50m drills + 4-6 x 50-100m accelerations
Tues: (am)
(pm) 4 x 400m @ 1 mile race rhythm (59-58-57-56) with 2-3 min recovery
Wed: (am)
(pm) 4-6 miles/7-10km @ 60-65% MHR. Normally sub-6 min mile pace.
Thur: (am)
(pm) 5 x 200m @ 800m race rhythm pace (26-27 sec) with 200m recovery jog in 2 min
Fri: (am) 4-6 miles/7-10km @ 65-75% MHR and 50m drills + 4-6 x 50-100m accelerations
(pm)
Sat: (am)
(pm) 1500m or 1 mile race, practicing fast finish, OR 3k @ 87-92%
Sun: (am) 10-12 miles/16-18km @ 60-70% MHR
Weekly Volume: 6-7 hrs of running incl. warm-up, strides & cool-down. 55-65 miles/90-110km.

Competition Period 1993-94. Phase II. (4-6 Weeks Post-Nationals. Often run in Europe)

Mon: (am)
    (pm) 4-6 miles/7-10km @ 50-65% MHR
Tues: (am)
    (pm) 2-4 miles/4-7km incl. 2 x 100m, 1 x 200m, 2 x 100m accelerations
    Recovery, as needed
Wed: (am)
    (pm) Race
Thur: (am)
    (pm) 4 miles/7km @ 50-65% MHR + travel
Fri: (am)
    (pm) 2-4 miles/4-7km + 50-100m accelerations
Sat: (am)
    (pm) Race
Sun: (am) 6-10 miles/10-16km @ 50-65% MHR

Weekly Volume: 3-5 hrs of running incl. warm-up, strides & cool-down. 30-40 miles/60-75km.

Sharon Stewart. 22 years old.

Target: 1988 National 800m. Olympic Qualifying time below 2:01.5
Date of Peaking: Early March.
Coach: Tony Benson

In 1983 Sharon was an 18-year-old 100m runner with a PR of 12.5 at high school. She began training in 1984 and went on to represent Australia at the 1986 and 1990 Commonwealth Games, the 1991 World Championships and the 1992 Olympic Games. She won three Commonwealth Games medals, three Australian 400m titles and two 800m titles and retired at 27 with PR's of 12.00 (1985), 23.36 (1986), 51.32 (1992) and 2:00.17 (9191) for events from 100m to 800m.

Data:
Career Volume   18,040km (11,202 miles)
Annual Volumes   1984 1034km   1985 1357km   1986 1723km
                           1987 2208km   1988 2475km   1989 2584km
                           1990 2536km   1991 2247km   1992 1876km
Average Volume   2004km (1244 miles)

The following points are worth noting about Sharon's career because despite her considerable successes, for which she can be very proud, Sharon is also a classic example of an athlete who maximized her potential in the event she preferred but underachieved in the event for which she was best suited physically. In Sharon's case the 400m was her Olympic event, but the 800m should have been her Olympic medal event. The conversion tables in Chapter 10 illustrate these things clearly.

1. Sharon's natural strength and the endurance gained from three years focusing on 400m allowed her to convert her 100m time to a 200m time as well as any male athlete.
2. Her 200m to 400m conversion was also very good in 1991-92 because her best 200m time off blocks during the season was only 23.7, yet she ran 51.32. This excellent conversion of 2.17 was due to the 800m training done in 1991, the year she ran 2:00.17.
3. Her conversion from 400m to 800m did not reach its potential, however. Prior to her 2:00.17, she had run 52.3 for 400m. This represents only 2.30 on the conversion table. Had she been able to achieve even an average conversion figure of 2.24 she would have run 1:57.1! A strong conversion figure of 2.21 would have given her a 1:55.6.

Sharon Stewart (No. 0085) won a bronze medal in the 1990 Commonwealth Games 800m.

4. Sharon would never have broken 49.0 for 400m to enable her to join the truly elite at this event because she did not have the necessary speed to run below 11.5 for 100m.
5. She never accumulated the 20,000km or 12,000 miles necessary for elite 800m running, but by 1992 her kilometers were well in excess of 400m requirements.
6. She never ran the 3000km or 2,000 miles necessary for elite 800m running in a year but every year from 1987 onwards exceeded the annual 400m requirements.

Sharon had plenty of speed to run 800 meters. After all, women have run 1:58-1:59 off 55-56 seconds for 400m. What she lacked was stamina.

Had she decided to make the 800m her sole priority after winning the 1988 national title in March, we would have maintained our focus on 400m speed and increased her mileage by 10k (6 miles) a week during 1988-89, 1989-90, and 1990-91. During 1991-92 the mileage would have been stabilized and the intensity increased by 1-2%. This would have ensured a time of 1:57-1:59 by the time of the 1992 Olympics. Her best Olympics would have been 1996, where, at 31 years of age, she would have been at the peak of her career.

Sharon's 1987 program is outlined below. This was the first year she focused on the 800m.

Base Period 1987-88. Phase I. (6 Weeks)

Mon: (am)
    (pm) 6-8km (4-5 miles) incl. 10 x 100m accelerations to 400m pace
Tues: (am)
    (pm) 10km (6 miles) @ 60-70% MHR
Wed: (am)
    (pm) 10km (6 miles) @ 60-70% MHR
Thur: (am)
    (pm) 10km (6 miles) @ 60-70% MHR
Fri: (am)
    (pm)
Sat: (am) 10km (6 miles) @ 60-70% MHR.
    (pm)
Sun: (am) 12km (7 miles) @ 60-70% MHR
Weekly Volume: 5 hrs of running including warm-up and cool-down, or 37 miles/60km.

Base Period 1987-88. Phase II. (8 Weeks)

Mon: (am)
    (pm) 6-8km (4-5 miles) incl. 10 x 100m @ 400m pace
Tues: (am)
    (pm) 10km (6 miles) incl. 20 min @ 10k pace or 80-85% MHR
Wed: (am)
    (pm) 12km (7 miles) @ 60-70% MHR
Thur: (am)
    (pm) 10km (6 miles) incl. 20 min @ 10k pace or 80-85% MHR
Fri: (am)
    (pm)
Sat: (am) 10km (6 miles) incl. 6k @ 80-90% MHR over a tough undulating course.
    (pm)
Sun: (am) 15km (9 miles) @ 60-70% MHR
Weekly Volume: 5-6 hrs of running including warm-up and cool-down, or 40 miles/65km.

Base Period 1987-88. Phase III. (10 Weeks)

Mon: (am)
    (pm) 6-10km (4-5 miles) incl. 4-6 x 150m @ 400m pace
Tues: (am) 5km (3 miles) @ 50-65%
    (pm) 10km (6 miles) incl 20 min @ 10k pace or 80-85% MHR
Wed: (am)
    (pm) 10-12km (6-7 miles) @ 60-70% MHR
Thur: (am) 5km (3 miles) @ 50-65%
    (pm) 10km (6 miles) incl. 20 min of 2 min fast, 1-2 min easy @ 87-92% MHR
Fri: (am)
    (pm)
Sat: (am) 10km (6 miles) incl. 6k surging up the hills on the undulating course.
    (pm)
Sun: (am) 15km (9 miles) @ 60-70% MHR
Weekly Volume: 5-6 hrs of running including warm-up and cool-down, or 45 miles/70km.

Pre-Competition Period 1987-88. Phase I. (5 Weeks)

Mon: (am)
    (pm) 5km (3 miles) incl. 500m - 400m - 300m OR 300m - 200m - 2 x 150m Recovery, as needed
Tues: (am)
    (pm) 8km (5 miles) incl. 20 min of 2 min fast, 1-2 min easy @ 87-92% MHR
Wed: (am)
    (pm) 10km (6 miles) @ 60-70% MHR
Thur: (am)
    (pm) 8km (5 miles) incl. 10 x 200m @ 1500m pace (33-34 sec) with 200m jog in 1:30
Fri: (am)
    (pm)
Sat: (am) 8km (6 miles) incl. 6k surging up the hills on the undulating course.
    (pm)
Sun: (am) 12km (6 miles) @ 60-70% MHR
Weekly Volume: 4-5 hrs of running including warm-up and cool-down, or 30 miles/50km.

Pre-Competition Period 1987-88. Phase II. (4 Weeks)

Mon: (am)
    (pm) 5km (3 miles) incl. 2 sets of 30m - 50m - 40m flying start sprints.
Tues: (am)
    (pm) 8km (5 miles) incl. 10 x 200m @ 800m pace (29-30 sec) with 200m jog in 1:30
Wed: (am)
    (pm) 8km (5 miles) @ 60-70% MHR
Thur: (am)
    (pm) 8km (5 miles) incl. 600m - 400m - 2 x 200m @ 800m pace (i.e., 60.0/400m pace) with as short a recovery as possible
Fri: (am)
    (pm)
Sat: (am) 8km (6 miles) incl. 10 x 130m steep hill (15 degrees) with jog/walk-back recovery
    (pm)
Sun: (am) 12km (7.5 miles) @ 60-70% MHR

Weekly Volume: 4-5 hrs of running including warm-up and cool-down, or 30 miles/50km.

Competition Period 1987-88. Phase I. (4 Weeks)

Mon: (am)
    (pm) 5km (3 miles) incl. 6 x 60m flying start accelerations.
Tues: (am)
    (pm) 6km (4 miles) incl. 600m - 400m - 2 x 200m @ 800m pace (i.e., 60.0/400m pace)
Wed: (am)
    (pm) 10km (6 miles) @ 60-70% MHR
Thur: (am)
    (pm) 6km (4 miles) incl. 3-4 x 300m OR 4-6 x 200m @ 400m pace
Fri: (am)
    (pm)
Sat: (am) 6km (4 miles) incl. 6 x 130m steep hill (15 degrees) with jog/walk-back recovery
    (pm) 200m, 400m or 800m Race. Normally a club event of no importance. Or time trial.
Sun: (am) 10km (6 miles) @ 60-70% MHR

Weekly Volume: 4-5 hrs of running including warm-up and cool-down, or 27 miles/45km.

Competition Period 1987-88. Phase II. Week Leading to Sharon's First National 800m Title.

Mon: (am)
    (pm) Rest
Tues: (am)
    (pm) 5-6km (3 miles) incl. 4 x 200m @ 400m pace with 600m walk recovery
Wed: (am)
    (pm) 4-5km (2-3 miles) easy jog
Thur: (am)
    (pm) Rest (travel)
Fri: (am)
    (pm) 3-5km (2-3 miles) + stretching and accelerations
Sat: (am)
    (pm) National 800m (Heats)
Sun: (am)
    (pm) National 800m Final. 1st 2:01.4. Very windy.

Despite qualifying for the Seoul Olympics the Australian selectors of the time did not include her on the team!

Weekly Volume: 3-4 hrs of running incl. warm-up, strides & cool-down. 20-30 miles/30-45km

Note: The year was abbreviated because Sharon hurt her knee skiing during the early Base Period.

Developmental Junior-Level Or College Athletes (non-specific to age but most commonly 19-24 years old; 400-800-1500m, with emphasis on 800m)

Michele Bucciohio. 39 years of age. Arcadia, CA. Asics Track Club.

Coach: Irv Ray

Previous Season's Bests: 400m—59.5, 800m—2:15, 1500m—4:32, 3000m—9:48, 5000m—17:18.

She ran: 400m—57.5, 800m—2:09, 1500m—4:19, 3000m—9:18, 5000m—16:27. Note: the 3000m time of 9:18 was an age-group world record.

Michele's times mirror the performances of a developing athlete. Her training would be appropriate for a developing female athlete of 19 to 24 years of age and gives an example of what a dedicated senior athlete can do.

Base Period 1995-96. Phase I. (10 Weeks)

Mon: (am)
    (pm) 40-45 min incl. 35 min @ 85% MHR
Tues: (am)
    (pm) 30-40 min @ 60-75% MHR + form drills and 4-6 x 50m accelerations
Wed: (am)
    (pm) 30-45 min incl. 4-6 x 3 min hill surges with 2 min recovery
Thur: (am)
    (pm) 30-40 min @ 50-65% MHR
Fri: (am)
    (pm) Drills, 4-8 x 100m accelerations
Sat: (am) Long run: 1-1:15 hr on a hilly course
Sun: (am) 30-40 min @ 50-65% MHR

Weekly Volume: 6-7 hrs of running including warm-up and cool-down, or 40-50 miles/75-80km.

Base Period 1995-96. Phase II. (10 Weeks)

Mon: (am)
 (pm) 7.5 miles (12km) @ 85% MHR + 50m drills & 4-6 x 50m acceleration
Tues: (am)
 (pm) 30-40 min @ 50-65% MHR
Wed: (am)
 (pm) 5 x 800m @ 10k pace or 87-92% MHR with 200m jog.
Thur: (am)
 (pm) 30-40 min @ 50-65% MHR
Fri: (am)
 (pm) Drills, 6-8 x 100m accelerations working towards 14.5 per 100m or goal 400m pace
Sat: (am) Rest OR Run 11-13 miles (17-21km) @ 65-75%
 (pm) Cross Country Race OR Rest (if the long run was done)
 (2-3 races would be needed as a lead-up to the National Senior XC.)
Sun: (am) 6 miles (10km) @ 50-65% MHR
Weekly Volume: 6-8 hrs of running including warm-up and cool-down, or 50-55 miles/80-90km.

Base Period 1995-96. Phase III. (10 Weeks)

Mon: (am)
 (pm) 7.5 miles (12km) @ 85% MHR OR 6-8 x 3 min @ 85-90% MHR with 2 min jog recovery
Tues: (am) 30-40 min @ 50-65% MHR
 (pm) 30-40 min @ 50-65% MHR + 50m form drills & 4-6 x 50m accelerations
Wed: (am)
 (pm) 23 min fartlek (15-30-45-60-90-120-90-60-45-30-15 sec sprints with equal jog recovery
Thur: (am) 30-40 min @ 50-65%Z≠HR
 (pm) 30-40 min @ 50-65% MHR
Fri: (am)
 (pm) Drills, 8-10 x 100m accelerations in 14.5 per 100m or goal 400m pace
Sat: (am) Run 12-14 miles (18-23km) @ 65-75%
 (pm) Cross Country Race OR Rest (if the long run was done)
Sun: (am) 6 miles (10km) @ 50-65% MHR
Weekly Volume: 8-9 hrs of running including warm-up and cool-down, or 55-65 miles/90-105km.

Pre-Competition Period 1995-96. Phase I. (4 Weeks)

Mon: (am)
 (pm) 6 miles (10km) @ 65-75% + Drills, 4-6 x 50m accelerations
Tues: (am)
 (pm) 16 x 200m @ 1500m goal pace (32-34 sec) with 200m jog recovery in 60-90 sec
Wed: (am)
 (pm) 30-40 min @ 50-65% MHR
Thur: (am)
 (pm) 2 x 120m, 2 x 100m, 2 x 60m @ 400m-800m pace
Fri: (am) 30-40 min @ 50-65% MHR
 (pm)
Sat: (am)
 (pm) 6-8 x 400m @ 68-70 sec with 2:30 to 1:15 min recovery
Sun: (am) Run 9-11 miles (15-18km) @ 50-65%
Weekly Volume: 6-8 hrs of running including warm-up and cool-down, or 45-55 miles/75-90km.

Pre-Competition Period 1995-96. Phase II. (4 Weeks)

Mon: (am)
 (pm) 6 miles (10km) @ 65-75% + drills, 4-6 x 50m accelerations
Tues: (am)
 (pm) 2 x 3 x 300m @ 3km race rhythm with 100m jog in 60 sec. & 5 min between sets
Wed: (am)
 (pm) 30-40 min @ 50-65% MHR
Thur: (am)
 (pm) 4 x 400m OR 2 x 800m OR 1 x 1600m of 50m sprint/50m float
Fri: (am) 30-40 min @ 50-65% MHR
 (pm)
Sat: (am) 2 x 3 x 400m @ 1500m race rhythm (68-70 sec) with 45 sec recovery & 10 min between sets
 (pm) OR Races over 800m to 5k
Sun: (am) Run 9-11 miles (15-18km) @ 50-65%
Weekly Volume: 6-7 hrs of running including warm-up and cool-down, or 45-50 miles/70-80km.

Competition Period 1995-96. Phase I. (4 Weeks)

Mon: (am)
 (pm) 6 miles (10km) @ 65-75% + drills, 4-6 x 50m accelerations
Tues: (am)
 (pm) 3 x 400m + 1 x 200m @ 1500m race rhythm—Recovery, as needed
Wed: (am)
 (pm) 30-40 min @ 50-65% MHR
Thur: (am)
 (pm) 3 x 200m + 1 x 100m @ 800m race rhythm
Fri: (am) 30-40 min @ 50-65% MHR

Sat: (am)
    (pm) Race: 800m, 1500m or 3000m to practice tactics
Sun: (am) Run 9-11 miles (15-18km) @ 50-65%
Weekly Volume: 5-6 hrs of running including warm-up and cool-down, or 35-40 miles/65-75km.

Competition Period 1995-96. Phase II. (4 Weeks)

Mon: (am)
    (pm) 20-30 min incl. drills, 4-6 x 50- 100m accelerations to 400m pace
Tues: (am)
    (pm) 200's or 300's @ race rhythm
Wed: (am)
    (pm) 20-30 min @ 50-65% MHR
Thur: (am)
    (pm) 400m OR 600m OR 800m @ race pace
Fri: (am)
    (pm) 20-30 min incl. striding and stretching
Sat: (am)
    (pm) Race
Sun: (am) Long run: 45 min
Weekly Volume: 3-5 hrs of running incl. warm-up, strides & cool-down. 20-25 miles/30-40km.

Ricky Etheridge. 20 years old. California Baptist University.
Milton Browne. 21 years old. California Baptist University.
Coach: Irv Ray
Previous Season's Bests (1997): Etheridge 400m—49.5, 800m—1:52.2, 1500m—3:48.8. Browne 400m—48.2, 800m—1:51.0, 1500m—4:10. Ricky is a 1500/800 type, Milton an 400/800 type. Two different athletes, both benefiting from strength/speed of *Run With The Best* training strategies. The results were dramatic, excellent examples of what motivated athletes can accomplish.

Season progression (1998):
Feb. 25 (NAIA indoor nationals):
    Etheridge 1:52.8 on 4x800 relay team
    Browne 1:52.2 on 4x800 relay team (California Baptist set an NAIA national record of 7:32.95.)
April 18 (Mt. SAC):
    Etheridge, 1st, 1:50.17 (48.2 in 4x400)
    Browne, 3rd, 1:50.65 (47.5 in 4x400)
April 23 (Fullerton Open):
    Etheridge, 1st, 1:50.76
    Browne, 2nd, 1:51.41
May 2 (Irvine Invitational):
    Browne, 1st, 1:50.51 (47.4 in 4 x 400)
May 9 (Occidental Invitational):
    Etheridge, 3rd, 1:47.66
May 16 (VO₂Max Invitational at USC):

Cal Baptist's 1998 NAIA Indoor National Champions in the 4x800 and distance medley relays: Ricky Etheridge, Nate Browne, Milt Browne, Neil Smart.

    Browne, 2nd, 1:47.79
May 30 (Footmark Invitational at USC):
    Etheridge, 3rd, 1:47.51
    Browne, 6th, 1:48.91

Base Period 1998. Phase I. (10 Weeks, July-mid-September)

Mon: (pm) 20 min warm-up run, 50m form drills
    4-8 x 100m accelerations, working toward sprints
    20 min cool-down run
Tues: (pm) 30-45 min run, 4-6 miles @ 70-75% of MHR. General conditioning pace
Wed: (pm) 25-35 min run, 60-65% of MHR. Recovery run
Thur: (pm) 1-mile warm-up + 20-35 min of unstructured fartlek run @ 75-85% of MHR
    1 mile cool-down
Fri: (pm) 20-30 min recovery run
Sat: (am) Endurance run—45-75 min or 7-10 miles @ 70-75% of MHR over dirt roads, trails, rolling to hilly
Sun: Rest
Weekly Volume: 35-45 miles.

Base Period 1998. Phase II. (10 Weeks, mid-September-November)

Mon: (pm) 20 min progressive warm-up + 50m form drills
    6-10 x 100m accelerations, working toward sprints @ 400m goal pace (12.0 per 100m)
    20 min cool-down run
Tues: (pm) Lactate threshold run @ 80-85% of MHR (2-mile warm-up + 20-35 min + 2-mile cool-down)
Wed: (am) 20-30 min recovery run
    (pm) 20-30 min recovery run @ 55-65% of MHR
Thur: (pm) 2-mile warm-up
    MVO₂ or cross country specific @ 87-

93% of MHR: 15-25 min of fartlek
or hill reps
2-mile cool-down
Fri: (am) 20-30 min recovery run
(pm) 20-30 min recovery run @ 55-65% of MHR
Sat: (am) 8-10k cross country race @ 90-95% of MHR OR 10-12-mile long run @ 75% of MHR over hilly terrain.
Sun: (am) 20-35 min, as athlete feels
Weekly Volume: 45-55 miles.

Base Period 1998. Phase III. (10 Weeks, December-mid-February)

Pre-Track Base Phase.

Mon: (am) 20-30 min easy run
(pm) 20 min progressive warm-up + 50m form drills
10 x 100m sprints at 400m goal speed (11.8-12.0) with 2-3 min recovery
20 min cool-down
Tues: (pm) 2-mile warm-up
Lactate threshold run @ 80-85% of MHR
6 miles—down to 5:30 pace
2-mile cool-down
Wed: (am) 20-30 min recovery run
(pm) 20-30 min recovery run at 55-65% of MHR
Thur: (pm) 2-mile warm-up
MVO_2 specific for track. 3 rotating weeks: 1. 10-12 300m hill, bounding (high knees) in 70-75 sec w/3 min recovery
2. 20 x 200m @ mile goal pace. 30-31 sec w/ 55-65 sec 200m recovery
3. 5 x 800m @ 2-mile goal pace (9 min), 2:15 per 800m w/2 min recovery
2-mile cool-down
Fri: (am) 20-30 min recovery run
(pm) 20-30 min recovery run @ 55-65% of MHR
Sat: (am) Long run (endurance) @ 65-75% of MHR, usually 3500-6500 ft elevation. Mountain roads, trails, working up to $1^{1}/_{2}$ to 2 hr runs, 14-16 miles
Sun: (am) 45-60 min @ recovery pace, 55-65% of MHR
Weekly Volume: 45-60 miles per week.

Pre-Competition Period 1998. Phase I. (4 Weeks, mid-February-March)

Mon: (pm) 20 min progressive warm-up + 50m form drills
4-6 x 50m-100m accelerations
20 min cool-down
Tues: (pm) 800m specific, i.e., 10-12 x 200m @ 800 goal pace (27 sec) w/2 min rest
Wed: (am) 20 min recovery run
30 min recovery run
Thur: (pm) 400m or 1500m specific:
1. 4 x 400 of 50m floats with 50m sprints @ 800m pace, usually @ 56-60 sec per 400m w/ 2-3 min recovery
2. 2-3 x 800m @ 2:00-2:08 w/4-5 min recovery between (50m sprints + 50m floats, progressively faster)
Fri: (am) 20 min recovery run
(pm) 30 min recovery run
Sat: Race of 1000m + 400m leg on relay
OR 1500m + 800m
OR Race simulation: 2 x 800 continuous of 300m @ goal pace (39-40 sec), 100m in 20 sec, 200m @ goal pace of 27 sec, 100m in 20 sec, 100m sprint (13.5). Total time: 2:01-2:02. (1:51-1:52 equivalence.)
Sun: (am) Long endurance run, 60-75 min @ 65-75% of MHR over easy terrain.
Weekly Volume: 45-60 miles.

Pre-Competition Period 1998. Phase II. (4 Weeks, March-April)

Mon: (pm) 20 min progressive warm-up + form drills
4-6 x 50-100m accelerations
20 min cool-down
Tues: (pm) 800m specific: 2 x 4 x 200m @ 800m goal pace (27.0-27.5) w/30 sec recovery. 10 min between sets
Wed: (am) 20-30 min recovery
(pm) 25-35 min recovery @ 55-65% of MHR
Thur: (pm) 400m specific: 100 @ goal pace (11.8); 300m @ goal pace (35-36 sec); 200m @ goal pace (23.5-24.0). Full recovery between.
Fri: (am) 20 min recovery run
(pm) 30 min recovery run @ 55-65% of MHR
Sat: 800m Race, practicing good race strategies
OR 800m Simulation @ goal pace: 500m @ 65-66 sec (coming through 400m in 52 sec); 100m float in 20 sec; 200m kick & finish @ goal pace (27.0 sec). Total time: 1:54 (1:48 800m equivalence)
Sun: (am) Long endurance run, 60 min @ 70-75% of MHR.
Weekly Volume: 45-60 miles.

Competition Period 1998. Phase I. (5 Weeks, April 20-May 24)

Mon: (pm) 20 min progressive warm-up + form drills
6-8 x 50-100m sprints/accelerations
20 min cool-down
Tues: (pm) 400m specific: 100-300-200-300 at 400m goal pace. Full recovery
Wed: (pm) 35-45 min recovery run
Thur: (pm) 800m pace rhythm: 3 x 200m @ 26-25-24 sec + 1 x 100m (12.5). Rest, as needed
Fri: (pm) 25-35 min recovery run
Sat: Race—800m at goal pace; 1st 400 in 52-53 sec; 600 in 1:19-1:20; last 200m, kick home in 27-28 sec
Sun: (am) Long endurance run. 45-60 min easy.
Weekly Volume: 35-45 miles.

Competition Period 1998. Phase II. (5 Weeks, May 25-June 21)

Preparation for USA National Championships, New Orleans.

Mon: (pm) 15 min progressive warm-up + form drills
6-8 x 100m sprints. Fast, feel good
10-20 min cool-down, as needed
Tues: (pm) 800m race rhythm: 1. 4-6 x 200m @ goal pace (26.5-27 sec) w/ 60 sec recovery; 2. 500m @ goal pace, 300m @ goal pace, 200m fast
Wed: (pm) 25-35 min recovery run
Thur: (pm) 400m pace rhythm: 100 in 11.2-11.8, 300m @ 34.5-35.0, 200m @ easy pace (23.5-24.5)—all full recovery
Fri: (pm) 20 min recovery run
Sat: Race: 52.0, 1:19 at 600m, last 200m in 26-27 sec
OR
Simulation: 500m @ 65 sec w/400m @ 52.0; 100m stride @ 20 sec; 200m @ 27-28 sec. Total time: 1:53-54 (1:47-1:48 equivalent)
Sun: (am) 45-60 min endurance run.
Weekly Volume: 35-45 miles.

Hector Begeo. 26 years of age.

Philippine national 3000m steeplechase record holder at 8:45 in 1987. Asian Games Bronze Medalist.
Target: to perform well at the Seoul Olympics
PRs: 800m—1:57.1, 1500m—3:54.0, 5000m—14:10
Coach: Tony Benson

Hector ran 8:35 in the semifinal. Missed the final by less than 1.0.

Hector Begeo was a three-time Olympian for the Philippines and a steeplechase semifinalist in 1988 (Seoul).

Base Period 1987. Phase I. (10 Weeks)

Mon: (am)
(pm) 16km (10 miles) steadily
Tues: (am) 10km (6 miles) easily
(pm) 16km (10 miles) easily through hills
Wed: (am)
(pm) 20km (12.5 miles) steadily
Thur: (am) 10km (6 miles) easily
(pm) 16km (10 miles) easily through hills
Fri: (am)
(pm) 10km (6 miles) incl. 10 x 100m accelerations
Sat: (am) 32km (20 miles) steadily through hills
(pm)
Sun: (am) 16km (10 miles) easily
Weekly Volume: 130km/80 miles.

Base Period 1987-88. Phase II. (10 Weeks)

Mon: (am)
(pm) 16km (10 miles) steadily
Tues: (am) 10km (6 miles) easily
(pm) 16km (10 miles) easily through hills
Wed: (am) 10km (6 miles) easily
(pm) 10km (6 miles) incl. 30 x 200m rhythm runs with 100m jog
Thur: (am) 10km (6 miles) easily
(pm) 16km (10 miles) easily through hills
Fri: (am)
(pm) 16km (10 miles) steadily

Sat: (am) 32km (20 miles) easily (if racing, run 16km easily in the morning)
(pm) 8km (5 miles) @ 85-90% OR Club XC race
Sun: (am) 16km (10 miles) easily (if racing, on Sat. run 32km through hills on Sunday)
Weekly Volume: 160km/100 miles.

Base Period 1988. Phase III. (10 Weeks)

Mon: (am) 10km (6 miles) easily
(pm) 16km (10 miles) steady to hard
Tues: (am) 10km (6 miles) easily
(pm) 16km (10 miles) easily
Wed: (am) 10km (6 miles) easily
(pm) 10km (6 miles) incl. 10 laps (4km/2.5 miles) of 100m sprint, 100m float
Thur: (am) 10km (6 miles) easily
(pm) 16km (10 miles) easily
Fri: (am) 10km (6 miles) easily
(pm) 16km (10 miles) hard
Sat: (am) 32km (20 miles) easily through hills
(pm) 8km (5 miles) easily
Sun: (am) 16km (10 miles) easily
Weekly Volume: 180km/112 miles.

Pre-Competition Period 1988. Phase I. (6 Weeks)

Mon: (am) 8km (5 miles) easily
(pm) 16km (10 miles) steady to hard
Tues: (am) 8km (5 miles) easily
(pm) 16km (10 miles) easily
Wed: (am) 10km (6 miles) easily
(pm) 10 laps (4km/2.5 miles) of 100m surge, 100m float. One steeplechase barrier on the straights)
Thur: (am) 8km (5 miles) easily
(pm) 16km (10 miles) easily
Fri: (am) 8km (5 miles) easily
(pm) 16km (10 miles) hard
Sat: (am) 32km (20 miles) easily through hills
(pm)
Sun: (am) 10 x 100m accelerations to 400m pace
Weekly Volume: 140-150km/90-95 miles.

Pre-Competition Period 1988. Phase II. (4 Weeks)

Mon: (am) 8km (5 miles) easily
(pm) 6 x 100m accelerations + 1 x 8:30 min running over water jump only
Tues: (am) 8km (5 miles) easily
(pm) 16km (10 miles) hard
Wed: (am) 8km (5 miles) easily
(pm) 20km (12.5 miles) easily
Thur: (am) 8km (5 miles) easily
(pm) 6 x 800m with 4 barriers @ race pace with 200m jog recovery
Fri: (am) 8km (5 miles) easily
(pm) 16km (10 miles) easily
Sat: (am) 10km (6 miles) incl.. 30 x steep 130m hill (15 degrees)
(pm)
Sun: (am) 32km (20 miles) easily through hills
Weekly Volume: 130-145km/80-90 miles.

Competition Period 1988. Phase I. (4 Weeks)

Mon: (am) 8km (5 miles) easily
(pm) 8km (5 miles) incl. 6 x 100m accelerations
Tues: (am) 8km (5 miles) easily
(pm) 2 x 3 x 1000m @ race pace with 30 sec between reps & 3 min between sets
Wed: (am) 8km (5 miles) easily
(pm) 20km (12.5 miles) easily
Thur: (am) 8km (5 miles) easily
(pm) 16km (10 miles) hard
Fri: (am) 8km (5 miles) easily
(pm) 10km (6 miles) easily
Sat: (am) 10km (6 miles) incl. 10 x steep 130m hill (15 degrees)
(pm) 8:30 min @ race rhythm with children's hurdles on the track in place of barriers
Sun: (am) 32km (20 miles) easily through hills
Weekly Volume: 130-145km/80-90 miles.

Competition Period 1988. Phase II. (Began 5 Weeks prior to the Olympic 3000m Steeplechase)

Mon: (am)
(pm) 8km (5 miles) incl 6 x 100m accelerations
Tues: (am) 2 x 1600m with 4 barriers on the track @ race rhythm with 5 min recovery
(pm) 8km (5 miles) easily
Wed: (am) 15km (10 miles) easily
(pm) 8km (5 miles) easily
Thur: (am) 8 x 300m @ 3km pace with 200m jog recovery
(pm) 8km (5 miles) easily
Fri: (am) 10km (6 miles) easily
(pm)
Sat: (am) 25km (15 miles) easily through hills
(pm)
Sun: (am) 8km (5 miles) easily
Weekly Volume: 90-100km/55-60 miles.

American High School Or Junior Athlete (14-19 Years)

Jeff McLarty: 18 years old, Ayala HS, Chino, CA, USA
1994-95: 1600m—4:29, 3200m—9:31, 5k XC—15:54.
1995-96: 1600m—4:19, 3200m—9:01, 5k Track—15:05.

Coach: Brad Peters

Jeff's goal race was the CIF Masters 3200m where he achieved his 9:01 and earned a full scholarship to the University of Arizona. An early indication of his improvement was a 15:23/5k XC run in Phase III of the Base Period.

His lead-up races to his goal race were as follows.
- Week No 1.   9:30 (3200m)
- Week No 2.   9:23 (3200m)
- Week No 3   9:11 (3200m)
- Week No 4.   9:01 (3200m)
    1st Place in his Goal Race.
- Week No 5   9:07 (3200m)

He ran his 5000m time of 15:05 in the US Junior National Championships. This was his first 5000m track race and he finished in fifth place.

Michelle Teodoro: 18 years of age, Gig Harbor Washington and Azusa Pacific University, CA
1994-95: 400m—59.5, 800m—2:11.8, 1500m—4:45 3200m—11:23, 5000m XC—19:48.
1995-96: 400m—58.5, 800m—2:10.2, 1500m—4:32, 3200m—10:03, 5000m XC—18:43.
Coach: Irv Ray/Scott Wilson

Michelle was 14th in the USA Junior XC Nationals and 12th at the NAIA XC Nationals. She was selected All-American indoor mile and outdoor 1500m.

The training of both athletes was very similar and both showed significant improvement. (Michelle did run less volume than Jeff.)

Base Period 1995-96. Phase I. (8 Weeks)

Mon: (am)
 (pm) 40-45 min @ 85% MHR
Tues: (am)
 (pm) 30-40 min @ 50-65% MHR
Wed: (am)
 (pm) 30-40 min @ 70-75% MHR over a hilly course
Thur: (am)
 (pm) 30-40 min @ 50-65% MHR
Fri: (am)
 (pm) Drills, 4-8 x 100m accelerations
Sat: (am) Long run: 1-1:15 hr on a hilly course
 (pm)
Sun: (am) 30-40 min @ 50-65% MHR
Weekly Volume: 6-7 hrs of running including warm-up and cool-down, or 45-55 miles/75-90km.

Base Period 1995-96. Phase II. (8 Weeks)

Mon: (am)
 (pm) Drills, 8-10 x 100m accelerations to 400m pace
Tues: (am)
 (pm) 40-45 min @ 85% MHR
Wed: (am)
 (pm) 30-40 min @ 50-65% MHR
Thur: (am)
 (pm) 40-45 min incl. 16-20 x 200m on grass @ 1500m pace with 200m jog.
Fri: (am)
 (pm) 30-40 min @ 50-65% MHR
Sat: (am) 15-20 min jog
 (pm) Cross Country Race OR 4 x 1200m @ 5k pace with 400m jog recovery
Sun: (am) Long run: 1:15-1:30 hr on a hilly course
Weekly Volume: 6-8 hrs of running including warm-up and cool-down, or 50-60 miles/80-100km.

Base Period 1995-96. Phase III. (8 Weeks))

Mon: (am)
 (pm) 45-60 min @ 85% MHR
Tues: (am) 30-40 min @ 50-65% MHR
 (pm) 30-40 min @ 50-65% MHR
Wed: (am)
 (pm) 45-60 min incl. 25-35 min of fartlek @ 87-92% MHR
Thur: (am) 30-40 min @ 50-65% MHR
 (pm) 30-40 min @ 50-65% MHR
Fri: (am) 30-40 min @ 50-65% MHR
 (pm) Drill, 4-8 x 100m accelerations
Sat: (am) Long run: 1:15-1:45 hr @ 65-75% on a hilly course
 (pm)
Sun: (am) Rest OR 30-40 min @ 50-65% MHR
Weekly Volume: 8-10 hrs of running incl. warm-up, strides & cool-down. 60-75 miles/100-120km.

Pre-Competition Period 1995-96. Phase I. (4 Weeks)

Mon: (am)
 (pm) 30-45 min @ 65-75% MHR + drills, 4-6 x 50-100m accelerations to 400m pace
Tues: (am)
 (pm) 3200m - 1600m - 800m @ 5k pace with 800m jog recovery
Wed: (am)
 (pm) 30-40 min @ 50-65% MHR
Thur: (am)
 (pm) 10 x 300m @ 1500m goal pace with 100m jog recovery
Fri: (am)
 (pm) 30-40 min @ 50-65% MHR
Sat: (am) 30-45 min incl. 20 min @ 87-97% MHR on a very hilly course
 (pm) Invitational race. 800m or 1500m + 3 x

114

800m @ 3200m goal pace
Sun: (am) Long run: 1:15-1:45 hr on a hilly course
Weekly Volume: 8-9 hrs of running incl. warm-up, strides & cool-down. 55-65 miles/90-110km.

Pre-Competition Period 1995-96. Phase II. (4 Weeks))

Mon: (am)
    (pm) 30-45 min @ 65-75% MHR + drills, 4-6 x 50-100m accelerations to 400m pace
Tues: (am)
    (pm) 10 x 200m @ 800m goal pace with 200m jog in 60-75 sec
Wed: (am)
    (pm) 30-40 min @ 50-65% MHR
Thur: (am)
    (pm) 4-6 x 200m @ 800m goal pace + dual meet. Race 800m or 1500m
Fri: (am)
    (pm) 30-40 min @ 50-65% MHR
Sat: (am) 15-20 min jog
    (pm) Invitational race. 800m or 1500m + 3 x 800m @ 3200m goal pace
Sun: (am) Long run: 1:15-1:45 hr on a hilly course
Weekly Volume: 7-8 hrs of running incl. warm-up, strides & cool-down. 45-55 miles/75-90km.

Competition Period 1995-96. Phase I. (5 Weeks))

Mon: (am)
    (pm) 20-30 min incl. drills, 4-6 x 50- 100m accelerations to 400m pace
Tues: (am) 20-30 min @ 50-65%
    (pm) 8-10 x 300m @ race goal pace with 200m jog in 60-75 sec
Wed: (am) 20-30 min @ 50-65%
    (pm) 30-40 min @ 50-65% MHR
Thur: (am) Rest OR easy jog
    (pm) 4-6 x 200m @ 800-1500m goal pace
Fri: (am) Rest OR easy jog
    (pm) 20-30 min incl. striding and stretching
Sat: (am) 15-20 min jog
    (pm) THE MAJOR RACE
Sun: (am) Long run: 45-60 min
Weekly Volume: 3-5 hrs of running incl. warm-up, strides & cool-down. 30-40 miles/60-75km.

Competition Period 1995-96. Phase II. (5 Weeks)

Mon: (am)
    (pm) 20-30 min incl. drills, 4-6 x 50-100m accelerations to 400m pace
Tues: (am) 20-30 min @ 50-65%
    (pm) 8-10 x 300m @ race goal pace with 200m jog in 60-75 sec
Wed: (am)
    (pm) 30-60 min @ 50-65% MHR
Thur: (am) Rest OR easy jog
    (pm) 4-6 x 200m @ 800-1500m goal pace
Fri: (am) Rest OR easy jog
    (pm) 20-30 min incl. striding and stretching
Sat: (am) 15-20 min jog
    (pm) Race
Sun: (am) Long run: 45-90 min
    (pm)
Weekly Volume: 3-5 hrs of running incl. warm-up, strides & cool-down. 30-40 miles/60-75km.

CHAPTER 25
TRAINING GUIDELINES

1. AEROBIC RECOVERY RUNNING [End-1]

Volume: 35-40% of weekly/annual volume
Speed: Easy running, including relaxed accelerations
Methods: Easy running at "conversation" pace
Distance: 15-45 min runs. 3-7 runs of 3-8% of weekly volume
Recovery: N/A
Heart Rate: 110-120 bpm (50-65% MHR)
Improves: Heart stroke volume
Muscle capillarization
General circulation
Develops: Speed (1%)
Anaerobic (3%)
Aerobic (96%)

Comments:
1. Begins the conditioning process
2. Enhances adaptation after training
3. Contributes to running economy.

2. AEROBIC CONDITIONING RUNNING [End-2]

Volume: 30-40% of weekly/annual volume
Speed: Marathon pace and slower
Methods: Long steady running
Distance: 1-2 runs of 12-25% of weekly volume
Two (2) runs not to exceed 35% of weekly volume
Recovery: N/A
Heart Rate: 120-140 bpm (65-80% MHR)
Improves: Heart stroke volume
Muscle capillarization
General circulation
The ability to use fat as a fuel
Muscular and skeletal strength
Develops: Speed (2%)
Anaerobic (5%)
Aerobic (93%)

Comments:
1. First step in adapting the body to fatigue
2. Continues the development of general running economy.

3. LACTATE THRESHOLD RUNNING [End-3]

Volume: Type A—may range from 12-20% of weekly volume. Type B—may not exceed 10% of weekly volume. Only one session of this type per week. LT training = approx 6-8% of annual volume

Type A: Continuous Fast Running [LaT1]
Speed: Half-marathon to marathon pace
Methods: Fast continuous running
Distance: 12-20% of weekly volume
Recovery: N/A
Heart Rate: 80-85% MHR
Improves: Heart stroke volume
Muscle capillarization
Develops: Speed (2%)
Anaerobic (5%)
Aerobic (93%)

Type B: Variable Pace Running [LaT2]
Speed: Train at current 10km pace
Methods: Intervals, repetition & fartlek
Distance: 2-3km/6-10 min surges (2-4 reps)
Recovery: Sufficient to resume at 10km pace
Heart Rate: 80-85% MHR, reaching 87-90% over the last 1-2 min of each repetition
Improves: Heart stroke volume
Muscle capillarization
The action of the Fast Oxidative Glycolytic (FOG) cells which are a type of fast-twitch muscle fiber that are powerful but don't use oxygen very well and fatigue fairly quickly
Develops: Speed (3%)
Anaerobic (7%)
Aerobic (90%)

Comments:
1. Introduces faster running
2. Continues to develop general running economy.

4. AEROBIC POWER RUNNING [END-4]

Volume: 3-8km or 2-5 miles
Speed: Based on current 5-10k pace.
Methods: Surge intervals
Distance: 30 sec - 4 min reps or 200-1200m reps
Recovery: 30 sec - 2 min or 100m-600m jog
Heart Rate: 80-90% MHR
Improves: Muscle capillarization
General circulation

Further enhances FOG's activation
Activation of Fast Glycolytic (FG) fibers which excel at producing short, fast bursts of speed.
The conversion FG's to FOG's

Develops: Speed (10%)
Anaerobic (25%)
Aerobic (65%)

Comments:
1. Enhances lactate threshold development & continues to improve speed
2. Prepares the athlete for MVO₂ and anaerobic power work.

5. MAXIMUM OXYGEN UPTAKE RUNNING [End-5]

Volume: May not exceed 10% of weekly volume or approximately 10k
Equals approx 6-8% of annual volume
Speed: Current 1500m to 10km pace, depending on the length of the repetition
Methods: Interval/repetition running & fartlek
Distance: 1-3% of weekly volume (using 2-10 bursts of 2-6 min efforts)
Recovery: Suffic(nt to resume at 5km pace
Heart Rate: Reaches 92-97% MHR in last 1-2 min of each rep
Improves: The rate of oxygen consumption
Introduces small amounts of acidosis into the blood
Develops: Speed (5%)
Anaerobic (15%)
Aerobic (80%)

Comments:
1. Further increases running speed
2. Continues to develop general running economy

NOTE: Remember, do not exceed 25-30% of weekly volume with hard training. Volume in terms of distance for aerobic intervals and repetitions may be thought of in terms of 2-4 times the athlete's racing distance. (Aerobic/anaerobic intervals and repetitions equate to approximately 2-2.5 times the race distance and pure anaerobic work to 1-2 times the race distance.

6. ANAEROBIC POWER RUNNING (Lat-1)

Volume: 2-5% of weekly volume (1-3 times race distance)
Speed: 800—1500m speed but may be as fast as 400m speed in very short repetitions
Methods: Reps of 50m—100m are done as done as sprint intervals and the longer reps are done with shorter recover(s than MVO₂ or lactic acid tolerance workouts.
Distance: 5 sec - 2 min or 50m-800m reps
Heart Rate: 180+ bpm (90%+ MHR)
Recovery: Pulse return to 135
Improves: The ability to deal with significant but not high levels of acidosis in the blood.
Develops: Speed (20%)
Anaerobic (40%)
Aerobic (40%)

Comments:
1. Develops race rhythm
2. Develops the ability to use O₂ efficiently.

7. LACTATE ACID TOLERANCE RUNNING [Lat-2]

Volume: A session involves between 4 and 12 min of near maximal running
Speed: Depends on the distance, e.g., 30.0 = 95-100%, 60.0 = 400-600m speed, 2:00 = 1500-3000m speed.
Distance: 30 sec - 2 min reps
Recovery: Recovery 2-4 times the work interval
Heart Rate: 200+ bpm (95-100% MHR)
Improves: Buffering capacity of the blood to enable the athlete to withstand the effects of lactic acid accumulation
Develops: Speed (15%)
Anaerobic (80%)
Aerobic (5%)

Comments:
1. Hydrogen ions released by lactic acid lower the pH of the blood, block the breakdown of glucose and prevent muscle contraction
2. Several weeks of LAT training Develops: the ability to produce creatine phosphate—a high-energy compound inside the muscles—increasing buffering proteins and the ability of the muscle cells to excrete acid in the blood stream
3. Excessive training of this type can adversely affect speed, explosiveness and running economy.

8. SPEED DEVELOPMENT RUNNING [Lat-3]

There are a number of types of speed training and according to the event (800m to marathon) will account for 1-5% of annual volume. The type of session used will also vary considerably.

a. Acceleration sprints [Lat-3a]

Volume: Normally about 1km
Speed: 70-100% of maximum speed
Methods: Begin moderately aiming to reach top current speed over the final 5-10m
Distance: 60-220m reps
Recovery: Walk-back recovery or jog 2-3 times the

distance run
Heart Rate: N/A
Develops: Speed (90%)
Anaerobic (5%)
Aerobic (5%)
Comment:
Develops smooth running, speed and speed endurance.

b. Sprint repetitions [Lat-3b]

Volume: Normally 800-1200m but may be as high as 1500m
Speed: It is essential to reach top current speed in the first 20-30m, then maintain a high-speed float to the finish.
Methods: Standing/flying start runs at maximal speed
Distance: 60-300m reps
Recovery: Complete or near complete
Heart Rate: N/A
Develops: Speed (80%)
Anaerobic (15%)
Aerobic (5%)
Comment:
Develops speed, speed endurance and introduces the sensation of lactic acid accumulation.

c. Power sprints [Lat-3c]

Volume: Normally 500m-1km
Speed: Maximum
Methods: Repeat standing or slow approach starts
Distance: 20-120m on the track, up hills and in sand or on sandhills
Recovery: Complete or near complete if using sets
Heart Rate: N/A
Develops: Speed/Power (75-100%)
Anaerobic (10-25%)
Aerobic (1-5%)
Comments:
1. Develops explosive power and strength endurance in both arms and legs
2. Introduces the body to lactic acid when training on the flat
3. Develops high levels of lactic acid if done on steep hills or in sand

d. Interval sprints [Lat-3d]

Volume: 800m-5km
Speed: Equivalent to the speed developed in the first 100m of a 400m race. It is essential to reach top current speed in the first 20-30m, then maintain a high-speed float to the finish
Methods: Sprint 50 or 100m/jog (float) 50-100m
Distance: 50 or 100m reps
Recovery: 50 or 100m jogs or "float jog"
Heart Rate: N/A (but expect it to be high)
Develops: Speed (20%)
Anaerobic (30%)
Aerobic (50%)
Comments:
1. Develops anaerobic power and lactic acid tolerance
2. Duplicates racing stress and develops the ability to kick.

Note: Heart rate is not considered because it will not reflect the intensity of effort due to the short duration of the work time. This is why acceleration, repetition and short-duration power sprints can be used on recovery days. Interval sprints are much harder and always constitute a major workout.

9. SPECIAL NEEDS RUNNING

a. Race Preparation Training

Race preparation training focuses on the four things an athlete needs in order to race well: rhythm, a feeling for racing conditions, an understanding of tactics, and a knowledge of the best way to train in order to be properly prepared for racing during the Competition Period.

These workouts vary greatly in their physiological impact. Some, like race maintaince, are normally non-stressful. Others such as race tactical may be very demanding. Sometimes a particular type of workout, say a race simulation, may fit an aerobic power definition. On other occasions it may be re-defined to become an MVO_2 workout.

Race Rhythm Training
Comments:
1. Develops race rhythm
2. Develops the ability to use O_2 efficiently
3. Develops a feeling for pace under increasing fatigue.

Race Simulation Training
Comment:
Duplicating race pacing conditions.

Race Tactical Training
Comment:
Duplication of racing experiences.

Race Maintaince Training
Comment:
These sessions aim to maintain form and fitness and to enhance race results.

b. Resistance Training

These workouts may fall into any of the five major aerobic components or the three major anaerobic components depending on the structure of the workout. Normally they would fall into the aerobic power to speed/power area.

Volume: 1-10% of weekly volume (1-5 times race distance)
Speed: As dictated by the resistance
Methods:
 a. Sprinting—short/high resistance bursts
 b. Rhythm—longer/lower resistance surges
 c. Bounding—attention to rhythm and form
 d. Continuous—sprints/surges with jog recover(s for 20-40 min
Distance:
 a. 70-130m (short/high resistance)
 b. 150-600m (long/low resistance)
 c. 100-300m (moderate/moderate resistance)
 d. 3-10km (sprint/surge continually)
Heart Rate: 180+ bpm (90-100% MHR)
Recovery: Dictated by the method being used
Develops: Speed (5-20%)
 Anaerobic (50-75%)
 Aerobic (5-45%)

Comment:
Resistance running, especially hills, is one of the best all-round forms of training. Hills are one aspect of training common to virtually every successful runner and are of very specific benefit to 800m performers.

c. Fartlek Training

These workouts do fall into any of the five aerobic components or the three anaerobic components depending on the structure of the workout. A well structured fartlek workout may impact four or more of the eight major components.

Volume: 5-20% of weekly volume
Speed: Fast-slow training
Methods: Repeated sprints and/or race pace surges. In a hard fartlek workout the athlete is required to alternate hard and easy efforts until too tired to continue productively. An easy fartlek workout is little more than relaxed striding interspersed with accelerations and race-pace runs.

Distance: 50m-5km sprints and surges
Heart Rate: 110-200+ bpm (50-100% MHR)
Recovery: Pulse return to 130-150 (65-75% MHR)
Develops: Speed (20%)
 Anaerobic (40%)
 Aerobic (40%)

Comment:
Ideal way to train if done properly.

d. Will Power Training

This type of training crosses all boundaries and (depending on the strength of the will to keep going) may require as much as three days recovery. It is simply a case of ignoring heart rate, pain or discomfort, distance, time or number of repetitions and pushing!

Any of the sessions mentioned under any other heading can be turned into a will power session. Will power sessions are normally done once every 4-6 weeks in the buildup period and perhaps twice in the Pre-Competition Period. They are rarely required in the Competition Period.

The aim is to conquer the "mental barrier" the mind creates to prevent the body from hurting itself. The result is that races become easier than training.

Comment:
Exhaustion is defined as one rep more than what's possible, but ceasing before form and technique drop to 80% of optimal. Keep in mind the words of Herb Elliott: "Most athletes have trained only to 70% when they think they are exhausted." Look in a mirror after the session and ask yourself, "Could I have done one more? Would my opponents have done one more?"

10. AUXILIARY TRAINING [Aux]

Running, bounding and hopping on stairs may form part of a middle distance runner's program, but hills and sand hills are probably better.

a. Non-Running Strength Training:
 General and specific strength is an important part of any running program and running alone will not provide this. Weight training, circuits and plyometrics are all important and must be considered.
b. Flexibility Training:
 Flexibility is also important and must be part of any routine.

CHAPTER 26
EXAMPLES OF VARIOUS TYPES OF WORKOUTS

AEROBIC RECOVERY RUNNING [End-1]

15-30 min easily, possibly including jogging, striding and even walking.

AEROBIC CONDITIONING RUNNING [End-2]

a. 5-35km (30 min—3 hrs) easy running
b. Aerobic-based fartlek, i.e., surges of 5-45 min with pulse rate around 150-170 bpm interspersed with easy jogs with pulse at 100-120 bpm.

LACTATE THRESHOLD RUNNING [End-3]

a. Continuous running @ 80-87% MHR
   - 4-6km or 3-4 miles or 20-25 min (for anyone who does not run beyond an hour)
   - 7-12km or 5-8 miles or 35-45 min (for those whose long runs are between 60 and 90 minutes)
   - 13-16km or 9-10 miles or 45-60 min (for those whose long runs are in excess of 90 minutes)
   - Marathon runners may occasionally do threshold runs of up to 90 minutes
b. Interrupted running @ 80-92% MHR
   - 25-35 min of 5 to 10 min repetitions with 1-3 min recovery.

AEROBIC POWER RUNNING [End-4]

a. 15-25 min @ 80-90% MHR
b. 5 x 800m @ 5-10k pace with 200m float recovery
c. 8 x 400m @ 3-5k pace with 200m float recovery
d. 12 x 200m @ 3k pace with 200m float recovery
e. 6 x 800m over 4 steeplechase barriers @ 3k steeplechase pace with 200m float recovery. (A float recovery means a loss of only 25-30% pace.)

MAXIMUM OXYGEN UPTAKE RUNNING [End-5]

a. 5-8 x 1k or 3 min reps @ 5k pace with 500m —1k or 1:30 —3:00 recovery
b. 3-5 x 1600m or 1 mile @ 5k pace with 400-800m or 3:00 —6:00 recovery
c. 6-10 x 600-800m or 1:30-3:00 min reps @ current 5km pace with 600-800m or 3:00-6:00 recovery
d. 2 sets of 3 x 1000m @ 3k steeplechase pace with 30 sec recovery between reps and 3 min between sets.
e. 15 min @ 3-5k pace alternating 2-3 min fast with 1-2 min easy
f. 3k or 2-mile Time Trials or races.

ANAEROBIC POWER RUNNING [Lat-1]

a. 10-15 x 200 @ 1500m pace with 200m jog recovery
b. 8-10 x 300 @ 1500m pace with 100m jog recovery
c. 6-8 x 400 @ 1500m pace with 200-400m jog recovery
d. 4-6 x 500 @ 1500m pace with 200-500m jog recovery
e. 4-8 x 800-1000m with 4 barriers and perhaps the water jump
f. 2-4 x 800m alternating 50m sprint and 50m float
g. 3200m or 2 miles alternating 50m sprint and 50m float.
h. 1-2 x 1600m alternating 100m sprint and 100m float
i. 4k-5k alternating 100m sprint and 100m float.

LACTIC ACID TOLERANCE RUNNING [Lat-2]

a. 5-10 x 30.0 (225-250m) with 2-3 min recovery
b. 4-8 x 45.0 (275-350m) with 3-6 min recovery
c. 3-6 x 60.0 (350-500m) with 4-8 min recovery
d. 2-4 x 1:30 (550-700m) with 5-10 min recovery
e. 2-3 x 2:00 (700-900m) with 6-12 min recovery
f. 10-20 x 70-130m sprints on a steep hill
g. 10-30 x 10-30 sec sprints up a 20-40m sand hill.

SPEED DEVELOPMENT [Lat-3] RUNNING

Acceleration Sprints [Lat-3a]
   a. 150-160-170-180-190-200-190-180-170-160-150
   b. 2-4 sets (180-150-120)
   c. 3-5 x 300m

Repetition Sprints [Lat-3b]
   a. 6 sets of 6 x 60m
   b. 2-3 sets 60-90-120-120-90-60
   c. 2-4 sets 120-90-60

Power Sprints [Lat-3c]
   a. 10-20 x 10-50m standing start sprints

b. 10-20 x 10-50m sprints up a steep hill
c. 5-15 x 30-60m flying start sprints
d. 5-8 x 30m sprint – 20m float – 30m sprint
e. 4-7 x 60m sprint – 30m float – 60m sprint
f. 8-12 x 70-130m steep hill sprints with full recovery

Interval sprints [Lat-3d]
a. 5-8 x 30m sprint – 20m float – 30m sprint
b. 3-6 x 60m sprint – 30m float – 60m sprint
c. 3-6 x 400m alternating 50m sprint and 50m float
d. 2-4 x 800m alternating 50m sprint and 50m float
e. 1-2 x 1600m alternating 100m sprint and 100m float.

SPECIFIC NEEDS RUNNING

Race Preparation Training
1. Race Rhythm Training
   a. See workouts a.- d. under Anaerobic Power section
   b. 800m: 600–400–2 x 200
   c. 1500m: 1000–600–2 x 400
   d. 3000m: 2000–1000–2 x 500
   e. 5000m: 3000–1500–2 x 1000
   f. 3kS/C: 2000–1000–2 x 500 with 4 barriers
   g. 800m: 200–400–600–400–200
   h. 1500m: 300–600–1000–600–300
   i. 3000m: 400–800–1500–800–400
   j. 5000m: 600–500–3000–1500–600
   k. 3kS/C: 400–800–1500–800–400 with 4 barriers
   l. 800m: 8 x 300m @ race pace with 2:00 recovery
   m. 1500m: 8 x 400m @ race pace with 1:30 recovery
   n. 2kS/C: 3-5 x 800 @ 2k steeplechase pace with 200 jog recovery
   o. 3kS/C: 6-8 x 800 (3km steeplechase pace) with 200 jog
   p. 3-10k: 2 x 3 x 1k @ race pace with 30.0 sec between reps & 3:00 between sets or 5k (400m surge with 200m float).

2. Race Simulation Training
   a. Time Trials
      - 600—650m (800m)
      - 1000-1200m (1500m)
      - 2000-2400m (3000m)
      - 2000-2400m with 4 barriers (3km S/C)
      - 3200-4000m (5000m)
      - 7-8km (10,000m)
      - 28-32km (Marathon)
   b. Surge Trials (100% of race distance with 75% covered at race pace including the last 100-200m sprinting), e.g.:
      - 800m: 200m-(100 float)-300m-(100 float)-100m sprint
      - 1500m: 400m-(200 float)-600m-(100 float)-200m sprint
      - 3k: 800m-(400 float)-1200m-(200 float)-400m sprint
      - 3k S/C: 800m-(400 float)-1200m-(200 float)-400 with 4 barriers
      - 5k: 2 sets of 500m-1k-200m/200m recovery + 400m fast
      - 10k: 3k-5k-1k with 1k recovery.

3. Race Tactical Training
   800m:
   - 200m (5-10 sec slower than race pace)/ 400m (race pace less 1-2 sec)/ 150m (relaxed)/ 50m sprint
   - 400m (race pace)/ 200m (relaxed)/ 200m sprint
   - 200m (race pace less 2 sec)/ 200m (relaxed)/200m (race pace)/ 100m (relaxed)/ 100m sprint

   1500m:
   - 400m (10-15 sec slower than race pace)/ 600m (slightly faster than race pace)/ 400m (relaxed)/100 sprint
   - 800m (race pace)/ 300 (relaxed)/ 200 (acceleration)/200 sprint

   3000m:
   Lap 1—10-15 sec slower than race pace
   Lap 2—3-5 sec faster than race pace
   Lap 3—10-15 sec slower than race pace
   Lap 4—20-40 sec slower than race pace
   Lap 5—10-15 sec slower than race pace
   Lap 6—race pace
   Lap 7—10-15 sec slower than race pace
   Last 200m—sprint

   5000m:
   Lap 1—10-15 sec slower than race pace
   Lap 2—3-5 sec faster than race pace
   Lap 3—10-15 sec slower than race pace
   Lap 4—20-40 sec slower than race pace
   Lap 5—10-15 sec slower than race pace
   Lap 6—3-5 sec faster than race pace
   Lap 7—10-15 sec slower than race pace
   Lap 8—20-40 sec slower than race pace
   Lap 9—10-15 sec slower than race pace
   Lap 10—3-5 sec faster than race pace
   Lap 11—10-15 sec slower than race pace
   Lap 12—20-40 sec slower than race pace
   Last 200m—sprint

   3000m steeplechase with 4 Barriers per Lap:

Lap 1—10-15 sec slower than race pace
Lap 2—3-5 sec faster than race pace
Lap 3—10-15 sec slower than race pace
Lap 4—20-40 sec slower than race pace
Lap 5—10-15 sec slower than race pace
Lap 6—race pace
Lap 7—10-15 sec slower than race pace
Last 200m—sprint (includes water jump)

10,000m:
This is merely an extension of the 5000m

Marathon:
This is covered by 5-45 min surges in the long runs.

4. Race Maintaince Training
- 10-15 min of 50-100m accelerations
- 4-8 x 200-300m at race pace with easy recovery jogs
- 15-45 min easy running interspersed with relaxed accelerations, jogging, walking and stretching.

Resistance Running Training
1. Hills
   - short steep x 10-20 reps @ 90% (jog/walk recovery)
   - long gradual x 5-10 reps @ 80% (jog recovery)
   - 3-6km sprinting 10-30 hills of all types
2. Sand
   - 10-30 reps x 20-50m sand hill (jog/walk-back recovery)
   - 30-60 sec surges in heavy sand (1-3 min recovery)
   - 3-6km of 1-3 min surges over sandy hilly terrain.

Fartlek Running Training
Fartlek typically trains all event areas simultaneously. A standard session of 20 to 40 minutes would entail using a random combination of some/all of the sprints and surges for 200m through to 5000m as listed below.
- 200m: 5, 10, 15 & 30 sec bursts
- 400m: 15, 30, 45 & 60 sec bursts
- 800m: 30.0, 1:00, 1:30 & 2:00 bursts
- 1500m: 1:00, 2:00, 3:00 & 4:00 surges
- 3km & S/C: 3:00, 6:00 & 9:00 surges
- 5000m: 5:00, 10:00 & 15:00 surges

Comments:
1. Recoveries are "as needed" to commence the next burst
2. If done in hilly terrain add the dimensions of resistance and raise the running economy factor

3. Aerobic versions may also be used, i.e., 8:00, 5:00 and 1:00 surges.

Will Power Running
Repeated surges for the various race target times, for example:
- 400m—45.0 (m)/50.0 (w)
- 800m—1:45 (m)/2:00 (w)
- 1500m—3:35 (m)/4:00 (w)
- 3000m—7:40 (m)/8:45 (w)
- 5000m—13:00 (m)/15:00 (w)

- 20-30 min of continuous running interspersed with repeated simulated mid-race (200-1600m) surges, allowing only 50-60% recovery, until exhausted
- 20-30 min of repeated 50-350m finishing sprints with a recovery jog to the point of starting the next sprint, e.g., jog to 200m, sprint 200m, jog 50m, sprint 350m, jog 250m, sprint 150m, etc., to exhaustion
- Repeated hill/sand hill sprints to exhaustion
- Repeated intervals to a set target time to exhaustion, e.g., 400's/sub 56.0 (=1500m race pace for men or =800m race pace women), etc. Recoveries are based on a pulse return to 126-132 bpm. Workout ceases when the pulse fails to return to 132 in 15 minutes
- Combinations of all of the above.

Comments:
1. Will power sessions do not always have to be anaerobically hard. An endurance run at, say, 75% MHR which is set 10-15km longer than what is normal is hard. So is a set of multiple repeats at an aerobic speed with a set recovery until the heart rate passes a set point, e.g., run the maximum possible number of 200's @ 10k pace with 200m recovery @ 10k pace + 20.0.
2. A special advantage of the aerobic will power interval-type session is that the committed athlete strives for greater and greater levels of relaxation at a given speed in order to keep the HR down and set a new personal best number of repetitions done.

AUXILLIARY [Aux] TRAINING

a. Bounding/Running Steps and/or Stairs
   One step at a time (Target—fast movement)
   Two steps at a time (Target—fast powerful movement)
   Max possible steps per stride (Target—power)
b. Single/Double Leg Hopping
   Alternate leg, i.e., left-left-right-right, etc.
   Interchanging leg, i.e., 3-5xL/leg-3-5xR/leg, etc.

- Single Leg
    i) L/leg only
    ii) R/leg only
- Double Leg
    i) 2-3 steps at a time
    ii) Max steps at a time

Target minimum "touchdown" time via active landings.

c. Strength Training

Workout A (General Strength)
1. Wide grip lat pulldowns (3 x 10 @ 50-80% body weight)
2. Narrow grip lat pulldowns (3 x 10 @ 60-90% body weight)
3. Bench press (3 x 10 with 70-90% body weight)
4. Dumbell swings (3 x 2-4 min)
5. Leg extensions (3 x 10 @ 40-70% body weight)
6. Seated leg press (3 x 10 @ 200-300% body weight)
7. Hamstring curls (3 x 10-20 @ 5-15% body weight)
8. Stomach crunches (3 sets targeting 100-200+ total)
9. Leg raises (3 sets targeting 50-100+ total)
10. Back extensions (3 x 10-20 with body weight).

Workout B (General No 2: 3 x 10 Reps)
1. Barbell bench press
2. Barbell behind-head press
3. Dumbell curls
4. Barbell upright rowing
5. Seated leg press.

Workout C (Circuit No. 1: 1-3 sets x 30-60 sec)
1. Push-ups (modified if backs/arms not strong enough)
2. Stomach crunches (as per General Strength)
3. Dips (modified if parallel bars unavailable)
4. Alternate lead leg lunges
5. Standing sideways leg raises
6. Single leg half squats
7. Back extensions.

Full recovery for explosive workouts or short recovery workouts for endurance.

Workout D (Circuit No. 2: 1-3 sets x 30-60 sec)
1. Pull-ups (modify, if necessary)
2. Leg raises (as per General Strength)
3. Sideways lunges (back straight)
4. Alternate leg bench step-ups
5. Burpees
6. Side Bends
7. Neck curls
8. Trunk twisting.

Workout E (Strength)
1. Military press (seated)
2. Half squat or lying leg press
3. Power cleans
4. Bench press
5. Dead lift

Begin with 3 sets of 10 @ 65-70%
Progress to 3 sets 7x (70-75%)—5x (80-85%)—1-3x (90-95%).

Workout F (Power)
1. Half squats or lying leg press
2. Bench press
3. Sit-ups
4. Power cleans
5. Step-ups.

Begin with 3 sets @ 60-70% x 15-20 sec
Progress to 3 sets x 40-50 sec.

Workout G (Plyometrics)
1. Standing long jump x 3
2. Standing triple jump x 3 (L/leg ~ R/leg)
3. Right leg ~ left leg hops x 3 (target max distance)
4. Double leg hops x 3 (target max distance)
5. Straight leg vertical jumps x 3 (target max height)
6. 30m bounding strides (target minimum number of steps)
7. 3 x double foot bounds over 3-5 hurdles (84-91cm)
8. 3 x L/leg ~ R/leg hops over 3-5 hurdles (76-84cm)
9. Double leg depth jumps (76-100cm) x 3 into sand pit.
10. L/leg ~ R/leg depth jumps (50-75cm) x 3 into sand pit.

The above equates to one set.

Workout H (Gym/Track Circuit)
1. 10 x [squats (body weight) + squat jumps w/ SB + squat jumps w/o SB]
2. 10.0 x dumbell swings
3. 10 x [step ups w/SB + step-ups w/o SB]
4. 10 x sit-ups
5. 10 x bench press
6. 10 x [split jumps w/SB + straight leg toe bounces]
7. 10 x dips
8. 10 x straight leg raises from wall hanging position]
9. 10 x military press
10. 3 x 3.0 fast- 3.0 jog- 3.0 fast. 1-2 min recovery

Take 3-8 min between sets. (SB = Sandbag—wrapped over shoulders)

Ten-time All-American Michelle Teodoro (No. 339) trained under Irv Ray at Azusa Pacific.

Workout I (Outdoor/Track Circuit)
1. Medicine ball—throw-ups x 10 + fast arm swings x 10
2. Squat jumps with SB x 10 + squat jumps w/o SB x 10
3. Sit-ups x 10
4. Single leg squats x 10 each leg
5. Push-ups (modified—women) x 10
6. Split jumps w/SB x 10 + split jumps w/o SB x 10
7. Back arches x 10
8. High knee-butt kick-quick feet x 3
9. Dips (modified) x 10
10. 50m tire/sled pull + 50m sprint w/o tire/sled x 2. Take 1-2 min recovery between runs. Take 3-5 min between sets.
(Acknowledgment to Efim Shuravetsky, Australian Institute of Sport coach, Melbourne)

d. Flexibility
1. Neck & shoulder rotations
2. Shoulder shrugs, both ways
3. Trunk circling (keep lower body still)
4. Knee rotations (keep upper body still)
5. Ankle rotations
6. Calf stretches (keep leg straight)
7. Achilles stretches
8. Quadriceps stretches (keep upper body straight)
9. Hamstring stretches
10. Gluteal/hip stretches
    a. Side-to-side lunges (don't lean forward
    b. Standing hamstring curls (keep active knee behind support leg knee)
    c. Standing clockwise leg circles (don't lean sideways)
    d. Standing anti-clockwise leg circles.
    e. Standing sideways leg raises (Keep upright)
11. 300-500 "toe crawls"
12. "Inside-to-outside" ankle rolling.

Do each exercise 10 times SLOWLY, breathing out as the stretch is applied, in as you relax. Remember, relaxation is an essential element of proper stretching. You cannot be distracted in any way, e.g., talking to other squad members. Yoga, tai chi, kung fu, etc., are all fine, and instructional videos are very helpful.

AFTERWORD
Using The *Run With The Best* Program In The American College And High School System

By Irv Ray

Now that you have read *Run With The Best* and worked through the worksheets I will share my experience of using the program since 1993 with you. The good news is that the results get better each year and the athletes run faster when it counts.

Prior to using the *Run With The Best* program I had coached only one All-American. Since then I have coached 49 All-Americans, six national championship teams, two national champion distance relay teams and two national 800m qualifiers for U.S. national championship meets, as well as the U.S. mile indoor champion in 1997. And this has all been achieved while coaching at small Christian colleges.

Success is unlikely to come without challenges however. For this reason it is essential that the coach remembers that his learning curve will be accelerated if he heeds the warnings contained in the book, because one or both of the authors either made the mistake referred to or knows a coach or athlete who made a similar mistake! To get the most from the *Run With The Best* program I suggest you pay special attention to the following:

1. **The concept of accumulated volume.**

    Prior to 1993 I rarely asked my athletes to complete long runs. Now these workouts are considered a core element the accumulation of the athlete's career volume and in maintaining the athlete's annual volume at the required level appropriate to his event. I also suggest you be creative and use supplementary aerobic training, such as water running, simulated climbing on stairmaster machines, swimming, or cycling to help build the aerobic base. These activities will be very beneficial while the athlete is still at relatively low volumes because they assist in enhancing the aerobic base and they initiate the athlete to the type of routine he will have to follow later in his career when two and three daily workouts will become normal.

2. **A year-round focus on speed development.**

    It is essential the coach allocate at least one workout per week to speed development. This is one very important component I omitted during 1993-94 because I thought the threshold running and hill bounding would be enough (see No. 6 below). I had overlooked Tony's advice that stimulating the alactic acid system by running fast 80-120m accelerations during the Base Period was more beneficial to speed improvement than ignoring it until later in the year. If the coach has forgotten the reasons for approaching speed from this perspective it is worth taking the time to reread Chapter 7.

    I now schedule a workout of 10 x 100m repetitions every week of the year. The 100m repetitions are run, initially, at 400m date pace, gradually moving to 400m goal pace as the season progresses. For example, if 400m goal time for the year is 52 seconds but the athlete is currently running 55 seconds, the coach will expect the athlete to gradually improve his average 100m time from 13.5-14 sec to 12.5-13 sec by the end of Phase 2 of the Base Period.

    The results of the once-a-week speed workout can be dramatic. For example, a first year freshman on my team, 19-year-old Chinyere Nduwke, had PR's of 61.0 for 400m and 2:30 for 800m in 1997. In 1998 she ran 57.5 and 2:15. More importantly, even if Chinyere never ran any faster over 400m, her new time indicates she can run 2:09 or faster for 800m in the future. A time of 57.5 for 400m also means she has the potential to run fast times at longer distances.

    Another example many coaches can identify with relates to a high school sophomore who appeared unable to run much faster than 4:48 for the mile and 10:18 for 2 miles. After including a weekly speed session for 12 months, his 400m PR dropped from 61 to 54 seconds. The result was a 4:31 for the mile and 9:48 for 2 miles and he now knows he can go much faster in all the middle and long distance races than he originally thought possible.

3. **Avoiding hard running surfaces whenever possible.**

    Schedule the bulk of the training runs on soft surfaces—dirt roads, trails, grass fields and parks, rather than paved roads and synthetic tracks. This practice was common years ago when less pavement existed and is still common to the Africans. It may mean the coach has to organize a 20-30-minute

Tony Benson   Steve Scott   Irv Ray

bus trip to a suitable venue. But it will benefit the athlete by reducing injuries, improving recovery time and providing a more enjoyable training environment. This, in turn, will mean that the quality of training is better.

4. The value of hills.

Over the last two years I have tried to incorporate as much hill running into the program as possible. All the "training to train" workouts can be accomplished in a hilly environment or on one particular hill of at least 200m. Some coaches may not have hills in close proximity to their school and it may mean driving to find suitable areas for this form of training.

The workouts I use are basically of two types. The first workout consists of running for 33 to 38 min on a long uphill mountain trail, alternating 3 min at 87-93% MHR and 2 min of recovery running. Naturally beginners and developing athletes do lower volumes, e.g., 22-27 min and 27-32 min respectively. We do this workout once a week four to five times towards the end of Phase I and III of the Base Period and I have seen it improve an average male athlete with a 2-mile PR of 9:15-9:30 by 15 to 20 seconds. The results are often even more dramatic with women, and a number of them with PR's in the 11:30 to 12:00 range improved to 10:30-11:00.

A word of caution here. This is a tough aerobic power workout and should only be introduced after the athlete has developed a very strong aerobic foundation, based on 1:00, 1:30 and 2-hour long runs and 20-, 35-, and 50-minute (or 4-, 7.5- and 10-mile) threshold runs.

The second workout I incorporated was a Lydiard-style hill bounding session. The athletes are instructed to run with a powerful arm drive and a high-knee or bounding type of leg action. We use a six- to eight-degree hill and run 300m repetitions. Initially the schedule requires the athlete to complete eight to ten repetitions and to build up from there to perhaps to 16 to 20 repetitions. I use this workout three to four times during the final 10 weeks of the Base Period to enhance the athlete's muscular and skeletal strength and increase his MVO_2 capacity in preparation for the Pre-Competition Period, with its heavy emphasis on track-specific workouts.

5. The importance of lactate threshold training.

This type of training has always been part of my coaching program but I was unsure of how to maximize its value, and my workouts were likely to be based on the interval concept, i.e., 3-5 x 5-8 min at 85-87% MHR. After speaking to Tony in 1993 I made the following changes to my program for 1993-94.

First, the threshold workouts became continuous running. Lydiard had threshold runs listed for Monday and Friday evening during his 10-week 100-mile-per-week period and Steve Scott regularly ran fast 10-milers around the streets of San Diego and a "strong" six- to ten-mile run is a consistent feature of a significant number of middle and long distance runners' programs.

Secondly, I scheduled threshold training in conjunction with the long run. An athlete who can only run for one hour at a general conditioning pace (65-

80% MHR) and/or 40 to 50 minutes for 10km cannot be expected to run 6-10 miles at 85-87% MHR.

I recommend coaches adopt the *Run With The Best* strategy of scheduling 35- to 50-min threshold runs for athletes capable of a 2-hour long run, 20-35 min for athletes who regularly run 1¹/₂-hr. long runs and either 2-3 x 5-8 minutes or 20 min continuously for athletes whose long run is only around one hour. As all middle and long distance runners should be doing long runs in excess of an hour, the threshold workouts associated with a one-hour long run can be thought of as transition sessions.

Thirdly, as I worked with the system, I found the stronger, more experienced athletes needed a higher level of challenge every second week after about 15-20 weeks of once-a-week threshold training. But, while the younger or lower-level athletes often showed dramatic improvement after short periods of exposure to threshold running, they gained the most benefit if they included a once-a-week threshold workout for 20-30 weeks.

The results achieved by Coach Bill Reeves at South Hills High School in West Covina, California, are a good example of what can be achieved if regular threshold workouts are introduced into the programs of very average male and female athletes. In 1996 Bill's girls' and boys' cross country teams won their respective league championships and advanced to the California Interscholastic Federation preliminaries. The girls reached the finals, the boys did not. In 1997 the team started with 2-mile threshold runs and gradually built these runs up to 6 miles. After approximately 20 weeks of training where threshold running replaced various forms of interval running, South Hills had the following results.

Girls	Boys
1st CIF Preliminary Meet	1st CIF Preliminaries
2nd CIF Finals	3rd CIF Finals—a little disappointing but the team improved at the State Meet
3rd California State Meet (Div. 3)	2nd California State Meet (Div. 3)

The value of the training can be judged by the fact that the boys' team did not have one sub-4:35 miler on the team. The benefits of the threshold training can also be seen in the improved mile times of the five runners the following track season.

Runner	Mile Time 1997	3-Mile X-C Time 1997	Mile Time 1998
No. 1	4:37	16:10	4:26
No. 2	4:43	16:06	4:31
No. 3	4:49	16:23	4:36
No. 4	4:55	16:31	4:40
No. 5	4:58	16:36	4:40

6. **Appreciating that balance in workouts is more important than content.**

I have already mentioned the importance of hill running and the value of the uphill surge session (see hill workout No. 1 above), but this workout was the undoing of some of my athletes in 1994-95. I introduced the workout in exactly the same way as I have done every year since, but that was the year you will recall I did not have them run the once-a-week 400m speed session. The result was the athletes did not peak as I believed they should have.

When I mentioned this to Tony towards the end of the season he was as mystified as I was until he realized that my Wednesday hill workout was a replacement workout for the fartlek type workout that he had used when training on Lydiard's program during 1970. Immediately the problem became clear. Tony pointed out that his fartlek workout included everything from 50m sprints to 1320-yard surges, as well as hill sprints over distances from 30m to 300m.

What had happened was I had brought the athletes into the Pre-Competition Period with plenty of stamina but short on basic speed. When the race-specific work was introduced they were able to tolerate the intensity of the workouts but they lacked the speed to use their stamina and race fitness to race at higher levels than previous years. The introduction of the once-a-week 400m speed workout changed all that in 1996, 1997 and 1998.

7. **Educating the athlete so he/she can take responsibility for their performances.**

The whole premise of the *Run With The Best* system is that it takes time to develop an athlete to full potential. The high school years are just the beginning of the journey. The middle distance athlete may just have accumulated enough volume in his event at the end of his college years, but the distance runner will still be very much in the transitional stage from development to senior level.

If all this is explained to the athlete he can then make a choice between an *anaerobically* oriented program that *may* make him marginally more competitive against his equally or more talented contemporaries in the short term, but will stunt his progress in later years, or a more *aerobically* orientated program that will ensure he or she will "run with the best" when it really counts in his middle to late twenties and early thirties.

Once the athlete makes his decision he must be held accountable for his actions. It is one thing to "talk the talk" but quite another to "walk to walk." Tony's years of experience taught him physical ability is but one small aspect of that thing coaches call potential and in the early years of our association he would often point out how few teenage stars went on to become great senior middle and long distance runners as opposed to the number who developed steadily over years.

The truth of this was demonstrated to me in 1996 when I had two talented male athletes whose training showed they were in sub-3:40/1500m condition but who failed to achieve times better than 3:47. Despite their avowed goal of the 2000 Olympics, when it came down to running the daily miles and training at paces that were uncomfortable, they were often missing from practice.

I now feel the coach has accomplished over 50% of his job once the athlete begins to realize that all training is *cumulative* and that speed forms the basis of all performance. The athlete then becomes more relaxed about his progress and can accept that what was not accomplished in the first or second year can be done in the third or fourth year and that small improvements over 400m or in a 7.5- or 10-mile threshold run will always translate to improved performance over 800m, 1500m, one mile, 3k, 5k, 10k, and so on.

In summary, the results I have experienced using the *Run With The Best* system have been dramatic, and each year, as my understanding of the philosophy that forms the foundation of the system increases, each generation of athletes I coach performs at a level slightly above the previous one at the same stage of development. Some athletes have already reached national level and a few have gone on to international level. But more importantly the relationships I have developed with many coaches across America have enabled numerous high school-age athletes of average talent to perform at levels they had not dreamed of twelve months earlier.

The boy who improves from 2:16 to 1:58 for 800m or the female 2-miler previously stuck on 12:00 who achieves a sub-11:00 time are the real success stories of our training system because at all these high schools are many kids with the potential to be outstanding athletes.

Tony Benson had proved the system works again and again, both in the Philippines and in Australia, while I regularly receive exciting success stories from all over this country from coaches we introduced to the *Run With The Best* program. We hope you will add to those stories so our athletes will achieve their potential and compete on equal footing with the rest of the world.

If you are interested in contacting either Coach Ray or Coach Benson to discuss these training principles or to learn more on how to successfully apply the *Run With The Best* program, contact:

Irv Ray
California Baptist University
8432 Magnolia Ave.
Riverside, CA 92504-4012 USA
Fax: 909/689-4754

Tony Benson
P.O. Box 117
Parkville, Vic. 3052
Australia
Fax: 61-3-9329-2165
Email: Bensons@blaze.net.au
Web Site: http://www.blaze.net.au/~bensons/

EXTRA WORKSHEETS (See Chapter 3)

WORKSHEET 1

Name:	Training Age: Yrs
Estimated Accumulated Lifetime Volume (Miles/Kms/Hours)	

WORKSHEET 2

Name:	Training Age: Yrs	Year:
Estimated Accumulated Lifetime Volume (Miles/Kms/Hours)		
PLANNED VOLUME FOR THE CURRENT YEAR (MILES/KMS/HOURS		

WORKSHEET 3

YEAR	ANNUAL TOTAL MI/KM/HR	PROGRESSIVE TOTAL MI/KM/HR	YEAR	ANNUAL TOTAL MI/KM/HR	PROGRESSIVE TOTAL MI/KM/HR
PRE-1998	1998		2004		
1999			2005		
2000			2006		
2001			2007		
2002			2008		
2003			2009		
			2010		

WORKSHEET 4

NAME:							
BASE PERIOD			PRE- COMPETITION PERIOD		COMPETITION PERIOD		
NO OF WEEKS:			NO OF WEEKS:		NO OF WEEKS:		
PHASE I	PHASE II	PHASE III	PHASE I	PHASE II	PHASE I	PHASE II	
WKS:	WKS:	WKS:	WKS:	WKS:	WKS:	WKS:	

WORKSHEET 5

NAME:	TRAINING AGE: YRS	YEAR:
PLANNED ANNUAL VOLUME (HOURS/MILES/KMS)		
BASE PERIOD	PRE-COMPETITION PERIOD	COMPETITION PERIOD
AS A % OF TOTAL VOLUME	AS A % OF TOTAL VOLUME	AS A % OF TOTAL VOLUME
IN HOURS, MILES OR KILOMETERS	IN HOURS, MILES OR KILOMETERS	IN HOURS, MILES OR KILOMETERS

WORKSHEET 6

NAME:	TRAINING AGE: YRS	YEAR:
PLANNED VOLUME		(HOURS/MILES/KMS)
BASE PERIOD	PRE-COMPETITION PERIOD	COMPETITION PERIOD
% (HR:MI:KM) = VOLUME =	% (HR:MI:KM) = VOLUME =	% (HR:MI:KM) = VOLUME =

PHASE I (%)	PHASE II (%)	PHASE III (%)	PHASE I (%)	PHASE II (%)	PHASE I (%)	PHASE II (%)

PHASE I (HR/MI/KM)	PHASE II (HR/MI/KM)	PHASE III (HR/MI/KM)	PHASE I (HR/MI/KM)	PHASE II (HR/MI/KM)	PHASE I (HR/MI/KM)	PHASE II (HR/MI/KM)

WORKSHEET 7

Base Period			Pre-Competition Period		Competition Period	
Phase I (Miles or Kms)	Phase II (Miles or Kms)	Phase III (Miles or Kms)	Phase I (Miles or Kms)	Phase II (Miles or Kms)	Phase I (Miles or Kms)	Phase II (Miles or Kms)
Weeks 1-10	Weeks 11-20	Weeks 21-30	Weeks 31-35	Weeks 36-40	Weeks 41-45	Weeks 46-50
1. 2. 3. 4. 5. 6. 7. 8. 9. 10. Total=	11. 12. 13. 14. 15. 16. 17. 18. 19. 20. Total=	21. 22. 23. 24. 25. 26. 27. 28. 29. 30. Total=	31. 32. 33. 34. 35. Total=	36. 37. 38. 39. 40. Total=	41. 42. 43. 44. 45. Total=	46. 47. 48. 49. 50. Total=

WORKSHEET 8

Name:						
Base Period			Pre-Competition Period		Competition Period	
Phase I	Phase II	Phase III	Phase I	Phase II	Phase I	Phase II
1.	11.	21.	31.	36.	41.	46.
2.	12.	22.	32.	37.	42.	47.
3.	13.	23.	33.	38.	43.	48.
4.	14.	24.	34.	39.	44.	49.
5.	15.	25.	35.	40.	45.	50.
6.	16.	26.				
7.	17.	27.				
8.	18.	28.				
9.	19.	29.				
10.	20.	30.				

WORKSHEET 9

TRAINING COMPONENT	ABBREVIATION
AEROBIC RECOVERY	END-1
AEROBIC CONDITIONING	END-1
LACTATE THRESHOLD	END-3
AEROBIC POWER	END-4
MAXIMAL OXYGEN UPTAKE	END-5
ANAEROBIC POWER	LAT-1
LACTIC ACID TOLERANCE	LAT-2
SPEED & POWER	LAT-3

WORKSHEET 10

DAY		BASE PERIOD	PRE-COMPETITION PERIOD	COMPETITION PERIOD
MONDAY	(AM) (PM)			
TUESDAY	(AM) (PM)			
WEDNESDAY	(AM) (PM)			
THURSDAY	(AM) (PM)			
FRIDAY	(AM) (PM)			
SATURDAY	(AM) (PM)			
SUNDAY	(AM) (PM)			

EXTRA WORKSHEETS (See Chapter 3)

WORKSHEET 1

Name:	Training Age: Yrs
Estimated Accumulated Lifetime Volume (Miles/Kms/Hours)	

WORKSHEET 2

Name:	Training Age: Yrs	Year:
Estimated Accumulated Lifetime Volume (Miles/Kms/Hours)		
PLANNED VOLUME FOR THE CURRENT YEAR (MILES/KMS/HOURS		

WORKSHEET 3

YEAR	ANNUAL TOTAL MI/KM/HR	PROGRESSIVE TOTAL MI/KM/HR	YEAR	ANNUAL TOTAL MI/KM/HR	PROGRESSIVE TOTAL MI/KM/HR
PRE-1998	1998		2004		
1999			2005		
2000			2006		
2001			2007		
2002			2008		
2003			2009		
			2010		

WORKSHEET 4

NAME:							
BASE PERIOD				PRE- COMPETITION PERIOD		COMPETITION PERIOD	
NO OF WEEKS:				NO OF WEEKS:		NO OF WEEKS:	
PHASE I	PHASE II	PHASE III		PHASE I	PHASE II	PHASE I	PHASE II
WKS:	WKS:	WKS:		WKS:	WKS:	WKS:	WKS:

WORKSHEET 5

NAME:	TRAINING AGE:	YRS	YEAR:
PLANNED ANNUAL VOLUME (HOURS/MILES/KMS)			

BASE PERIOD	PRE-COMPETITION PERIOD	COMPETITION PERIOD
AS A % OF TOTAL VOLUME	AS A % OF TOTAL VOLUME	AS A % OF TOTAL VOLUME
IN HOURS, MILES OR KILOMETERS	IN HOURS, MILES OR KILOMETERS	IN HOURS, MILES OR KILOMETERS

WORKSHEET 6

NAME:	TRAINING AGE:	YRS	YEAR:
PLANNED VOLUME			(HOURS/MILES/KMS)

BASE PERIOD			PRE-COMPETITION PERIOD		COMPETITION PERIOD	
% (HR:MI:KM) =			% (HR:MI:KM) =		% (HR:MI:KM) =	
VOLUME =			VOLUME =		VOLUME =	
PHASE I (%)	PHASE II (%)	PHASE III (%)	PHASE I (%)	PHASE II (%)	PHASE I (%)	PHASE II (%)
PHASE I (HR/MI/KM)	PHASE II (HR/MI/KM)	PHASE III (HR/MI/KM)	PHASE I (HR/MI/KM)	PHASE II (HR/MI/KM)	PHASE I (HR/MI/KM)	PHASE II (HR/MI/KM)

WORKSHEET 7

Base Period			Pre-Competition Period		Competition Period	
Phase I (Miles or Kms)	Phase II (Miles or Kms)	Phase III (Miles or Kms)	Phase I (Miles or Kms)	Phase II (Miles or Kms)	Phase I (Miles or Kms)	Phase II (Miles or Kms)
Weeks 1-10	Weeks 11-20	Weeks 21-30	Weeks 31-35	Weeks 36-40	Weeks 41-45	Weeks 46-50
1.	11.	21.	31.	36.	41.	46.
2.	12.	22.	32.	37.	42.	47.
3.	13.	23.	33.	38.	43.	48.
4.	14.	24.	34.	39.	44.	49.
5.	15.	25.	35.	40.	45.	50.
6.	16.	26.	Total=	Total=	Total=	Total=
7.	17.	27.				
8.	18.	28.				
9.	19.	29.				
10.	20.	30.				
Total=	Total=	Total=				

WORKSHEET 8

Name:						
Base Period			Pre-Competition Period		Competition Period	
Phase I	Phase II	Phase III	Phase I	Phase II	Phase I	Phase II
1.	11.	21.	31.	36.	41.	46.
2.	12.	22.	32.	37.	42.	47.
3.	13.	23.	33.	38.	43.	48.
4.	14.	24.	34.	39.	44.	49.
5.	15.	25.	35.	40.	45.	50.
6.	16.	26.				
7.	17.	27.				
8.	18.	28.				
9.	19.	29.				
10.	20.	30.				

WORKSHEET 9

TRAINING COMPONENT	ABBREVIATION
AEROBIC RECOVERY	END-1
AEROBIC CONDITIONING	END-1
LACTATE THRESHOLD	END-3
AEROBIC POWER	END-4
MAXIMAL OXYGEN UPTAKE	END-5
ANAEROBIC POWER	LAT-1
LACTIC ACID TOLERANCE	LAT-2
SPEED & POWER	LAT-3

WORKSHEET 10

DAY		BASE PERIOD	PRE-COMPETITION PERIOD	COMPETITION PERIOD
MONDAY	(AM) (PM)			
TUESDAY	(AM) (PM)			
WEDNESDAY	(AM) (PM)			
THURSDAY	(AM) (PM)			
FRIDAY	(AM) (PM)			
SATURDAY	(AM) (PM)			
SUNDAY	(AM) (PM)			